The Environmental Promise of
Democratic Deliberation

The Environmental Promise of Democratic Deliberation

ADOLF G. GUNDERSEN

THE UNIVERSITY OF WISCONSIN PRESS

The University of Wisconsin Press
114 North Murray Street
Madison, Wisconsin 53715

3 Henrietta Street
London WC2E 8LU, England

5 4 3 2 1

Printed in the United States of America

Figures 4.1, 4.2, 4.3, 4.4, 4.5, and 4.6 courtesy of *Environment*, volume 33, number 8, pages 12–14, 32–34, October 1991. Reprinted with permission of the Helen Dwight Reid Educational Foundation. Published by Heldref Publications, 1319 Eighteenth Street, N.W., Washington, D.C. 20036–1802. Copyright © 1991. Figure 4.7 courtesy of *The Christian Science Monitor*. By Susan B. Tyner in *The Christian Science Monitor*. Copyright © 1987 TCSPS.

Library of Congress Cataloging-in-Publication Data
Gundersen, Adolf G., 1958–
    The environmental promise of democratic deliberation /
Adolf G. Gundersen.
    280 p.   cm.
    Includes bibliographical references and index.
    ISBN 0-299-14480-1   ISBN 0-299-14484-4 (pbk.)
    1. Environmental policy—United States—Citizen participation.
2. Democracy—United States. I. Title.
HC110.E5G86   1995
363.7'058'0973—dc20   94-36212

Contents

Figures

Tables

Acknowledgments

As the reader will see, neither my sensibilities nor the conclusions of this study are of the ivory tower sort. Carrying out this study likewise depended far less on contemplative isolation than on the active collaboration and support of a wide range of friends, colleagues, and acquaintances.

The project would never have gotten off the ground without the enthusiastic encouragement of Karoline Kirst. I had been wandering among the academic trees when the idea of it first came to me; she realized it meant that I was starting to see the forest again—or at least my own forest.

My parents, Rachel and Cameron Gundersen, provided both constant encouragement and a peaceful and productive field station from which to conduct many of the interviews. They were also a great help in locating potential participants. Perhaps only they can see the degree to which this study represents a hybrid of their many influences on me.

Gene Becker, my "philosophical twin," managed to combine enthusiasm for and skepticism about the project from beginning to end. He also found time to edit an earlier version of the entire manuscript. Many other friends made an important contribution to the finished product, especially Judith McCaslin, Mary Kay Wilcox, Eric Gorham, Jim Hein, and Thornton Jacobs. Jay Dadmun supported my study in more ways than I can recount, but especially by making sure that I deliberated about other things from time to time. To Frank Baumgartner and Gretchen Casper, my ever-supportive colleagues and friends, I owe 52 percent (at last count). I gave up trying to keep track of what I owe Marguerite Burns long ago. But I can safely say that the final version of the book would have been impossible without her.

Professor Bryan Norton of the Georgia Institute of Technology responded in a friendly and helpful fashion to my critique of environmental ethics. His view of environmental ethics in large part inspired the interpretation that I present in chapter 5. John Witte, R. Booth Fowler, Ed Portis, Kenneth M. Dolbeare, George Graham, and Russell Gardner, all supplied me with instructive and constructive commentaries. What follows is much the better for the attention they gave the manuscript at various stages of its development. I owe a special thanks to Russell Hanson, who not only read the manuscript with great care but also spurred me to make a number of important changes and additions.

My participants gave liberally of their time (some 240 hours in all) and hospitality. To protect their privacy, I do not use their real names in the text, and so cannot name them here. But I very much want to acknowledge their contribution. They gave freely, not only of their time, but of their thoughts as well. The interview was not easy. It was often enjoyable, but always demanding. Still, no one gave up after the first session; all saw it through to the end. These individuals neither expected nor received remuneration of any type, and yet were willing to spend hour after hour with me knocking heads on questions that have no easy answers. I can only hope that my book lives up to their expectations.

Finally, my advisor and teacher of 15 years, Charles W. Anderson, lent me not only encouragement and advice but also a constant challenge: What do you *really* want to learn? It was only after the interviewing process was well advanced that I saw it was all quite simple: I wanted to do precisely what I was asking my participants to do—invent a political theory of the environment. Once that was clear, the rest followed rather easily. But I simply would never have looked for what I found had it not been for Professor Anderson's ability to sense that there was something more to what I was doing, and his unwillingness to be satisfied with description and explanation. I cannot claim to have solved the environmental problem, but my having been able to sketch an answer at all is owed in great measure to this most remarkable teacher.

I am deeply thankful to all these individuals for their many and varied contributions. This study would have remained a distant glimmer in my eye without them. And, if that glimmer now sparkles at all, it is in no small measure due to their efforts. For that which remains lackluster—or simply wrong—in what follows, I alone claim full credit.

The Environmental Promise of
Democratic Deliberation

Introduction

Quite possibly the fate of our civilization, our posterity, our species, even of the biotic community itself, rests portentously upon the answer to that question: "Are we ready for an ecological morality?"
—Ernest Partridge, "Are We Ready for an Ecological Morality?"

Our environmental crises are now too numerous to list, too profound to dismiss. We know that the environment is a mess. The question is what to do about it. The burning issue is no longer: Environment—yea or nay? Rather, it is: How do we implement our collective yea? Individual enlightenment will not be enough. We must act, and act *collectively*. Our collective yea to the environment must be translated into collective action. There is no shortage of advice about how this might be done. Policy experts and political activists have environmental schemes aplenty. But those schemes do little good if no one is willing to act upon them. We have an environmental problem not because we have the wrong values or because we lack institutional creativity. We have an environmental problem because we have largely failed to connect our values with our institutions. To solve our many environmental problems, our first step must thus be to reconnect our environmental values with our institutions. Our first environmental priority must be to reinfuse our capacity for collective action with environmental purpose.

There is now virtual unanimity among philosophers and theologians of all stripes that we must value nature more than we do at present. As we shall see in chapter 4, this consensus appears to be echoed by the public as a whole. Hence the most pressing environmental question is how to get from here to there, a question made all the more pressing by the very urgency of our multiple environmental dilemmas. But focusing on individual change is doomed to failure because of the very nature of those dilemmas. The environment, however good we deem it to be in the final analysis, is a collective good. As numerous theorists

3

before me have argued, this makes preserving and restoring the environment a political problem.

What kind of politics is suitable to the greener world we desire, believe in, and pray for? We do not need a more orderly or disciplined politics, for order and discipline can be, and too often have been, placed in the service of environmental destruction. We do not need a more caring and compassionate politics, for human benevolence is too small a shield to cover entire ecosystems, much less the whole biosphere. We do not need a more self-reliant and autonomous politics, for environmental protection requires cooperation. We do not need even a more respectful politics, for the problem is not honoring boundaries, but helping each other redraw them. No, what is needed is a more *thoughtful* politics. Thought must build on care, independence, and respect. But only thought can compass both human society and the natural environment. And only thought can link the two.

We thus face the following choice: either we narrow the political circle to the environmentally thoughtful, or we stimulate environmental thought among the broader public. Not only does preserving democracy require that we reject the first alternative, but also, as I explain in chapter 2, there are good grounds for believing that an elitist strategy would fail. However, stimulating environmental thought is not enough. If it is to do any good, it must be political. That is, it must take the public into account. My own answer to the environmental challenge, then, is simple enough: *Create more opportunities for citizen deliberation about environmental issues in order to encourage more and better collective answers.* Doing so need not require a frenzy of meeting attendance. Thinking in public, as we all know, is not the same thing as thinking about public issues. The distinction was well known by the ancient Athenians: They regularly penalized those whose speeches were thought to be self-serving. And much of the deliberation that fueled their highly participatory democracy took place not in the Assembly, Council, or law courts, but in the agora, the public square adjacent to those places (Hansen 1991). If expanded deliberation represents a viable solution to our environmental ills, we must expand our own agora, or invent an equivalent.

I should warn the reader from the start that this work presents neither a full-blown environmental-ethical theory nor a systematic political theory. Instead, it tries to bridge the chasm that still to a large extent separates these two bodies of thought. I combine political theory and environmental ethics at each step in developing an "environmental-political theory." First, although I defend a specific normative conception of the environment, which I term *environmental rationality*, that conception contains an explicitly *political* component. Second, although I argue that we need to rethink our view of political deliberation, that argument rests to a substantial degree on evidence drawn from citizens' deliberation about primarily *environmental* dilemmas. Third, and most crucially, I argue that political deliberation and environmental rationality are linked: political deliberation enhances environmental rationality. The theoretical bridge between environmental ethics and political theory I construct here thus runs from democratic deliberation to environmental ethics.

The interviews I conducted are a test of the strength of that bridge, of the strength of the link between deliberation and environmental rationality. What they show is that deliberation can bear a lot of traffic.

The Citizen as Student

No theorist works alone. As the opening chapter makes clear, I am far from the first to argue that our manifold environmental crises are at root a political problem requiring a political solution.[1] Furthermore, my argument derives whatever force it has from those who are usually cast as the objects of political theory: everyday people. The general theoretical case for expanded political deliberation is by now a familiar one (see Spragens 1990; Fishkin 1991). In the discussion that follows, 46 citizens confirm it in real life. As they show rather convincingly in chapter 6, these very diverse citizens responded to deliberative opportunities by becoming more rational or, more precisely, more environmentally rational. Deliberation tended to improve these citizens' understanding of the social value of the environment and simultaneously improve the fit between their environmental aims and the means they chose of realizing those aims. Given the opportunity to engage in political deliberation on environmental questions, citizens *do* learn. Hence expanding such opportunities holds a very real promise for environmental solutions.

The Citizen as Teacher

Because the interview style I employed was broadly Socratic, it resulted in learning, not only on the respondents' part, but on mine as well. All students are potential teachers; all citizens are potential political theorists. And some of those I talked to fulfilled that potential in eloquent, moving, and, yes, persuasive, ways. In one sense this was unsurprising: environmental philosophy is a new and rapidly growing field. No one can yet say of it that everything has been thought of before. Yet the persuasive force of these citizens' theoretical insights usually had little to do with novelty and everything to do with their very real and present humanity. As I have said, no theorist works alone; I only wish more theorists could benefit from as many collaborators as I had on this project.

True, no one I met could come close to John Muir's eloquence in elucidating the transcendent significance of a woods orchid. But a Vietnam veteran showed me the healing potential of fire asters. And a care-ridden welfare mother in Milwaukee's inner city showed me that wild places enrich the lives of more than just Sierra Club elitists. True, no one I spoke with could match Aldo Leopold's ability to weave science, philosophy, and poetry into a full-blown environmental ethic. Yet I was repeatedly reminded of the importance of sharing the burdens of environmental restraint in an equitable way. True, none of my respondents could equal Murray Bookchin's philosophical inventiveness in defending small-town democracy. Yet more than one participant suggested that the case for the decentralization of environmental decision-making might require reformulating John Stuart Mill's harm principle in order to protect whole communities as well as individual citizens.

A Neo-Aristotelian Approach to the Environmental Problem

The environmental prescription I advocate here—expanding the occasions for public deliberation on environmental issues— may lead some to label my position neo-Aristotelian. In fact, I have followed Aristotle in more than stressing the importance of the agora. As I noted above, I share Aristotle's view that widening the circle of argument usually produces better arguments, hence the inclusion of my respondents as participants in the dialogue about how best to order society's relationship to nature.

I also share Aristotle's view that political institutions and the quality of the citizenry are mutually determining. Advocating new political machinery makes sense only if one is confident that citizens are now, or can become, capable of operating it. Hence the prescription I reach in the initial chapters is really the starting point rather than the conclusion of my argument. By themselves, the considerations adduced there in favor of expanded environmental deliberation add up to a "deliberative hypothesis." The interviews I conducted, which I discuss in the following four chapters, amount to a test of that hypothesis. Those chapters are all devoted, in different ways, to answering this question: Can the American public make good use of expanded opportunities to deliberate about environmental policy? Together, the answer they give is strongly positive: because my citizen participants made such good use of the deliberative opportunities with which I presented them, we can be reasonably confident that the American public as a whole will take advantage of enlarged opportunities to deliberate on environmental policy issues.

The middle chapters show that this group of Americans was both willing and able to make use of the deliberative opportunity represented by the interview. These chapters also explain in some detail why this was so. Chapter 3 explains that participants are puzzled, more than anything else, by environmental issues and are looking for answers. There is also a widespread consensus, detailed in chapter 4, on the need for more environmental policy. This puzzlement and search predisposed my participants to environmental deliberation. The widespread policy consensus, paradoxically rooted in the wide variety of values people find in nature, strongly suggests that my participants' deliberative inclinations are widely shared by the public at large. Building on what was said about the nature of participants' puzzlement in chapter 3, chapter 5 pinpoints the primary barrier to heightened environmental policy commitment: the common tendency to think of environmental problems in purely individual terms. Not only does this tendency fly in the face of the popular view that the environmental crisis is yet another phase in the moral decline of Western civilization; it also suggests that deliberation, not exhortation, is the shortest path to strengthened environmental commitment. Chapter 6 confirms that analysis. It shows that participants generally increased their commitment to collective solutions to environmental problems over the course of the interview. It also maps out the various cognitive paths they took in arriving at that commitment.

Finally, Aristotle was an eminently practical political thinker; he paid close attention to institutional arrangements. Following his lead on this score seems more reasonable the more urgent our environmental dilemmas become. For this reason, I conclude in chapter 7 by suggesting a range of specific changes that can be made in the short and medium terms to expand the agora.

No political theory is complete until it has achieved a kind of balance between the true or the good and the existing limits on citizens' potential to achieve that end. Theory must be true discursively or rationally. Yet it must also take account of the human reality it aims to shape: *it must answer in the end to the people it is meant to guide.* It answers better if it has first listened.

1 _____

Democracy, Deliberation, and the Environment

> I know of no safe depository of the ultimate power of the society but the people themselves; and if we think them not enlightened enough to exercise their control with a wholesome discretion, the remedy is not to take it from them, but to inform their discretion.
> —Thomas Jefferson, letter to W. C. Jarvis, September 28, 1820

Present a random group of Americans with a copy of the original Declaration of Independence and a newer Declaration of Dependence on the Environment and invite them to sign whichever document they agree with. What would you see? Chances are very good, I think, that the great majority would unhesitatingly and enthusiastically sign both. Now, hold the mental image of these like-minded citizens affirming their values by affixing their signatures to the two documents, and you have as good a symbol as you are likely to find anywhere of America's environmental problem. America's environmental problem is this: we believe in democracy and in protecting the environment, but only very rarely do we pause to ask if these two commitments can be reconciled, much less how. Like the citizens in my sketch, we gladly sign both documents, never sorting out their possible conflicts, tensions, and implications. Are democracy and environmental protection compatible? Why? How? These essential questions are left unanswered in our enthusiasm to express our belief in self-government and our love of nature. We seem to believe that raw commitment can compensate for anything we might lack in logic, conceptual clarity, or institutional dexterity. To make matters worse, whatever success we do have in reconciling the two commitments seems very often to depend on a gross simplification of what each commitment alone might entail. We really do tend to think that "Consent of the Governed" and "environmental protection" are "self-evident." But it does little good to think carefully about how democracy and environmental protection are related if one has not also given careful consideration to the meaning of each of those terms. Just what is democracy? Why should we value it? Or, what does environmental protection really mean? Why is it important? Democratic theorists and environmental philosophers can help us answer such questions, can help us decide what we mean when we say yes to democracy, yes to the environment. Still, in the end, even that is not enough. What we need most of all is a coherent picture that not only includes answers to both sets of questions but also integrates them. We need, in short, a conceptual bridge capable of directly connecting democracy and environmental protection. This book constructs just such a bridge. But it also goes beyond this construction: it presents the results of a stress test I ran on a real-world prototype of that bridge.

The general concept that I develop here to link democracy and environmental protection is deliberation, or the process by which individuals actively confront challenges to their beliefs. Individuals hold beliefs about many things, of course. They can, likewise, deliberate about many things, both private and public. When they respond to challenges to beliefs that touch on collective or public aims and activities, they are engaging in what I call *public deliberation*. Because, as I will argue in the next chapter, environmental protection has an essential public component, *environmental deliberation* is always public deliberation. Environmental deliberation is thus a subset of public deliberation, and public deliberation is itself a subset of a more general deliberation. No matter what its content, though, deliberation always involves the individual in what is fundamentally the same kind of activity: confronting challenges to her or his beliefs. All that distinguishes one kind of deliberation from another is the focus of the activity, the kind of beliefs being challenged.

How, then, does deliberation conceptually bridge democracy and the environment? More specifically, what is the link between democracy and deliberation, on the one hand, and the environment and deliberation, on the other? The relationship between democracy and deliberation is rather straightforward. Not all democracies are deliberative; not all deliberation takes place in democracies. Deliberation and democracy thus stand in what philosophers call a contingent relationship to one another. If democracy and deliberation are to be linked, either democracy must become deliberative or deliberation must become democratic. From what I have said so far, we can be sure that, in any given society, people will deliberate about many things. It also follows that the more citizens are involved in deliberation about public aims and activities, the more democratic deliberation becomes, and the more deliberative democracy becomes, the more society approximates a *deliberative democracy*. A deliberative democracy is a thinking democracy. It is not satisfied with either the equal protection of individual interests or an active, involved citizenry, though it values both. Instead, it challenges citizens to move beyond their present beliefs, develop their ideas, and examine their values. It calls upon them to make connections, to connect more firmly and fully with the people and world around them.

Deliberation's connection to the environment is more direct. Environmental deliberation, like all deliberation, involves, first, a challenge to the individual's beliefs and, second, a thoughtful response by the individual. Environmental deliberation, like all public deliberation, casts the individual in the role of citizen responding to challenges to his or her public beliefs. Environmental deliberation is unique only in its subject matter: environmental protection, or the collective pursuit of environmental aims. Environmental deliberation can begin as a challenge: Come and see what lies at the end of your own thinking about environmental protection. Environmental deliberation can also start out as an invitation: Cross over from the amorphous, undifferentiated territory of "rule by the people" to the realm of "rule on behalf of environmental values." Whether solicitous or confrontational in its tone, environmental deliberation encourages individual citizens to take the next step, to connect their own lives, beliefs, and activities with the collective pursuit of environmental ends. Environmental deliberation, in short, connects the people, first with each other and then with the environment they wish not simply to visit, but also to inhabit.

If we now keep this link between deliberation and the environment in mind and then recall that deliberation can, at least in theory, be linked to democracy as well, we arrive at the first of this book's two theses: *the more deliberative democracy becomes, the smaller will be the gap that separates the people from the environment.* We can close the gap that now exists between democracy and the environment by encouraging citizens to deliberate about environmental protection. The theoretical bridge I propose between democracy and the environment can be realized in practice by citizens establishing their own links to the environment through deliberation.

This first thesis is clearly a theoretical one: deliberation successfully bridges the gap that now separates democracy and the environment, or democratic theory and environmental ethics. But my case for the environmental promise of deliberative democracy rests on more than purely theoretical foundations. I also subjected this theoretical bridge between democracy and the environment to a systematic stress test to see if it would hold up in practice. It did. I offered a highly diverse group of 46 citizens an opportunity to deliberate about environmental protection for several hours. All but one seized the opportunity. The rest were not only willing to deliberate but also connected more broadly and firmly with the environment as a result.

The results of this stress test, which take up the middle chapters of this book, suggest that the theoretical bridge between environment and democracy that I detail here not only looks good on paper but can also actually hold up under the weight of living, breathing, thinking citizens. My second thesis is thus neither wholly empirical nor strictly theoretical. It is based on real empirical evidence, but uses the deliberative theory I develop to generalize beyond that evidence. This second thesis is: *from an environmental perspective, deliberative democracy is as practically relevant as it is theoretically compelling.*

Combined, these two theses lead me to be optimistic about American democracy's capacity to come to terms with the environment, perhaps relentlessly so. The theory advanced (and tested) here offers what I believe to be a cogent and eminently practical answer to the question, What is to be done about the environment? And it does so in a way that not only considers the value of democracy, or even preserves democracy as part of the answer, but also sees in democracy—deliberative democracy—our very best environmental hope.

With this rough sketch in mind, it is time to look more closely at the links between deliberation, democracy, and environmental protection.

Foundations: A Dyadic Model of Deliberation

Considered in static terms, say, the way a civil engineer might look at a bridge, deliberation spans the gap between one individual and another, between the individual and the various communities of which she is a member, and between the individual and the larger world around her. But in practice this linkage is always the result of a dynamic thought process, in which the individual actively accepts a challenge to his beliefs or takes up an invitation to rethink them. Deliberation enriches and refines individuals' beliefs, it connects individuals more firmly and widely to the world beyond the individual self. But deliberation does not accomplish these things on its own. Deliberation cannot occur without both challenges and active respondents.

Deliberation does not just happen. It occurs only when people are willing to make connections, to go places their thoughts have not yet taken them. They must be willing to make the trip. If deliberation is to be an ongoing process, rather than an occasional foray, people must be willing to make the trip repeatedly. They must see the mental travel that deliberation entails, not as a holiday, but as a way of life. Deliberation leaves monuments to its activity everywhere, in our minds and in the real world, but however many times it visits these places, it is never willing to say, "Here I rest, and will no further."

On this view, deliberation is quite clearly an active, even strenuous, process. Moreover, it is deliberation that makes practice (i.e., deliberate action as opposed to mere activity or behavior) possible. Deliberation does not equate thought with action, but sees action that is divorced from thought as the ultimate form of alienation. Thoughtless action is action disconnected from everything but instinct and habit, divorced from the self, society, the environment, the cosmos. Without deliberation, action is mere movement without direction or meaning. It is sleepwalking through a Kafka novel we never finish writing.

Will deliberation always translate into thoughtful action? No, of course it won't. No one seriously thinks that what we believe in always dictates how we act. But the greater part of philosophical heritage, the historical record, and a wealth of psychological research all argue that beliefs make a big difference.[1] Equally important, we need to remember that the only alternative to inducing people to make their own connections to the realm of political activity is to coerce them into such activity, to force them to make leaps in directions they may not wish to go or even see clearly if at all. To do so would be, in a word, antidemocratic. It would be to give up on the prospect of moving from democracy to the environment, for it would obliterate democracy in the process. It would amount to an admission that such an ongoing process is beyond us. But we should not be willing to throw in the towel so easily. We can be skeptical about humans' ability to perfect themselves without giving up our belief that they can improve themselves. We ought to acknowledge that the people, in their less-than-infinite wisdom, make mistakes. But that doesn't mean that they cannot make fewer tomorrow. Thomas Jefferson was right: if we think the people insufficiently enlightened, the remedy is not to take away their control of public affairs; it is to "inform their discretion." If the people and enlightenment, prudence, or truth appear to reside in different countries, the answer is not to extradite them forcibly, but to encourage them all the more strongly to make the trip on their own. That ongoing project is not beyond us. In fact, it is well within our grasp.

Deliberation can serve as the bridge between democracy and the environment, preserving both. That is my central claim here. In the following two sections we will see how deliberation connects with democracy on the one side and the environment on the other. Now I want to look more closely at the deliberative process itself, the process through which I am claiming that citizens will be able to connect with the environment.

Deliberation is a kind of thought travel or the traveler's thought in motion. Although we need to remember that deliberation is essentially a neverending, dynamic process, we can freeze it in time to look more closely at its constituent components. Like travel, any particular deliberative act has a beginning, a middle, and an end. Deliberation always begins with a departure from one's accepted beliefs, from where one is now. One may be challenged to leave or invited to leave, or one's thoughts may simply have the mental equivalent of wanderlust. Whether the reason is a call from afar or simply restlessness, however, the result is the same: one abandons passive belief and embarks on a mental journey elsewhere; one makes the connection with something new, something beyond the confines of the beliefs one simply used to inhabit. This does not mean that the deliberative traveler necessarily changes his or her beliefs, any more than the typical traveler sells his or her abode before every trip. It means only that one has sallied forth literally to experience new beliefs.

While underway, the deliberative traveler is no mere observer of new territory, new beliefs. Her or his goal is not simply to *record* new mental scenery. The search is for an enriched understanding, not a bigger library of video cassettes. The thoughtful traveler must do more than seek out panoramic vistas. She or he must engage them, reflect upon them, and come to some conclusions about them (knowing all the while that future trips may alter those conclusions). Deliberative travel is more than a matter of seeing new things; it is a matter of consciously integrating what one has seen with the beliefs one had at the start of the trip.

Deliberation begins as a challenge to one's existing beliefs. Responding to the challenge requires that one either resolve the conflict posed by the challenge or remain conscious of the conflict. Both types of response require the active exercise of reason. Deliberative challenges call upon us either to reason about what we know or to acknowledge what we can't know or for the present simply don't know. Deliberation does not presume that all conflicts can be resolved rationally. Many conflicts can be resolved rationally (such as the free-rider problem); others cannot be (such as the present scientific dispute over global warming); still others perhaps never will be (such as the age-old argument about the existence of God). Deliberation requires only that reason be brave enough to sally forth and modest enough to admit its own failings. Mere rationalization, for example, fails on this definition, for it involves disguising or avoiding challenges rather than meeting them head on. Deliberation may be exhilarating, but it probably shares more with backpacking than with sightseeing.

Deliberation in general thus requires an active, reasoned response. Public deliberation is no different, except that here both the challenge and response touch upon collective aims and pursuits in particular. Deliberation depends on direct responses, meeting challenges head on. Public deliberation involves challenges to public beliefs. To count as public deliberation, responses to those challenges must likewise be public in character. Since individual preferences, tastes, personality style, and upbringing are all purely individual factors, invoking one (or all) of them stills falls short of qualifying as *public* deliberation. Notice that citing only facts which pertain to oneself as an individual also fails to qualify as "reasoning." More than perhaps any other kind of deliberation, public deliberation means movement. Public deliberation, including the environmental deliberation that will occupy most of our attention here, is a form of travel, not a simple description of where one stands right now.

What lies at the end of the deliberative traveler's journey? That is impossible to say with any great precision. Itineraries will vary. Some travelers will decide to stay in the new places they discover. Others will conclude that their original beliefs were where they wish them to remain and will decide to return home. But even those who opt for a round trip will not be coming back to their starting place. They will be changed by their travels. They not only will have experienced more of the world but will also have worked to integrate the new with the old. Old beliefs may remain unaltered, but, as a result of the thought travel involved in deliberation, they will not be held in the same way. As a result of experiencing alternative ways of looking at things, even beliefs that remain unchanged will be held with a deeper understanding of their implications, their meaning, and their importance. Like all trips, round trips mean leaving home. And if the travel is truly deliberative, the return trip will be made out of a conscious choice to make home the destination, a choice made not after "all things are considered" but after "more things are considered." The round-trip traveler returns home not with new conclusions but with better arguments—not with new beliefs but with better-grounded beliefs. Deliberation can thus paradoxically mean leaving one's home in order to give it better foundations.

Perhaps more frequently, however, the deliberative traveler will decide to relocate as a result of his travels. He will change the content of his beliefs. Those changes may involve very large moves—to a new continent, as it were. But such moves are probably rare, or happen as the result of numerous shorter trips. Most deliberative acts lead to changes akin to moving just around the corner, moves which are not necessarily any more profound than the kind of changes experienced by the traveler who decides not to move at all. But *all* deliberation results in change. One cannot deliberate without also changing either what one believes, or how one believes it, or both. In the same way that taking a trip leads us either to appreciate home all the more or, perhaps, to relocate, deliberating means accepting an invitation to change ourselves.

Deliberation, like travel, is an active process. It is thought in motion. It is movement, and movement entails change. Even when thought comes full circle, its compass is greater. But neither deliberation nor travel are random motion. Both involve departures, itineraries, and destinations. For both the deliberator and the ordinary traveler, these three elements are inseparable. To deliberate means to accept an invitation or challenge to explore new terrain. This invitation or challenge is the crucial structural element in deliberation; it is the bridge to the realm of the new, of the unexamined. Without that bridge we have no way of experiencing what is "over there." However, the bridge only potentially connects us to what is on the other side. To get there actually, we must travel across the bridge. We cannot begin to explore without first crossing the bridge. Once we do, once we accept the challenge and cross over its bridge to the other side, how and what we explore there is largely up to us. Similarly, deliberation is a willing departure from our present beliefs and requires a bridge into new areas of thought, but what our thought sees and experiences once there—thought's "itinerary"—is largely up to the traveler. If the deliberator's itinerary is largely open-ended, so too is his destination. He may move beyond the first bridge and cross others; he may stay put on the other side; he may return home. We know only that he will be changed from his travels—that, however many mental leaps he takes along the way, he will be more, not less, connected with the world as a result of his trip.

Deliberation, to sum up what I've said so far, is an active response to a challenge to one's beliefs. It is traveling across a mental bridge and actively confronting what one finds on the other side. It is a kind of mental connection. For the connection to take hold, only two things are necessary: a challenge and a response. It is for this reason that deliberation is at root, not a group process, but a two-party process. Deliberation is dyadic, dialogic—like a conversation, not a series of speeches. Even when one deliberates alone, this dyadic structure remains in place. All that has changed is that one has assumed both deliberative roles: challenger and respondent. The deliberative traveler is never alone, but always conversing—with another person, a book, a TV program, a landscape, or simply with herself.

With this general picture of deliberation in mind, it is time to narrow our focus, to return to the two things I am claiming can be connected by deliberation: democracy and the environment. I begin with democracy. The next section goes on to discuss the environment, the other endpoint of the particular deliberative bridge that I wish to build.

Connecting Deliberation to Democracy

If "democracy" means "rule by the people," "deliberative democracy" means "deliberative rule by the people" or "rule by a deliberative people."[2] However one chooses to put it, the motivating ideal at the heart of deliberative democracy is clear: thoughtful rule by the people. Even understood as an ideal, this may not sound especially revolutionary. Yet it is, at least when compared with more conventional views of democracy. These tend to fall into two broad camps which generally divide according to whether they see representation or citizen participation as more central to democracy. (I discuss both views at length in chapter 2.) First, both representative democrats and participatory democrats equate democracy with the exercise of power by the many. They differ only on the question of whether power should be exercised directly (the participatory view) or through intermediaries (the representative view). The deliberative democrat sees this dispute as largely beside the point. What matters, from his perspective, is not how many people are actually in on pulling the levers of public power, but how thoughtfully those levers are approached. This suggests the second important way in which deliberative democracy departs from more traditional conceptions of democracy. If the levers of public decision-making are approached only after an extended process of deliberation, it follows that they will be pulled thoughtfully as well. The decisions that result will, in a very direct sense, embody the thought that went into their making. The representative democrat, on the other hand, is satisfied if the people are satisfied, if the machinery of representative government gives the people what they want. The participatory democrat is typically more demanding, and expects that participation will result in a regard for fellow citizens, civic consciousness, and so on. But few (if any) participatory democrats argue that participation in public affairs leads to any other kind of learning, any other kind of connections between citizens and the world they inhabit. Deliberative democracy shares with participatory democracy the belief that politics can be transformative, that it can change people, can link them together. But deliberative democracy's agenda is not restricted to communal impulses. The curriculum it has in mind is not limited to establishing connections with one's neighborhood; it begins with one's backyard and is literally as extensive as the cosmos.

If deliberative democracy's curriculum is limited only by the imagination of its citizenry, so too is its classroom. It is here that deliberative democracy most clearly differs from both traditional and contemporary views of participatory democracy. (Representative democrats are by and large happy to leave citizens as they found them.) According to participatory democrats, the magic of participation can be worked only *in public*. One must participate—act within the public sphere—if one is to reap any psychological or ethical rewards. Public squares, town meetings, neighborhood groups—these are where the wonders of democratic politics are worked. This view is, in some ways, very close to my own. It stresses learning, active citizens, and broadened perspectives. But it is severely cramped in its appraisal of not only what citizens are capable of learning but also of how they learn.

Participatory democrats, admirers of public spirit, have for too long looked for that spirit only in public. They have equated public consciousness with being in public, participation with physical and temporal proximity, connections between citizens with citizen meetings. For all their psychological subtlety, participatory democrats all too often forget that theirs is a psychological theory, not an architectural one. The changes they expect to follow from participation happen, ultimately, not in the town square, but in the hearts and minds of citizens. I, too, believe that such changes take place from deliberation. But I believe we can, and occasionally should, bypass the town square. We can speak directly to citizens, even those who, like most of us, never set foot in the town square. And when we do, we need not limit our discussion to the parochial concerns of our neighborhood. We speak more broadly than this every day. We need only do more of it and do it better.

Deliberation is a mental bridge between the individual and her or his surroundings. Democratic deliberation occurs anytime a citizen travels across such a bridge between herself and the world of the people. It requires only a challenge and the citizen's response. The challenge—and this is the key point here—can come from anywhere: from the newspaper or television, from one's neighbor or friend or spouse or coworker, from one's experience on or off the job, from the Sunday service, even from within. Deliberation about public ends need not take place *in public*, though it certainly can and does. (Political participation can stimulate public deliberation—deliberation about public affairs—

both in public and in private. Likewise, private deliberation about public affairs can stimulate political participation and further public deliberation in public settings.) Deliberative democracy aims to infuse public affairs with thought, but it recognizes that no public sphere, however expansive, can contain it, much less expand it. Thought travels along many bridges, not just one. And yet all bridges ultimately come down to a link between two points: where I am now and where someone or something suggests I go.

All of this may strike us as rather commonsensical. In a sense that is true: deliberation is neither rare nor somehow ineffable. Yet the image of citizens routinely sprouting and crossing mental bridges in all directions is surely an arresting one. Among other things, it leads to a couple of rather striking political conclusions. The first is that we must radically alter our very definition of "politics." Democratic deliberation can occur anywhere, anytime a citizen takes up a challenge to his or her beliefs about public ends. Hence politics becomes coextensive, not just with the narrow realm of collective action per se, but also with deliberation about collective action. The fact that democratic deliberation can occur anywhere there are citizens willing to deliberate about politics (alone, in pairs, or in groups) does *not* mean that "everything is political." Sometimes citizens will conclude that this or that is not really a public question at all. But the the fact that deliberation can happen all around us does mean that politics is happening all around us. Only those who systematically heed the injunction not to argue, even with themselves, about politics (and take absolutely no part in public decision-making) succeed in depoliticizing themselves entirely. In a deliberative democracy, politics is coextensive with the publicly oriented deliberations of the citizenry, wherever they occur. Even casual observation tells us that, in fact, these deliberations occur almost everywhere.

The second feature about this portrait of deliberative democracy is as hopeful as it is startling. Like the expanded concept of the political just discussed, it follows from the essentially dyadic, conversational nature of deliberation. If deliberation is, as I have said, essentially a process of challenge and response, then deliberation is alive, if not well, in American democracy right now. If that is so, stimulating deliberation, improving the deliberative side of deliberative democracy, will be very much more like nurturing a live plant than like breeding a new strain altogether. Deliberation is democratic as long as it connects with the demos, as long as it takes the public as its object. Democratic deliberation is deliberation with a specific starting point: collective aims and pursuits. But for the deliberating citizen, this connection with the people is of course conceptual, not literal. No one could ever shake so many hands, much less converse with all those one greets. Because the connection is established internally, not in some exterior place set aside for the event, all that is necessary is an invitation or challenge. The rest is done by the citizen. Arenas, town squares, meeting places are all rendered unnecessary. We need not limit ourselves to building new public fora; we can also concentrate on encouraging citizens to build and cross bridges of their own.

If deliberation is essentially a two-party process between the challenger and respondent, it makes sense to build on the innumerable relationships that already exist in society between citizens, because these relationships are the place where deliberation already occurs or can be encouraged. The architectural foundations or, rather, architects of a more deliberative politics are already among us. We need not place our hopes exclusively in the magic of public places, in their ability to reinvent the citizen. We already have citizens who deliberate, and many others who lack only the opportunity to do so. We need only stimulate deliberation in those places it already works— or can work. If we remember that deliberation is like a conversation, not a series of speeches, we will focus our efforts on improving and expanding our conversations, not on giving speeches. Doing so will mean not only more deliberation but also a more vigorous democracy.

A democracy can be deliberative only if the people actually deliberate. This is the added challenge that deliberation poses to the democrat. Yet this is a challenge, not a utopian wish. We know that at least some people deliberate at least some of the time. I was doing so, when I typed this chapter into my computer; you are doing so now as you read it. The challenge is in *broadening* deliberation, in making it truly "of, by, and for the people." This, too, is as workable as it is appealing. It is a far simpler matter to get the individual citizen to confront one challenge at a time in a place of her or his own choosing than to convince her or him to confront a crowd of (sometimes angry) challengers all at once. Typical citizens are more willing to leave their beliefs "at home" and venture into the public realm if allowed to do so on their own terms. Deliberative democracy seeks to shield deliberation wherever it arises, seeks to give it the (mental) space it needs to flourish. Sometimes public places will do. Other times, however, they will be too crowded, or the heat of public argument will simply cause deliberation to wilt. Then we are faced with a choice: give up on public deliberation, or encourage it to go on in private. Participatory democrats all too readily choose the former. Deliberating in private does not mean that one cannot deliberate about public matters. Ask a political theorist if that is so; ask a president.

Deliberation's link to democracy ultimately comes down to individual citizens' willingness to deliberate. The more we are prepared to grant that citizens can deliberate even outside the confines of public assemblies, the more prepared we will be to admit that they can be invited to deliberate in many settings, and the more reason we will have to suppose that they really are willing to deliberate. The wider and more varied our conception of the public sphere, of the places in which public action *and* thought occur, the more firmly deliberation will be anchored in the people. But we have not been willing to make this concession. We tend to unreflexively equate deliberation with deliberative bodies. But if we expand our conception of "the political" so as to admit political (i.e., public) thinking wherever it occurs, we can see that deliberation can be anchored in democracy one citizen at a time, and that for each citizen this anchor may catch hold at any number of different points. Even when in groups, citizens deliberate, if they deliberate at all, one at a time. The point bears repeating: democratic deliberation does not rest upon a specific kind of group, locale, or organizational structure, but upon individual citizens. Individual citizens deliberate about the public; the public per se has never had a thought in its life.

It is time we jettisoned the idea that political thinking occurs only in political settings. Ever since Socrates, our political attention has been far too focused. This narrow focus has succeeded in illuminating public forums, public bodies, and public meetings with a penetrating beam of light. But in the process we have missed the big picture. It is time to bring up the house lights and look around. When we do, it will not take long before we begin to see that we need not wait for everyone to have a chance to mount the public stage for deliberation to begin. For all of us it can start right now. We don't even need to leave our seats.

Connecting Deliberation to the Environment

If democratic deliberation begins with an individual citizen, where does it go from there? That question really combines two separate questions. First, can we be sure that citizens will travel across their deliberative bridges to the environment in particular? And second, if they do, what will they find on the other side? These are both important questions. To the first question, I answer, yes, we can be very confident, not only that citizens can be encouraged to deliberate about public matters in general, but also that they can be encouraged to deliberate about environmental protection in particular. (I will return to the second question—What are they likely to conclude?—a bit further on.)

Will citizens make use of expanded opportunities to deliberate about the environment? Again the answer lies with the individual citizen, with her or his willingness to respond to challenges to her or his beliefs about environmental protection. But surely that resource exists in great abundance in late twentieth-century America. No special or particular kind of interest in the environment is required, just *an* interest. How many citizens of this country lack such an interest? Not many. For some the interest in environmental protection may be rooted in health concerns; for others the environment may be an essentially aesthetic issue; still others explicitly link environmental protection to their religious beliefs. Some people may trace their interest in the environment to early childhood experiences; others, to caustic air in the parking lot; still others, to a studied belief in the importance of biological diversity. The very variety, not to mention strength, of these interests is the bedrock upon which democratic deliberation can confidently rest in the environmental realm.

At the theoretical level, then, we can be confident of citizens' willingness to connect their deliberations to the issue of environmental protection because they need only an interest in environmental protection to do so. (As we will see in chapter 3 and again in chapter 5, there are also good empirical reasons to think that citizens have such an interest.) Environmental deliberation, like democratic deliberation more generally, requires active thinking. But active thinking can take place virtually anywhere, anytime. Because it is bounded neither by architecture nor by institutional structure, environmental deliberation requires neither new town halls nor new organizations. It requires only a challenge to one's environmental beliefs, and a willingness to take up that challenge. To stimulate environmental deliberation we need only issue more and better challenges. Citizens will meet environmental challenges because, in the end, the environment matters to them.

The variety of citizens' environmental interests parallels the variety of paths citizens can follow in their deliberations. In the preceding section I argued that, although political participation can stimulate public deliberation, citizens need not be gathered together in groups in order to deliberate. Now we can see that the freedom of movement we have extended to the would-be deliberator has an interior analog: even citizens whose interests do not coincide exactly are free to deliberate with one another. In fact, they are likely to do so, because they are likely to challenge one another's beliefs.

If the citizen's willingness to deliberate about the environment is encouraged regardless of where it arises, regardless of the institutional or social setting, it is less likely to be strained or filtered, diluted or weakened, than if it is continually channeled into (or sanctioned by) certain privileged institutional arrangements. The more places deliberation is encouraged, the more likely citizens will be to deliberate. Deliberative democracy is ecumenical: no deliberative forum is considered more "holy" than any other; deliberative democracy takes all comers who profess a belief in the importance of the subject under deliberation. In the environmental realm, the vast majority of us are, in this sense, believers.

There is, then, every reason to believe that, given a chance, people will deliberate about the environment—that among the many deliberative trips people take, some of those trips will connect people to the environment in particular. We now need to ask, what happens then? I have already said enough about deliberation to answer that question in general terms, at least. If deliberation has occurred, if one has actively responded to a deliberative challenge, I said, one of two changes will have occurred: either the content of one's beliefs will be changed, or the way in which those beliefs are held will be altered. Upon deliberating, either one "relocates," or one better appreciates "home." When the subject is the environment or, more precisely, our collective treatment of the environment, deliberation will cause us either to change our environmental beliefs or to have a firmer, clearer hold on them. If we think about the environment, we are being more thoughtful than if we don't, and the thoughts we have are fuller than the thoughts we had before. Upon reasoning, we are more reasonable, more rational, than we were before. Upon reasoning about the environment, we will be more environmentally reasonable, more environmentally rational, than we were before. All deliberation yields some form of rationality; environmental deliberation yields what I call environmental rationality.

When citizens deliberate about environmental protection, their beliefs will change or be altered—not randomly but in certain clearly definable ways. However variable, however unpredictable its effects, deliberation (if it has actually occurred) can be counted upon to lead citizens to think about the environment in a more rational way; their environmental rationality will be enhanced or sharpened from the experience of deliberation. Environmental rationality, then, is the key product of environmental deliberation. Specifically, environmental deliberation leads citizens to think of our collective pursuit of environmental ends in a more *collective, long-term, holistic,* and *self-reflexive* way. Environmental rationality involves all four of these components. Consequently deliberation can enhance environmental rationality by sharpening the citizen's thinking in any one or more of these different areas. If, upon deliberating, one has a better understanding of the collective nature of environmental problems, one has become environmentally more rational. (Hence environmental rationality embodies a specifically political component.) If one's beliefs are challenged and one comes to appreciate better the interconnectedness of environmental problems, their holistic nature, one's environmental rationality has been enhanced. Taking a longer-term perspective also amounts to enhanced environmental rationality, as does a clearer grasp of one's environmental values. Environmental deliberation can also (and actually does), of course, yield gains in two or more of these thought areas simultaneously. In chapter 6 I shall have much more to say about what each of the components of environmental rationality involves and how they are stimulated. For now, the important thing to remember is that, in my view, environmental deliberation is not likely to involve a random walk through the environment. Instead, I firmly believe that, upon deliberating, citizens will see and embrace greener pastures. I believe it because I have seen it happen.

Will the Deliberative Bridge to the Environment Hold Up? A Stress Test

Deliberation can help us work out the relationship between our belief in democracy and our belief in protecting the environment. It can also help us deepen our understanding of democracy and of environmental protection. Not only can deliberation be the bridge that links "we the people" to the environment; it can also help us explore the terrain on both sides of that bridge. It can improve our political understanding even as it promotes what I have termed environmental rationality. We need only encourage citizens, wherever they find themselves, to initiate the kind of travel that this bridge allows.

Still, all of this may strike us as rather utopian or perhaps a bit too theoretical. Can we really expect to have a citizenry of theorists? "Castles in the air," we might think. Can we expect citizens to be building and crossing thought bridges continually? "Another ivory tower scheme," we may be tempted to say. Yet the theory I have just laid out did not spring fully formed from my brow. Nor was it invented *ex nihilo* at the keyboard. Neither is it a pearl of wisdom plucked from between the covers of the Harvard classics. And it is certainly not the kind of theory that is meant to float like an ethereal beacon of shimmering light above the real world of people and practice. The fact is, rather, that my theory not only addresses the real world, but also *arose directly out of* the real world of living, breathing, thinking people. I did not so much design the deliberative bridge I have been discussing as discover it. I discovered it during the course of some 240 hours of deliberative interviews with a carefully selected group of 46 live representatives of the very citizenry whose deliberative travel I hope to encourage. Deliberative democracy is an ideal. But it is one that I distilled out of interactions with real people. I found the deliberative ideal there; I did not invent it. It is thus an ideal that already exists among us in nascent form; it is neither foreign to us nor beyond us. Though it is an ideal, deliberative democracy is already part of us, a potential waiting to be more fully realized. Nor is that all. The same group of citizens who inspired the theory did something else. They gave it a trial run. With my help, they subjected the theory of deliberative bridge-building to a systematic stress test.

Not only did I arrive at my conclusions about deliberative democracy in an unusual way, one that consciously preserves the link between practice and theory, I also took a further step, one that is even more unusual among political theorists: I tested my conclusions. The same interviews that provided grist for my theoretical mill also served as a test of the theory they inspired. This is how it worked. I individually invited 46 citizens to establish deliberative bridges to the environment in a one-on-one interview setting. The results tell us something about how Americans actually deliberate right now, and they tell us a great deal about Americans' deliberative potential. My participants were not a scientific sample of the American public; they were too few in number. But they did represent the American public, certainly more accurately (and no less deliberatively, I might add) than does the present U.S. Congress, for example. Interviewing 46 participants allowed me to deliberate with Americans from many different backgrounds, from many different walks of life, and with a wide range of beliefs about environmental protection and about politics more generally (see Appendix, pp. 211–235).

Not only did this widely varied group of participants cross the deliberative bridges I built for them as we talked; they did so with relish. And, once on the other side, they really did find greener pastures: their beliefs were more environmentally rational as a result of the interview's deliberative exchanges, and they were more willing to support collective action on behalf of the environment. In only one case did the interview fail to encourage deliberation; in only one out of 46 cases was my invitation to deliberate steadfastly refused. In all 45 of the cases in which this invitation was accepted, the deliberative bridge was crossed, and crossed repeatedly. It held up despite my participants' widely different environmental and political starting points, different gender roles, and different religious, ethnic, and class backgrounds. It held up despite their varied occupational concerns and educational levels. It held up despite differences in their motivations and personalities. It held up in the city, the country, and various places in between. No two interview participants crossed the deliberative bridge at the same rate; no two ended up in precisely the same place. But all—save one—crossed, and all of those who did were more environmentally rational for having done so. The interview, which lasted anywhere from 3 to 12 hours, was enough of a deliberative challenge to encourage 45 out of 46 participants to sharpen their environmental beliefs, either by thinking more collectively, more holistically, from a more long-term perspective, or more self-reflexively. These changes, in turn, led nearly two-thirds of my participants to strengthen their belief in collective action (even of the governmental variety) to improve the environment. In 45 out of 46 cases, the citizens I invited to deliberate were actually willing to do so. And in not one of those cases did they fail to become more environmentally rational. Not even Underwriters' Laboratory gets results like that.

Democratic Deliberation: Bridge Building without Blueprints

In this introductory chapter I have sketched a picture of a new kind of society, a society in which citizens are encouraged to deliberate about public matters, not just in public, but also at home, at work, even at play. Such a society, a deliberative democracy, would promote deliberation between individual citizens, not just between groups of citizens. In a deliberative democracy, public deliberation would be especially democratic, in two senses. First, it would include everyone, everywhere, as a deliberator. Democratic deliberation encourages all citizens to deliberate about public affairs, not just those active in traditional political roles. And even politically active citizens would continue to deliberate about politics even after they had left the public stage. Democratic deliberation takes democracy seriously in another sense as well: it excludes no citizen's interest as inherently unfit for deliberative attention; as long as an interest is related in some way to public aims and projects, it is a fitting subject for democratic deliberation. In fact, the more democratic deliberation becomes, the more often citizens deliberate and the more they deliberate about. For this reason we can be sure that citizens of a deliberative democracy would deliberate about many things, the environment included. Finally, we can expect that, as a result of their deliberations, citizens' beliefs will be clearer and deeper. When those deliberations touch upon the environment, they will promote environmental rationality and, with it, the collective pursuit of environmental aims.

Each of the chapters that follows fills in some of the details missing from this sketch. In the next chapter I return to my original starting point: the problem of linking environmental protection to democracy. Americans are right, I argue there, to affirm the value of "government by the people" and simultaneously acknowledge our dependence on the environment. Yet I also argue that not just any government by the people, not just any democracy, will do. Reasonable environmental protection depends on a reasonable brand of democracy—deliberative democracy. The next four chapters discuss the results of the stress test I discussed above. My interview findings show, first, that Americans *are* in fact willing to deliberate about the environment. They also show why. These are the subjects of chapters 3 and 4. Chapter 5 elaborates further on this explanation, underlining the importance of Americans' shared interest in discovering environmental solutions. After presenting a more systematic definition of the concept of environmental rationality that I claim is the product of democratic deliberation on environmental issues, chapter 6 provides a full report on the results of the stress test discussed above. It explains the nature and extent of the changes that led from the deliberative interviews I conducted. Most important of all, it shows how the positive changes in participants' environmental commitment resulting from the deliberative interview were at root the product of a heightened environmental rationality. It argues, in short, that deliberation encourages environmental rationality and that environmental rationality encourages environmental policy commitment. The results discussed in chapter 6 show that deliberative democracy is no pipe dream. Deliberation works, works surprisingly well, and works for just about everyone.

The final chapter offers some suggestions for improving or encouraging democratic deliberation. Deliberation is not an all-or-nothing affair. But if it is to deserve the label "democratic" it must engage all of us. I close by suggesting a number of ways we can expand deliberation's reach, both within the traditional political realm and outside it. But no one should expect me or anyone else to present him with a point-by-point manual that, if followed, will magically democratize deliberation or render democracy more deliberative. If people are at all persuaded by my case, they will see that such a program is not only beside the point but also contradicts the very essence of democratic deliberation—the essence being that all of us must seek out deliberative opportunities wherever we can find them. If we truly believe in deliberative democracy, we must not limit ourselves to someone else's idea of where, when, why, or with whom deliberation ought to occur.

When all the missing details are added, a fuller picture of deliberative democracy and its relationship to environmental protection develops. This picture was both inspired and tested by real citizens, yet it remains a theory. It is still very much a schematic drawing, not a detailed plan of action or blueprint for a new society. No one can say with any confidence just what a truly deliberative democracy will look like in detail, or in just what direction it will choose to go. That will depend on the nature of the deliberative opportunities that citizens create for themselves and on the uses that citizens make of these opportunities. As much as we might like to, we simply cannot forecast either of these very exactly. No single person, however great his or her theoretical insight, can identify all the places that deliberation occurs, much less all the places it might be successfully encouraged. Nor can anyone predict the exact course of citizens' future deliberations. In the environmental realm, for example, I believe that we can gauge its general trajectory. But that is a long way from being able to foretell its destination 20 (or even 5) years from now. Deliberation springs from unpredictable sources and flows to unpredictable places. If we wish to stimulate it, we will need to keep our eyes open and strengthen it where we find it. After that, we need only follow its course. Gravity will do the rest.

2

The Deepest Ecological Question of Them All: Whence Democracy?

> There has been just one really new thing since the Gigantosaurus. That new thing is Man, the first creature in all the immensities of time and space whose evolution is self-directed.
> —Aldo Leopold, "The River of the Mother of God"

For more than 2,000 years, political philosophers have been telling us how to organize our social worlds. However valuable their advice, it is no longer enough, for now the natural world upon which our social worlds depend is in jeopardy. If we ignore the environmental threat in our pursuit of a social utopia, we are sure to land ourselves, and countless other species, in the only utopia ever known to us, which is literally nowhere. Few now doubt this rather obvious fact. Unfortunately, fewer still take it into account when describing the Good Society. Worse still, those who are most aware of it, professional philosophers, tend to forget that their visions of the Good Environment depend quite directly on how society is organized. Hence political philosophy requires environmental philosophy, which in turn requires a political philosophy. The sum total might be called a political philosophy of the environment or an environmental political philosophy or perhaps a cosmosophy. My central goal here is to advance and defend just such a philosophy. It prescribes enriched public deliberation as a political antidote to our interrelated environmental problems. Because it sees in those problems a burgeoning crisis, it recommends widespread and forceful moves to encourage a more thoughtful public.

The theoretical argument I advance here is broadly similar to that advanced by a growing school of political theorists who see political deliberation as the key to a revitalization of liberal politics. But to their reasoned arguments mine adds the voices of a carefully selected group of 46 citizens, recorded over the course of some 240 hours of intensive discussion over a wide range of environmental issues. The central contribution of these citizens was to show that deliberation of the kind I recommend actually works. As will be seen in chapters 5 and 6, for most of my participants deliberation clearly encouraged what I term environmental rationality and, consequently, a more environmental outlook. I witnessed no conversion experiences among this intentionally mixed group of citizens. But more modest forms of learning were so commonplace as to be nearly universal. No one I talked with became fully rational or was absolutely enlightened by the interview experience. But nearly all were *more* rational, *more* enlightened at interview's end. Likewise, as might be expected, some individuals learned more than others. But far more important, from the standpoint of political theory, was that almost everyone learned something from the few hours of deliberation in which I engaged them.

The interviews also provide some rather straightforward explanations about why environmental deliberation worked as well as it did. In the first place, as I show in the next chapter, these Americans perceive the environment as involving not a program to be followed but an issue to be solved, not a platform but a problem. For most people, environmental deliberation is seen as necessary because there are no obvious environmental answers. For most people, the issue of the environment involves a question, not an answer. As chapter 4 explains, the puzzlement over this question is the result of a widely shared constellation of three beliefs: (1) a strong commitment to environmental preservation; (2) the perception that others share that commitment; and (3) the belief that radical political restructuring in the name of environmental ends is either unnecessary, unworkable, or undesirable. The first of these beliefs, of course, gives people an interest in deliberation. The second leads people to believe that deliberation is possible, that others share their basic environmental interests. The third means that deliberation is necessary.

The interviews I conducted thus constitute, primarily, a kind of test of the deliberative hypothesis in recent political theory and, secondarily, an explanation of the positive results I obtained. But why be interested in deliberation at all—especially in the environmental realm? The remainder of this first chapter explains why.

The environmental ethicist who argues for reining in our environmental policy is now an endangered species (if such a species can ever be said to have evolved at all). As I will show in chapter 4, the citizen who takes that position may be fairly labeled a threatened species. The great majority of us really *are* environmentalists, at least in the sense of endorsing an expanded environmental regime. True, there are disagreements about means, even about principles, as we shall see. But there is almost unanimous agreement, among ethicists and citizens alike, that we need to do more. We need more environmental restraint, less human disturbance. With apologies to Marx, we might say that philosophers have described the world in various ways; the point, we have come to recognize, is *to preserve it*. The burning question now, as one of my participants put it, is, "How do you go about it?" The answer, as another concluded, is, "We need to work together." But working together is not so much a guarantee of the right answer as it is the answer itself. The key is not to discover the right theory of environmental protection, but to ensure that society discovers it.

The Philosophical Consensus

Wandering among the trees of environmental philosophy, one has to be impressed by the diversity and vigor of the arguments one encounters over metaethical foundations. Even more than their political counterparts, environmental philosophers are fascinated with ultimate principles, with the search for a stable and definitive starting point for normative inquiry. The disagreements appear to be profound. Callicott's biocentric holism and Passmore's anthropocentric individualism appear to be as different as an oak and an aspen. But one cannot help noticing something else: all these theories are clumped closely together. They constitute a forest, not a random sprinkling of trees. And this forest's most impressive characteristic is neither diversity nor competition but its lush color: green.[1]

Preferring to dwell on the issue of the ultimate source of environmental value, few environmental ethicists have advanced anything remotely resembling a full axiology.[2] That is, the question of how environmental values fit with other values remains largely unexplored. Yet no one seriously argues that we should take environmental values less seriously than we do now. Not all trees are green, of course. But all forests are. The point is even more significant than it is obvious. To my knowledge, no environmental philosopher has ever seriously challenged the view that more environmental restraint is necessary. Economists never agree on what the interest rate should be (or even on the degree to which it should be manipulated). Legal scholars don't assume that more or less judicial activism is a good thing. Nor are political theorists likely to agree that the Good Society requires more or less individual freedom. The big normative questions are fundamentally open in those spheres in a way that they simply are not in environmental philosophy. Pope John Paul II was right when he declared recently,

"Theology, philosophy, and science all speak of a harmonious universe, of a 'cosmos' endowed with its own integrity, its own internal, dynamic balance" (1990; see also Naess 1989: 87).

Citizens' Consensus: More Environmental Policy

In one sense at least, the pope was preaching to the converted. I doubt very much whether any of my respondents would have resisted his message. Clearly most endorsed not just a greater collective effort on behalf of the environment, but also an expansion of environmental *policy*. Coming from a culture historically wary of government, they were confronted with a choice far more difficult than that between collective action and inaction in general. The choice I gave them was not between more and less environmental cooperation, but between more and less *state* environmental action. As difficult as the choice was, most willingly opted for greater governmental intervention in society on behalf of environmental goals, for an expansion in environmental policy. As I show at greater length in chapter 4, this was indicated in two separate ways. First, the immediate responses to both general and specific questions were generally pro-expansion. Second, those responses held up to varied and repeated challenges aimed specifically at undermining the view that any expansion is needed.

Whether responding to general philosophical questions or to quite specific environmental dilemmas, my respondents generally (and often quite strongly) endorsed an expansion of present environmental policy. There was universal agreement on both the need to save the environment and to keep it intact. And not a single individual questioned the legitimacy of state intervention in the environmental realm as a whole. Similarly, in an intentionally varied sample, no one advocated an environmental policy retreat. Only about a quarter were satisfied with the present level of state involvement. Among those, several endorsed the environmental policy status quo, partly out of the paradoxical belief that greater efforts were unnecessary because the government was already acting to solve new environmental problems. Likewise, only 1 in 10 could think of even a single instance in which the government had attempted to do too much in the environmental realm.

Several other, more specific, responses also indicated a consensus on the general direction of environmental policy. First, no one objected to teaching environmental subjects in public schools on the ground that they were too controversial or too "political." Other objections were made, but none on the basis of the view that teaching environmental issues would conflict with anyone else's fundamental values. Second,

even the least environmentalistic of my respondents endorsed a handful of the environmental reforms I suggested, some of which are as
radical as any that have yet been cooked up by theorists. Most respondents argued for many or most of those reforms. The way in which
respondents portrayed the typical anti-environmental position was also
illuminating. In virtually every case, those holding weaker environmental views were seen as lacking any rational foundation, and then
were dismissed as venal or simply selfish. Finally, when asked to sum
up their view of environmental issues at the close of several hours of
discussion, the emphasis was almost universally on maintaining or
improving environmental policy—even among the few who wanted its
growth curbed.

These are all important indices of the public's view. But they take on
far greater significance when one remembers that they withstood virtually constant scrutiny, when one remembers that they held up to
varied and repeated challenges aimed specifically at undermining the
view that any expansion is needed. I challenged participants' value
positions, their political theories, and their facts. Over and over again
I reminded them of the costs that environmental policies entail. Hence,
what resulted were not opinions, at least not in the usual sense. Nor
were they full-blown theories of environmental protection. However,
I can be reasonably sure that the public is convinced of the need, not
just for more environmental cooperation, but also for an activist environmental *policy*. Public opinion may be a moving target, but the
public's convictions are not. For the foreseeable future, their convictions
will favor an expansion in environmental policy.

Democracy and Environment: Friends or Foes?

If philosophers have not yet decided how deeply ecology
should go, they at least agree that we should go more deeply than we
have to date. And the public appears to agree. The real question is:
How? Where that question has been asked, it has usually been put this
way: Would environmental ends be better served by a broader democracy or a narrower one? That question has drawn two radically different
responses. On the one side are those who argue that less democracy
(i.e., less widespread political participation) means more environment
(i.e., greater environmental restraint). Within this group there are two
quite distinct positions. The first advocates a broader role for markets;
the second urges expanding the power of environmental hierarchies.
Implicit in the latter position is the further claim that the resultant environmental gains will more than make up for the consequent loss in

individual autonomy and popular control. On the other side are those who argue that the cause of the environmental crisis is a lack of democracy. From this point of view it follows that the solution to the environmental problems of democracy is more democracy.

As heated as this debate has sometimes been, it has generated but little light. True, advocates of hierarchy and democracy have conclusively demonstrated the inadequacies of the market alternative: environmental decisions must be political. But these advocates have been unable to demonstrate the superiority of their own political solutions. The reason, I will argue, is simple: what counts environmentally is not *who* makes decisions but *how* they are made.

That theoretical conclusion sets the stage for the interview results which are at the heart of my argument. If, as I argue below, environmental decisions must be political, and if they must also be made democratically, then the central environmental issue becomes one of improving people's capacity for making those decisions. Is expanded citizen deliberation the answer? The interview results, as we shall see, show that, if it is not the answer, it is at least the right direction. In order to appreciate that fully, however, we must first know that we are answering the right question. In what sense is democracy the environmental issue par excellence?

Democracy as Environmental Foe I:
The Neoclassical Critique

The neoclassical environmental critique of democracy can be stated in one sentence: markets are the most efficient means of conserving the total stock of scarce resources. The price mechanism is held to be a uniquely efficient means of matching resource availability and consumption, not only because it is able to provide more sensitive information about the status of resource supplies than, say, bureaucracies are capable of providing, but also because it creates constant incentives to use those resources which are most abundant.[3] Even assuming for the moment that all of this is true, markets alone can never produce satisfactory environmental outcomes for one simple reason: they inevitably lead to negative externalities, which must be dealt with politically. It is not that the neoclassical position denies the existence of externalities, or "neighborhood effects." Hayek, for example, readily admits that "the close contiguity of city life invalidates the assumptions underlying any simple division of property rights" (1960: 341). The problem is that, from an environmental point of view, all the world is a city: externalities are not the exception but the rule. The environment is perhaps not perfectly inelastic, but it transmits many more effects across much greater distances than the neoclassical position typically assumes. And the greater our technological prowess, the more likely this becomes. Ecologist Barry Commoner estimates, for example, that while the American economy grew by 126 percent between 1946 and 1970, the total volume of pollution produced in the United States increased by a factor of between 2 and 20. The difference was produced by technological innovation (Commoner in Paehlke 1989: 59; see also Stone 1987: 30–31). Yes, these externalities can, with some difficulty, be internalized in the price structure, but only by political means (Boulding 1966: 14; Freeman et al. 1973, in Baldwin 1985: 94; Porritt 1984: 35). Even if economists were to succeed in integrating all environmental externalities into price schedules by pricing trees, clean air, species, and views of the Grand Canyon, all the affected buyers and sellers would have to agree collectively that those "scientific" calculations are fair or acceptable. Such agreement presupposes an institutional framework; it presupposes politics. Hence, the more markets are expanded, the more environmental externalities are produced and the greater the need for political intervention. Environmentally, markets are in this sense parasitic on politics.

Even if we ignore this fundamental problem, markets fail as an environmental solution. In fact, William Ophuls was closer to the truth when he termed the market an environmental villain (Ophuls 1977: 168). First, and most fundamentally, scarcity almost never prices all consumers out of the market; market-imposed limits on consumption are less than absolute. The market recognizes neither the short-term need for positive bans on consuming "resources" like endangered species and wilderness areas nor the long-term need for an upward limit on overall resource use in order to guarantee sustainability (Ophuls 1977: 43). In short, markets do not recognize that "there is a limit to how much of the ecosphere can be converted into technosphere" (Daly 1976: 243). Another way of putting the same point is to say that markets cannot limit our use of the ecosphere because they are designed to respond to our wants, which are in principle unlimited. In fact, the more efficiently they translate wants, the more of an ecological threat they become. The immediate point is not that it is crass to put Yosemite and the spotted owl, or the environment more generally, up on the auction block. Rather it is that, once sold, there is no guarantee that these purchases will not be used. A related problem is that, because raw materials typically constitute only a small fraction of the finished cost of goods in the marketplace, large price increases produce only disproportionately small conservation gains (William A.

Vogely in Baldwin 1985: 92). As economist Herman Daly has argued, "prices cannot limit aggregate throughput" (1976: 251). Or, to borrow nineteenth-century ecologist George Perkins Marsh's metaphor, the market cannot prevent us from burning up our cottage to keep the home fires blazing (in Ophuls 1977: 13).

At the same time, markets begin to reward conservation only when resources are almost exhausted. Hence, resources necessary even two generations from now have an effective market value of zero. And once resource exhaustion becomes apparent, consumers may attempt to get a jump on anticipated price rises, thus aggravating scarcity still further. Alternatively, they may ignore rising prices because of habit, prior investments, convenience, or the prestige associated with consuming certain nonrenewable resources (Ophuls 1977: 169–170; see also Bartlett 1986: 237). To all of this the advocate of the neoclassical position is likely to reply that it is ludicrous to think we would consume our way to extinction. Consumers, they might argue, are capable of imposing limits on themselves individually. In the end, the neoclassical liberal might object, there is nothing to prevent environmentally minded individuals from demanding—and getting—more and more environmental goods (i.e., goods whose consumption or nonconsumption directly or indirectly benefits the environment). Unfortunately, there is. In fact, there are at least three such barriers.

The first is simply that the purchase of environmental goods normally produces positive externalities. Environmental goods are perhaps the archetypal public good (Ophuls 1977: 148–149). If I insulate my house, your grandchildren will have more oil to heat theirs. If I ride my bike to work, your air stays cleaner. If I donate to the Nature Conservancy, your chances of seeing a scarlet tanager are improved. Although this kind of shared benefit no doubt appeals to many people, to many others it seems unfair. No consumer is alone in the marketplace. Most want not only a good price but a good deal. They want to know that they are getting as much and spending as little as the next person. This is likely to be true even of individuals expressing ethical convictions rather than economic preferences in the marketplace. The concerned environmentalist may believe deeply in a greener world, but it is hard to act on one's convictions in isolation. When everyone else joins in, on the other hand, doing the right thing no longer seems like such a sacrifice. In the end, the more accurate the neoclassical portrait of the calculating consumer, the less likely it becomes that markets will promote environmental ends.

The second systematic bias against market demand for environmental goods is their cost relative to nonenvironmental goods, whether they be raw materials or manufactured products. Renewable resources are inherently more environmentally sound than nonrenewable resources. Now, because the supply of nonrenewable resources is limited, only a long-term decline in demand will keep prices from increasing. But such a decline is at best difficult to foresee and at worst unlikely to materialize. In most cases economic rationality dictates erring on the side of safety by overpurchasing nonrenewables. Environmental profligacy is the result (Robert D. Hamrin in Paehlke 1989: 141, 221). In the case of consumer goods, short-run cost differentials have the same end effect. Hand-crafted, organic, or recycled products are generally more expensive than existing alternatives. Hence even those with the appropriate environmental "preferences" must be willing and able to pay a premium to express them in the marketplace (Bookchin 1989: 22). And the ranks of such consumers are likely to dwindle over time when resource scarcities slow economic growth and market-generated inequalities accumulate.

But let us give the neoclassical position the benefit of all doubts. Assume for the moment that our populace is oblivious to free-riders, ignores uncertainties, *and* has an insatiable demand for all the right environmental goods. Would a free market respond to this demand? Perhaps it would, but only to a very limited extent. Markets are simply incapable of supplying most environmental goods. There is no firm which can supply clear skies and clean tap water, protect endangered species, and limit oil exploration in the Arctic. Many other natural resources are increasingly controlled by either corporate or national monopolies (John Kenneth Galbraith in Baldwin 1985: 92; Sandbach 1980: 212; Wenz 1988: 91). Hence even if we accept Hayek's dictum that "all resource conservation constitutes investment and should be judged by precisely the same criteria as all other investment," we must still have a *collective* method for applying that criterion (Hayek 1960: 374). If social utility warrants producing those goods, a public institution must ensure their provision and distribute the resulting costs. Once again, to use William Ophuls' phrase, "there is no escape from politics" (1977: 161).

Both history and the nature of our contemporary environmental problems confirm this theoretical analysis. Left to themselves, markets have led to one tragedy of the commons after another. Where the environment has been preserved, it has largely been the public's doing, by acting collectively. Markets are responsible for most of the damage; political authority of one kind or another is responsible for most of the repair and preservation. Most of us know this already. We acknowledge it every time we say "environmental protection." That, we think rightly, is a collective aim and a collective task. Unrestrained markets have left a train of environmental disasters in their wake; politics has repeatedly been called upon to clean them up. As we have grown wiser, we have begun to call upon politics to avert environmental disasters before they arise. And we have been right to do so. Political authority, whether exercised by government or "private" associations, has averted some environmental disasters and cleaned up many others.

American environmental history is simultaneously an indictment of unrestrained markets and a vindication of the power of collective action. Americans are now, and always have been, more environmentally committed when acting together than when acting alone. Acting individually, Americans pushed the bison to the brink of extinction; acting collectively, we not only brought it back but also preserved a part of its original range. Acting individually, we now threaten 500 further species; acting collectively, we have offered these species some degree of protection and have saved a number of others. Acting individually, Americans came, saw, and tamed some 96 percent of this country's land mass; acting collectively, we set aside the rest as wilderness. Acting individually, we drove atmospheric lead to toxic levels; acting collectively, we have eliminated lead from the air entirely. Acting individually, Americans are the world's most prodigious consumers; acting collectively, Americans have been enthusiastic supporters of environmental protection and perhaps the world's most enthusiastic environmental activists. And the examples could go on. In truth, this list, juxtaposing instances of market-induced environmental havoc and collective success in protecting the environment, can be lengthened almost indefinitely (Hays 1987; Fox 1985; Nash 1989; Hargrove 1983; Wyant 1982; Wisenhunt 1974; Ekirch 1963).

Of course, one is free to say, as true believers often do, that markets have not really been given a fair chance to show what they can do. To that I say, what's fair? Are we simply to gamble our air, water, scenery, wildlife, and wilderness on a theory? Not unless that theory—a theory that we have seen is radically flawed—can muster some awfully convincing empirical evidence in its support. We cannot compare the environment produced by a future devoid of political authority, on the one hand, with an environment produced by a future devoid of markets, on the other. That would be impossible because, obviously, such a future hasn't arrived yet. All we can do is compare our more market-oriented past with our more politically oriented present. And, when we do, it won't take us long to see that the neoclassical view is at least as flawed in practice as it is in theory.

My position, then, is that increasing our reliance on market solutions to environmental problems is an obvious invitation to ecological disaster. Markets ignore the huge negative externalities associated with pollution. They respect neither wilderness nor species nor the ozone layer. And they necessarily put profitability ahead of sustainability. Markets systematically overproduce material goods and systematically underproduce environmental goods. From an environmental point of view, it is less accurate to speak of market failures than of the failure *of* the market. And that is true even if judged according to neoclassical criteria alone. An auction system exists for relatively few environmental goods. Fewer still are exclusionary. Still fewer escape monopoly control. And of those that are left, how many produce neither positive nor negative externalities? It seems clear that it is not enough to challenge the conclusion that markets have become maladaptive, perhaps threatening. At a very minimum, we can say that the interconnectedness of the biophysical world has doomed *Homo economicus* to extinction. The preservation of the environment—on which our self-preservation ultimately depends—requires that we abandon the cooperation of the private contract for that of public decisions. Evolutionary history has yet to produce an irony so profound: our species' ability to live *with* nature turns out to depend quite directly upon that human characteristic which most sets us apart *from* nature: our capacity to modify social behaviors consciously. There are but two fundamentally differing views in regard to how this might best be accomplished.

Democracy as Environmental Foe II: The Neo-Hobbesian Critique

The first of the two views on modifying social behaviors, as the neo-Hobbesian label suggests, stresses centralized power. It rejects both markets and democracy as inadequate or positively inimical to environmental ends. Only a more hierarchical organization of society, it is argued, can adequately preserve the environment. The neo-Hobbesian case is thus built around two central claims. The first is that hierarchy is either inherently environmentalistic or can be made so. The second is that the resulting environmental gains will be worth the cost in individual freedom on the one hand and individual autonomy on the other.[4] In the end, because the first claim fails, the second becomes moot.

The neo-Hobbesians are the original authors of much of the environmental critique of markets reviewed in the preceding section. But they take aim at democracy, as well. Democracy is held to be inherently anti-environmental because it moves slowly, moves blindly, fragments decisions, and favors the short-term over the long. Others claim simply that popular values are insufficiently environmental and so must be corrected by those more sensitive to them. Hierarchies, it is agreed, can be made immune from all these defects.

The first proposition in the neo-Hobbesian critique is that democratic processes prevent timely environmental action. As Joseph Petulla puts it: "The history of environmental regulation is the evolution of a cumbersome, federal-state-local vehicle of overlapping jurisdictions, conflicting goals and political imbroglios. . . . ." Moreover, Petulla goes on, "environmental legislation seems to be enacted only as crises occur . . ." (1987: 6, 49; see also Ophuls 1977: 120). It is a classic complaint: the more we talk, the less we are aware of what needs to be done and the less still that we actually accomplish. This critique of democracy has always bothered me intensely because it mistakes speed for efficiency, doing for doing well. And in the environmental arena, this equation is especially dubious. Many environmental effects are seen only long after the causes that produced them have ceased operating. Bioaccumulation of toxic chemicals and the depletion of the ozone are but two examples of this phenomenon. Many others simply cannot be predicted ahead of time because of the interconnectedness of ecological systems. Very often, then, environmental wisdom depends on patience, not speed.

But patience alone is of no avail, a neo-Hobbesian might object. If wisdom is to be of any real use, it must be coupled with action. And here, surely, hierarchies have the edge. The army cannot tell us when to fight, but once hostilities ensue, an efficient chain of command is certainly an asset. Or is it? Ironically, the history of modern warfare itself suggests otherwise. The more mobile warfare has become, whether in the jungles of Southeast Asia or on the sands of Iraq, the greater the premium on reconnaissance and the initiative of individual combatants. Meanwhile, organizational theorists and political economists alike have for some time argued that where the decision-making milieu is characterized by either endemic change or highly variable circumstances, hierarchies tend to be less efficient because they are slow learners (Douglas and Wildavsky 1982: 100, 126, 196–198; Hage and Clignet 1982; Reich 1983; Piore and Sabel 1984). Hence, whether one sees environmental degradation as a highly mobile enemy or views the environment as a dynamic, complex system, one is led to the conclusion that the efficiency of environmental policy often has an *inverse* relationship with the degree of hierarchy involved in making and enforcing it (see Porritt 1984: 88–89).

Second, neo-Hobbesians claim that democracy is (at least presently) at odds with the technical expertise that is a necessary ingredient in enlightened environmental decisions (Ophuls 1977: 162; see also Greenwood 1989: 273). But this proposition surely exaggerates the importance of technical expertise in environmental policy making. Technical expertise is no guarantee of positive environmental outcomes. As Robert Dahl has argued recently, "No intellectually defensible claim can be made that policy elites (actual or putative) possess superior moral knowledge or more specifically superior knowledge of what constitutes the public good. Indeed, we have some reason for thinking that specialization, which is the very ground for the influence of policy elites, may itself impair their capacity for moral judgment. Likewise, precisely because the knowledge of the policy elites is specialized, their expert knowledge ordinarily provides too narrow a base for the instrumental judgments that an intelligent policy would require" (1989: 337, see also 68–69). In addition, Dahl points out, most "complex matters," such as environmental policy, involve significant elements of uncertainty and judgments about the acceptability of risks and trade-offs. On such matters, he concludes, "we have scant reason for trusting ourselves to policy elites" (1989: 338; see also Lindblom 1990: 10–11, 221, 247–248; Spragens 1990: 202, 215; Porritt 1984: 89).

But that is not all. Although it must be admitted that the technical capabilities of hierarchies will generally be superior to those that enter into democratic processes, that is clearly not always the case. The technical advantages of hierarchies are a direct function of scale and complexity. Granted, most environmental problems are both large in scale and very complex. But simple problems, whatever their scope, are as easily handled by democratic structures as by hierarchical ones. And the expertise that democratic processes can bring to bear on purely local problems will almost always exceed the expertise available to hierarchies because what counts in local problems is in-depth knowledge of a reduced geographical area (see OECD 1988: 229; see also Fox 1971). What is more, unless markets are eliminated entirely, the present tendency for environmental administrators to rely on producer groups for technical information will continue to prejudice their objectivity (Chubb 1983).

Third, it is claimed that democracies tend to work against a synoptic or holistic view of environmental problems (Petulla 1987: 10, 174, 184; Brenner 1973; Ophuls 1977: 191–195). According to Walter Truett Anderson, "the whole style of American politics is non-ecological" because of its "fix on single issues" (in Paehlke 1989: 211). The problem with this argument is that, although pluralist democracies probably do tend toward incremental decision-making (Braybrooke and Lindblom 1963), a fairly extensive body of literature shows that hierarchies seem constitutionally incapable of anything else. In fact, the more hierarchical an organization, the more overriding its concern with self-preservation, the narrower its view of problems and potential solutions, and the more incrementally it tends to move (Douglas and Wildavsky 1982: 126, 93; Lindblom 1990: 251–255; see also Fox 1971).

Fourth, there is the claim that democracies are short sighted. Political competition, just as surely as market competition, leads inevitably to the overexploitation of resources. Disjointed incrementalism, for its part, achieves short term adjustment only at the cost of long-term stability (Ophuls 1977: 192). Again, however, it is hard to show, either theoretically or empirically, that hierarchies possess any great advantage on this score (Douglas and Wildavsky 1982: 100, 126). Finally, it is sometimes claimed, or at least implied, that the American public is just not environmental enough, that the environment must be put in the hands of those who can be counted on to protect it. This is simply an environmental version of the ancient complaint that the demos is insufficiently enlightened to manage its own affairs. Petulla's main complaint with democracy, as we have seen, is that it tends to produce partial solutions when it produces solutions at all. But the principal remedy he proposes—a professional class of environmental managers whose task will be to integrate the environmental "interests" of corporations, environmental groups, and the public as a whole—belies his belief that professionals are worthier of our environmental trust than our fellow citizens are because, if that were not true, it would make little sense to suggest that their power be enhanced (Petulla 1987: 127ff., see also Heilbroner 1974).

However, such trust is clearly misplaced. In the first place, it is hard to imagine the values of such a hierarchy ever advancing very far beyond those of the elected officials to whom it would ultimately be responsible. If one envisions a structure like the Federal Reserve Board or the Supreme Court or even a fourth branch of government, one must still describe how it is to be staffed. No one has yet provided a blueprint for an academy that would graduate only committed environmentalists. In the second place, as Weber observed early in this century (and Allison and others have reminded us since), hierarchies generally tend to value their own survival at least as much as, if not more than, the substantive ends they were designed to serve: "Throughout the world policy elites are famous for the ease with which they advance their own narrow bureaucratic, institutional, organizational, or group interests in the name of the public good. The freer they are from public scrutiny and public judgment, it seems, the more likely they are to be corrupted—not necessarily in a venal way—by the familiar temptations of power" (Dahl 1989: 338; see also Douglas and Wildavsky 1982: 91ff.). Hence it is not only difficult to show—even theoretically—how an environmental technocracy can be made more prudent than the public: it is next to impossible to show how such a group could be kept from being corrupted. The neo-Hobbesian response cannot (as at least one of its advocates concedes) answer the old question: Who guards the guardians? (Ophuls 1977: 161; see also Paehlke 1989: 174–176; Dahl 1989: 26, 76).

On the other side of the coin we have a public that, as I show in chapters 4 and 5, is both committed to greater environmental restraint and, if not "enlightened," very clearly capable of (and even takes a certain delight in) reasoning about environmental dilemmas. Environmental elitists thus both exaggerate the potential environmental rationality of a class of environmental managers and underestimate the public's present environmental rationality. Still more damaging to elitists' case, they fail even to consider the public's *potential* environmental rationality. The argument for an environmental elite requires more than an empirical demonstration (now lacking) that a "rationality gap" exists (Cotgrove 1982). It requires that we accept that gap as inevitable or unbridgeable. But we have precious little reason to do so. Human history may not be the record of Reason making itself manifest in the world, but it certainly shows that human reason is restless. Rapid evolution (some would say revolution) has marked Americans' environmental rationality in the postwar period (Nash 1989). There seems little reason to think that this process will cease or even slow down. Indeed, as chapter 6 shows, given the right opportunities, citizens themselves can accelerate it: in deliberating about environmental dilemmas, they can and actually do become more environmentally rational.

Two final theoretical criticisms of the neo-Hobbesian position apply to all five of the above arguments. The first is that any major shift to a more hierarchical organization of environmental decision-making is likely to require mass participation (Barnet in Paehlke 1989: 75). The second is that even after they are firmly ensconced, hierarchies are ultimately constrained by the public's values (see chapter 3). As Petulla himself recognizes: "When public support wavers, environmental action and research flounders" (1987: 173). No hierarchy can function without authority. True, one can attempt to manufacture consent. But that is neither ethically acceptable nor likely to be very successful, especially in a culture in which a historical distrust of political authority has more recently threatened to harden into out-and-out cynicism. Unless one assumes a kind of environmental coup d'état, the public will continue to exercise considerable leeway in the implementation of environmental policy. Hence the environmental buck ultimately stops there, not in the civil service or even in the Oval Office.

Given these many theoretical shortcomings, it is little wonder that the historical record is so unkind to the neo-Hobbesian case. It is probably no coincidence that the greatest environmental villain of all time is the socialist bureaucracy responsible for the environmental devastation of Eastern Europe and much of the former Soviet Union.[5] "The lack of any public accountability for polluting, notably in the form of independent environmental groups, meant that production-happy planners had a heyday" (French 1990a: 6; see also McLaughlin 1990; Fox 1971). The results were widespread and almost uniformly damaging. According to one summary, "there is good reason to speak of the formation of an *united front of ecological degradation between Scandinavia and the Black Sea* (Wolfson 1992: 63, emphasis in original). One Soviet ecologist recently observed that glasnost and perestroika, on the other hand, have meant "more possibilities, and more and more people are involved in this political process to influence the bureaucracy to do something to solve Soviet environmental problems. It's a new trend in our country; before this, everything was governed from above" (*IES News*, July 1989: 2). Dr. Bedrich Moldan, Czechoslovakia's first noncommunist environmental minister, echoed that view upon assuming office: "I'm optimistic because I believe that the first prerequisite for really solving our ecological problems is true democracy. Without public participation—without an educated and engaged public—you cannot do anything" (*Sierra*, May/June 1990: 40). On this side of the Atlantic, the Canadian government's unenviable environmental record has been at least partly a function of closed decision-making processes (Schrecker in Paehlke 1989: 176). And our own federal bureaucracy hardly exemplifies the environmental guardianship envisioned by the neo-Hobbesians. More often than not it has been moved to action only at the urging of an anxious public (Joppke 1990; Hays 1987).

The neo-Hobbesian view thus fails on two counts: it grossly exaggerates both the environmental threat posed by democracy and the environmental promise of hierarchy. And, even if its portrayal of the two political forms were accurate, it would still be unable to tell us how much democracy we are to give up in the name of environmental hierarchy.

Democracy as Environmental Friend:
Small Is Sustainable

Rejecting both market and hierarchical solutions, the third position looks to participatory democracy as the ultimate answer to environmental problems. Bioregionalists, social and deep ecologists, Greens, and advocates of "appropriate technology" would all agree that Small is Sustainable (to broaden E. F. Schumacher's dictum, "Small is Beautiful"). If there is a single political theme that unites radical environmental theorists, it is that participation is good for the environment. Participatory environmentalists generally argue not only that democratic participation is good in and of itself, but also that it offers the best hope for the environment. I will dwell only on the latter claim, for there is little new in the defense of participation per se. Although I believe one must in the end reject the case for participatory environmentalism, it contains some profound (if partial) truths. I emphasize this at the outset because the participatory position has often been misrepresented as a kind of sophomoric nostalgia for a bucolic past that was long lost even when Rousseau pined about it. One ought not dismiss the participatory case so lightly.

Participatory environmentalists' first claim is that smaller political-economic units are environmentally efficient. They can be more labor intensive, can rely more heavily on renewable inputs, and, because final usage takes place closer to the source of production, they are able to minimize transportation costs (Tokar 1987: 27, 112; Sale 1985: 69; Sandbach 1980: 183; Morris 1989; Bookchin [1969] 1986: 8). The point at first seems inarguable. And in some cases local usage could easily be built into productive systems. Energy is one such area (Commoner 1976; Lovins 1977; Lawrence Solomon in Paehlke 1989: 81; Baldwin 1985: 120). Agriculture may be another (Daly and Cobb 1990). But the more general claim stands only if one also assumes that a market *between localities* does not replace the market between firms and individuals that was left behind. And history suggests that this would be difficult, if not impossible, to resist. One need only recall the history of the Italian Renaissance or the Hanseatic League: towns, no less than individuals, seem to have a propensity to "truck and barter." Moreover, were one to impose such a regime in any but the most incremental fashion, wholesale dislocations would result (see Dahl 1989: 47, 302). The people in Madison or Billings might get by. But where would Detroit grow the wheat for its Wonderbread? How would the Nebraska corn farmer repair his Ford? The criticism can be widened. Participatory environmentalists often seem to ignore their own ontological commitments when it comes to thinking about society and politics. If "everything is interrelated," humans are most so: economically, culturally, politically, and socially. To achieve a world of small communities will require ripping apart this complex, and in many ways quite valuable, web of relationships.[6]

Discipline and transition problems aside, there are a host of good ecological reasons to be suspicious of radical political decentralization. At its most extreme, political decentralization can mean granting local political units a large measure of control over the local economy. Hence the slogan, Local production for local use. But to succeed, such a program would almost certainly require some degree of *geographical* decentralization. Cities cannot support their own basic needs; they depend on the surrounding countryside. But spreading the population out might well lead to a general rise in per capita resource use (Paehlke 1989: 245–250). And it would most certainly consume vast amounts of one especially critical resource—land. Open land is important not only for food production but also for wilderness, wildlife habitat, and recreation. In addition, the benefits to be gained by diluting low-level pollutants would probably be more than offset by the increased difficulty of recycling inorganic wastes and processing toxic chemicals (Sandbach 1980: 192; Paehlke 1989: 245–250). Hence "local production for local use" may occasionally make sense. But it is doubly utopian, and would come at a cost in open space and other resources that many, probably most, environmentalists would consider unacceptable (see Paehlke 1989: 99).

Participatory environmentalists' psychology is weak on another score. They claim that self-interest dictates that localities protect their own surroundings. This is true enough. People, as Aristotle noted long ago, do tend to take care of their own. Although Aristotle had private property in mind, the same may be fairly said of environmental stewardship: "Despite the increasingly transient nature of today's human populations, people still have a vested interest in the town or township in which they pay property taxes, and in the county or regional municipality in which many decisions about waste management and land use are made" (Alexander 1990: 164). And there is at least some research to support this intuition. An early Environmental Protection Agency study showed that, indeed, local units of government, once encouraged to be involved in environmental management, tend to develop a strong sense of environmental responsibility (Baldwin 1985: 279). But won't that same self-interest lead communities to ignore their neighbors? As the Yugoslavian experience showed, "In a decentralized economic order, whether socially owned or not, interests are likely to attach themselves to a particular enterprise or economic sector rather than to some abstract notion of a general good" (Dahl 1989: 303). Hence localism only displaces the so-called tragedy of the commons to a larger commons. The tragedy is prevented *within* communities only to recur with a vengeance *between* communities. The rise and tremendous growth of the so-called NIMBY (Not In My Back Yard) movement only underscores this obvious theoretical point.[7]

Surprisingly, participatory environmentalists' appreciation of this problem is no greater than that of the neoclassical economists they criticize. Although they certainly recognize the problem, they grossly underestimate how profound and pervasive it would be in a decentralized society (see, for example, Capra and Spretnak 1984: 221). Local production for local consumption is somehow supposed to alleviate this problem (Porritt 1984: 136). As a result, although they are willing to admit that localities would have to be linked *"confederally"* (Bookchin [1969] 1986: 10, emphasis in original) or through some kind of "network" (Sale 1985: 50), participatory environmentalists suggest that these links could be loose, ad hoc, or even "entirely voluntary" (Tokar 1987: 98). But that is most certainly not the case. Are neighboring communities less likely to dump on each other than firms and individuals? It hardly seems so. In fact, 2.5 millennia of Western history (beginning with classical Greece and including even the Roman Empire) suggest that they are *more* likely to do so (Hansen 1991: 57, 116, 189, 269; Starr 1982; Dahl 1989: 23, 229–230, 302, 318–319, 322). Modern social psychology only reinforces that view (Billig 1982). In fact, our hard wiring may even guarantee such a result. As Sale himself notes, the first law of evolutionary ecology is the survival of the fittest *community* (Sale 1985: 82). The same logic, then, undermines both libertarian and communal decentralization. The more decisions are left to the market, the more negative externalities must be internalized by some collective authority. From an environmental point of view, the more society is decentralized, the more it requires hierarchy. Or, to dispense with the paradox, environmental protection will always require some degree of hierarchy.

A third argument on behalf of participatory environmentalism is that localities are closer to Earth than organizational entities that have broader jurisdictions. This is held to lend them a distinct advantage over higher levels of government in monitoring the environment (Ophuls 1977: 38; Tokar 1987: 29; Porritt 1984: 50–65). No one is in a better position, we are told, to gauge the nature and extent of emerging problems and the impact of attempted solutions than those who actually live with them (Sale 1985: 50–65). Once again the intuitive appeal of this claim fades upon closer scrutiny. The environment consists of relationships, not points on a map. Looked at ecologically, the local environment extends across the state, nation, continent, and, finally, the globe. True, local residents are in the best position to monitor their own impact on their own local environment. But the more isolated they become, the less they will know about how their community affects and is affected by other communities. And, even if they are capable of monitoring those effects, they are powerless to do anything about them.

Participatory environmentalists' final argument is their most provocative: local control is environmentally educative. Not only does participation strengthen individuals' commitment to the environment; it also tends to take the place of environmentally harmful activities like mindless consumption (Paehlke 1989; Tokar 1987: 148; Bookchin 1991: chapter 12; Bookchin [1969] 1986: 4; Bookchin 1987: 71; Devall and Sessions 1985: 169, 197; Naess 1989: 63, 97, 135–137, 142–143, 205; al Kouri 1990). The first part of this claim, that consumption will yield to social interaction, is neither logically necessary nor psychologically compelling. Logically, one's level of consumption is not limited by the number of hours one spends in meetings. As it now stands, in fact, just the opposite is true of Western democracies, where political participation is positively correlated with consumption (as measured by socioeconomic status [Verba et al. 1978]). Psychologically, we ought not to expect much therapeutic relief from political participation. To begin with, there is the almost universal phenomenon just cited: the biggest participators are also the biggest consumers. Clearly participation in existing democracies hasn't curbed consumption. But even in a radically decentralized society it is unlikely that the predicted change would occur. To begin with, let's remember that politics can be as dissatisfying as it is satisfying. For many people, politics is not only dissatisfying but also distasteful. Some people are political animals. Many others are not. For the latter, participation is likely to produce anxiety, stress, even shame. Other people are indifferent to politics: it's simply a bore. Then there are those who temporarily have other priorities: like caring for a sick relative, falling in love, or fixing the carburetor. For people in these situations, obligatory participation is likely to produce resentment or outright anger. Anxiety, boredom, resentment—these need not lead to a shopping binge, but they are not likely to prevent one either.

This leaves us with one final claim on behalf of participatory environmentalism: namely, that participation strengthens individuals' ethical commitment to the environment. Unfortunately, it is here that this school is shortest on specifics (see Ophuls 1977: 223). Bookchin perhaps comes closest to a theory of participatory environmental education in an early piece where he claims, "A relatively self-sufficient community, visibly dependent on its environment for the means of life, would gain a new respect for the organic inter-relationships that sustain it" ([1964] 1988: 17). But notice that this theory is based on the questionable assumption of self-sufficiency. Bookchin has also argued that the advent of communal politics will put an end to human exploitation and with it environmental exploitation (Bookchin [1969] 1986: 4; Bookchin 1987: 71).

But how and why this is to occur is never spelled out. That is a pity, because it is to these very questions that we most need answers. Still, it is unlikely that the vision of small-town democracies advanced in outline form by Bookchin and others fares any better on this point than it did on the others. This is because the educative potential of face-to-face meetings is radically diminished, if not eliminated altogether, wherever they involve clear conflicts of interest. Adversarial situations cannot always be transcended. But face-to-face democracy tends to aggravate differences rather than ameliorate them (Mansbridge 1983; see also Dahl 1989: 20–21). The two sides wall themselves off in an effort at psychological self-defense until, in the end, they are not unlike the inmates in a prisoners' dilemma. Reasoned discourse fails; the opposing sides no longer communicate at all. If the community is operating by majority rule, the minority will simply not be heard. If decision-making is by consensus, the minority will be heard, but no action will be taken. The result in either case is, if not positively disastrous as it occasionally was in ancient Greece (Ophuls 1977: 228), certainly less than optimal, less rational than had mutual deliberation continued. This brings us to the final section.

Democracy: Deliberation, Not Participation

Neither market nor hierarchy nor participatory democracy, then, can alone deliver the good environment. Adequate environmental protection, or "environmental rationality" (as I call it in chapter 6), entails restraint. None of these pure forms can guarantee that. To the extent that they are environmental, markets are parasitical on the other two forms. That is, markets presuppose collectively established parameters or a governance structure. Meanwhile, unless reined in by a higher authority, town meetings will simply provide repeat performances of the tragedy of the commons. (The same, incidentally, can be said of nongovernmental or "spontaneous" forms of social cooperation [Ostrom 1990], which are susceptible to functional, rather than territorial, parochialism.) And unless that larger authority is itself reined in, it will do the environment little good. Clearly some mix of the three forms is called for (see also Douglas and Wildavsky 1982: 185, 196–198). And our present environmental regime is just such a mix. But is it the best we can do? I think not. However, improvements depend less on altering the proportions of the mix than on improving the quality of the ingredients. Since both markets and hierarchies are relatively inert, we need to focus on the quality of the democratic element. What we need, in short, is not *more* democracy but *better* democracy.

What kind of democracy is most likely to overcome the environmental defects of the three pure institutional forms just considered? Recall that markets fail environmentally because they are atomistic and have a limited temporal perspective. Hierarchies are neither responsive nor responsible. And pure democracy suffers from a limited spatial perspective and an inability to deal with conflict. Can any form of democracy hope to remedy all these shortcomings simultaneously? No. But one type is likely to come closest: a representative democracy which systematically encourages its citizens to deliberate actively about environmental issues. If this is true, our first environmental priority must be to expand democratic deliberation, not participation.

I explained just what I mean by "democratic deliberation" in a conceptual or theoretical sense, in the last chapter; I shall return to it in chapter 6 (see especially pp. 163-165). And what such a conclusion might imply in the way of reforming the concrete world of the here-and-now, I suggest in chapter 7. Still, my own advocacy of democratic deliberation is inseparable from the specific definition I give the term, so it is important at each step to be clear about how I understand that phrase. Recall from chapter 1 that "democratic deliberation" means "the process by which citizens actively justify or defend their political views, *no matter where this process occurs.*" I emphasize the latter part of the definition to remind the reader that this conscious process can (and most often does) occur in private. Likewise, spurring democratic deliberation involves encouraging citizens to deliberate about public matters even when they do not find themselves literally in public.

Now, to return to the issue of organizational structure, it seems clear that representation is still the best available answer to the defects of local participation, whether economic or political. In a representative system, parochialism is self-defeating. And conflicts of interest are diluted. Historically, representative democracies have at least partly succeeded in containing violent conflict between competing localities ("the chronic disease of city-states") through universal legal systems (Dahl 1989: 318). In the process, a space is opened up for continued deliberation on the one hand, and public paralysis is avoided on the other. Representative democracy also recognizes that distance can be a help to deliberation as well as a hindrance. The answer to the prisoners' dilemma is communication. But it may not always be enough to put prisoners in the same cell. They may simply refuse to speak to one another. Representative democracy offers an alternative solution to the problem: let the prisoners speak to each other through their lawyers. Even if they are unable to resolve the conflict, nothing will have been lost in the process.

Representative democracy also entails collective decision-making, the chief failure of markets. It is likewise responsible in a way hierarchies cannot be. This is a distinct advantage. We can reasonably assume that the public is (and will stay) environmentalistic for the foreseeable future. Public convictions are the ultimate environmental guarantee in a representative democracy (Spragens 1990: 169). No such guarantee applies to environmental hierarchies. As Weber noted long ago, even benign hierarchies tend to confuse means with ends; they almost inevitably come to see their own continued existence (and expansion) as their chief function. The organization becomes more important than the task it was created to accomplish (see Douglas and Wildavsky 1982). Moreover, even if hierarchies could be counted on to promote environmental ends first, it is unlikely that they could do so as efficiently as more democratic structures. That sounds paradoxical. Hierarchies have for a long time been nearly synonymous with efficiency. But a more sophisticated understanding of efficiency shows it to be a function of organizational *fittedness* to the task at hand. In sectors characterized by rapid change, complexity, and customization, cooperative organization tends to be superior. One has to ask, Is making environmental policy more like stamping out microcircuits, or more like designing computer systems?

From an environmental point of view, then, representative democracy is absolutely indispensable. The institutional framework best suited to environmental decision-making is thus already largely in place. What needs to be changed is the way that framework is used. It must be guided by a more collective, holistic, and long-term view. My central thesis is that the best way to encourage such a view systematically is *to expand citizens' opportunities to deliberate actively about environmental issues*. If expanded deliberation does encourage such a perspective, as I argue in chapter 6, it will not only vastly improve the rationality and responsiveness of our environmental institutions; it will also help minimize environmental conflicts. Consequently, the environmental promise of democratic deliberation is immense. In what follows, my participants make clear that this promise is far from being empty.

3

Americans in Search of Environmental Protection

> Who can *disagree* with the things that various . . . I don't know, Isaac Walton League, you know, whatever some of those ones are . . . Who can disagree with what they're *for*? The problem arises as to how do you get there? How do you get there from *here*? How do you go about it?
>
> —developer Jim Needham

As we will see in the next chapter, the environmental policy norms of the citizens I interviewed were decidedly, but not decisively, progressive; their progressivism, strong as it was, was almost never programmatic, much less polemic or dogmatic. Like Jim Needham,* virtually all were both convinced that something must be done about the environment and unsure just what that something might be. Only a handful believed that they (or anyone else) had the answers. Almost everyone I talked with argued that American environmentalism ought to evolve, yet very few could tell me how. At the same time, they were usually willing to take time to puzzle through policy dilemmas—by soliciting information, by acknowledging suggestions, and by responding to alternative points of view. These Americans wanted answers to our environmental problems. They were not offering ready-made solutions, much less environmental platforms or programs. While not particularly surprising, that finding provides crucial support for my contention that expanding citizens' opportunities to deliberate about environmental protection is our best hope for speeding the evolution of American environmentalism, because it strongly suggests that most Americans are ready and willing to make active use of these opportunities. People don't deliberate when they

---

* The reader should be aware that, in order to protect their privacy, I have used pseudonyms in place of my respondents' names here and throughout what follows.

51

already have a workable answer; they deliberate when they have a problem. And that is precisely how this group of citizens defined the environment.

The Environment: Problem, Not Program

Neither historians nor sociologists have been particularly successful in describing, much less explaining, Americans' environmental policy beliefs. This can be explained partly as a result of their exclusive focus on one or another side of what is, by definition, a "compound" norm, made up of both an environmental norm and a political norm.[1] It is also a problem of methodology: the use of preestablished categories and quantitative explanations tends to displace close attention to what and how people actually think. Consider historian Roderick Nash's thesis that the new environmentalism is just the next stage in Americans' continuing extension of rights (1989).[2] Despite the ostensibly political concept he employs, he fails to explain which rights Americans are willing to cede to nature. At the same time, the notion of rights hardly fails to capture either the number (38) or complexity of the reasons my participants employed in justifying their environmental policy beliefs (see chapter 5). Likewise, that variation and complexity flies in the face of both structuralist arguments that environmentalism can be reduced to attitudes toward risk[3] and historical views that it is rooted in such "new values" as beauty, health, and permanence.[4]

As we shall see later on, most scholars have simply failed to appreciate the tremendous complexity of Americans' environmental policy thinking. More important still is the fact that the scholars have failed to appreciate that Americans themselves perceive their own thinking that way. At least among the citizens I interviewed, who spanned the range from ardent Green to wealthy developer, the environment represents not a new value or even set of values, not an abstract philosophy or ideology, not an ensemble of policy imperatives, but a societal dilemma. If there had been one statement to which all 46 of my participants would have agreed, it would have been something like: We have to *do* something about the environment. What "we," "something," and "the environment" meant to each, of course, would have varied tremendously, but the larger point remains: for these citizens, often for very different reasons, the environment represents first and foremost a dilemma, an issue, a predicament. And that inference is not merely a global impression, subject to the vagaries of the interviewer's memory or wishful thinking. Regardless of how I interpreted the interview results, the conclusion to which I was led was invariably the same: for most of us, the environment signifies less a program than a problem.

The Environment as Problematic

How did participants frame environmental policy, that subset of political action, when they began the interview? The short answer is that, if one counts spontaneous generalizations alone, more than half of the 46 suggested that some kind of answer is needed in regard to environmental policy or that we need to be working toward solutions. Of the remaining 20 participants, 6 were selected specifically because of their active involvement in environmental groups, 2 were developers, and 1 was a crop duster. Thus, of those without a predictably explicit orientation, approximately two-thirds approached environmental policy with more questions than answers. As can be seen below, expressions of uncertainty spanned a spectrum running from the argument that there are rarely any yes/no answers to environmental questions (or that environmental problems have to be dealt with on a case-by-case basis) to admissions that the environment poses a tough question, which was answered with a resigned, "I just don't know."

I asked Michael Cerutti, a middle-aged letter carrier and an environmental progressive, how he thought we ought to solve the solid waste problem, which he had identified as one of the two most significant environmental issues at the local level:

> As much as I hate it and think it's a pain in the neck, I think we got to do it: recycling. We're doing it—at a small level. But I think if everyone does it, it all adds up. And again, that's got to be done slowly. You can't stuff it down people's throats. People got to learn themselves how to do this, and they've got to be shown what they do is helping. . . . Most people will cooperate.

William Noone, a town planner, when asked if it would make sense to impose a complete ban on developing wetlands within his planning area, replied:

> It's not a yes-or-no answer. But if I had to answer yes or no, I would say no. . . . I think you have to look at the total needs of the community and how those needs can be satisfied. Looking at the impacts of different alternatives to satisfying those needs, certainly there is an environmental impact in utilizing floodplains and wetlands. But there is also an environmental impact in not using them. And you have to make a judgment on which impacts affect the community the greatest.

How do you assess which are greatest, and what the environmental impact from not developing might be?

That depends on what you're trying to satisfy.

Glen Thorne, environmental affairs officer at a regional utility, argued that the criteria to be employed in deciding whether to develop a given wetland are "clear and obvious" and that decisions ought to be, and generally are, made by consensus. But when asked where he would draw the line on developing wetlands, he continued, "Drawing the line is only possible on a case-by-case basis. I think you just have to study and decide."

Elizabeth Naess, a middle-aged, suburban homemaker who was often impatient with my probing and later complained that the interview "took longer than necessary," nevertheless admitted in a kind of backhanded way that she didn't have all the answers. The substantive portion of the interview began with the question, What are the most important environmental issues in this area? Her response: "The most immediate, I expect, is getting a decent landfill and teaching people how to go about dealing with a landfill." A bit further on in the interview, I asked Naess why her community had such a problem with solid waste. Her answer:

People are trying to sell things, and we get more and more packaging, and we've gotten more and more chemicals. It's just a matter of evolution.

Do you see any ready solution? If you were to solve the problem, how would you do it? Or maybe you don't have a ready answer to the problem.

Oh, we could do a lot better with packaging. We could package things in paper. . . . That's a start. It's a hard problem because no matter where you put the landfill, it's in somebody's back yard, and you can't put them close to water. . . .

Frederick Lorenz, an upper-level administrator for the state of Wisconsin, and among the most thoughtful and politically astute individuals I met during the course of my interviewing, also cited solid waste as a major local problem. His solution:

Recycle nonferrous metal (such as this beer can). Secondly, you pull glass out of the trash. Thirdly, incinerate garbage where a secondary benefit (electrical energy) can be obtained from it—while using scrubbers to make sure there is no loss in air quality. None of these is too much to ask of people. I honestly think that we're headed in the right direction. Are we there yet? No. Will we ever be there? No. We got to keep working at it.

That all sounds definite enough. But a few minutes later I asked him about developing wetlands. His answer was one he would repeat often during our discussions.

I don't know. I don't know an answer to that.
Perhaps, if it were roads that were to be built, they could be raised on piers?
OK, on piers the effect on the wetlands is going to be minimal.
But aren't the aesthetics ruined?
That's a valid complaint. As is true with most activities, one has to look at the greatest good. . . .
But then how do you determine what the greatest good is in that instance?
I'm glad you asked that question, because the answer to that is something for which we have an absolutely *marvelous* structure in place in this country. It's called a democratic republic. Whether it's at the state level or at the federal level, every two years, if the folks think that the people who are in leadership positions are not representing us appropriately, we can throw the rascals out. And that is just neater than hell.
So in the case where there's no absolute answer, you just have to let the people decide?
Yes. This is not an issue I would go to the stake for, as I might the doctrine of the Trinity.

Louise Fredericks, an office manager at a large insurance firm, cited agricultural chemicals as the most important local environmental problem. I asked her how she thought they ought to be dealt with:

Regulate it. Well, ban it would be better.
So we do that, say. We're not going to grow as much food, are we?
I think that's debatable, but I could be wrong.
So then the price will go up. That's OK?
Not really. That's OK for me, but it probably isn't OK for a lot of people that can't afford to buy food right now, anyway.
So then we have to have some kind of income transfers to these people, right?
[sighs] I guess we'd have to have some kind of income transfer.
But that wouldn't solve the problem of rising food prices for everyone. Basically our standard of living would be lowered.
Yes. Maybe it's the whole economic situation that's messing us up. It won't be solved. Human nature will never solve the economic situation. It just goes through cycles.

Does that mean that we just give up?

No. We have to keep trying. Definitely we have to keep trying. We can't give up.

Betsy Schon, a middle-aged home-care provider and a religious fundamentalist who "loves" living in a small house amidst western Wisconsin's rolling hills, cited wildlife loss and water pollution as the two most important environmental problems in her area. When I asked how she thought they ought to be resolved, she replied simply: "I don't know. But they should *definitely* be addressed."

Schon's anxiety was echoed across the state in Milwaukee's inner city by Deena Champney. Concerned with radon, acid rain, the ozone layer, and salt run-off, she too expressed a kind of unfocused resolve: "I don't know. If they can stop smokers in planes . . . I don't have all the answers. I have a lot of questions. My *answers* might be wrong."

The kind of uncertainty expressed in the above passages was not, as I noted in the case of Frederick Lorenz, limited to those who were relatively unaware, unconcerned, or unsophisticated. Tim Behringer, to pick but one example, was none of these things. The grandson of a forester, an avid outdoorsman who described duck-hunting as "something like a religion" to him, and a biologist well-schooled in environmental sciences, he was perhaps my single most careful participant. Every question was examined from several angles, the conflicting values weighed carefully, and the various solutions tested mentally. Yet Behringer consistently expressed dissatisfaction with his own solutions, deferring ultimately to the wisdom of his neighbors. On the question of wetlands, one would have expected Behringer to have enunciated a clear and forceful position. He had, he told me, expended a great deal of energy in fund-raising efforts for Ducks Unlimited with the aim of purchasing new wetland areas. After considering several sides of the issue of development versus wetlands, he concluded with a statement that was to become the hallmark of our discussion: "I think a lot of these things are frankly settled very well by consensus once, you know, all the proposals are looked at." This is certainly a principled kind of uncertainty or self-doubt, one that brings to mind Aristotle's epistemological metaphor of the superiority of the feast attended by many guests. But it is uncertainty, nevertheless.

I later asked participants point-blank to characterize their environmental beliefs in a general way. Taken as a whole, their responses only reinforce the message contained in the passages just quoted. Despite the fact that these questions followed directly upon our having sorted through 19 specific environmental policy dilemmas, only eight participants (four of whom were environmental activists) went so far as to suggest a clear program of action. The rest were either unsure or exceedingly vague about what should be done, or mentioned no plan or policy changes whatsoever.[5]

The relevant questions in this section were four:

1. The word "environment" means a lot of different things to different people. When *you* hear the word "environment," what do you think of?
2. What is your general orientation toward environmental issues?
3. How much environmental protection do *you* think is enough? In which kind of situations do we need to protect the environment and when is it OK to use it however we want? Why?
4. What *kind* of environment should we strive to achieve and maintain?

Although open-ended in form, surely these questions amounted to an invitation to set forth an environmental agenda, or at least to announce one. That so few of my participants accepted that invitation must therefore mean that such an agenda simply does not exist for most people. The range of responses illustrated below is thus in one respect far more striking than those just cited, all of which were drawn from discussions focused on finding answers. Here the range runs from the uncertain to the vague to those who claimed to have no answer—and then beyond, to those who had not yet begun to consider answers. For them, the environment represents a problem, and little else.

Betty Mikels is a vivacious, energetic woman approaching middle age, enthusiastic about having recently begun a second career in real estate, and long active in the Republican party. She placed herself (quite accurately, as it turned out) "right in the middle" on environmental issues. When I asked how far environmental protection ought to go, she replied:

> I don't know. I would say in areas that have not been tapped yet for obtaining some of our natural resources (like oil or mining or whatever), areas that have not been touched yet, I think there should be real tight controls to protect the environment. I don't know. I guess as far as the existing situations are concerned . . . If there are enough controls on it, forcing the companies and everything to be aware of air pollution and everything . . . I guess I don't know. It's kind of a hard question.

If the environment was perfect, what would it be like?

Ideal? I don't know, I don't know. You'd have green trees and clean air and no algae in the lakes and . . . I don't know.

Let me try asking the question a different way. What are we trying to accomplish with environmental protection, anyway?

Just protecting the earth, I think. Just protecting the earth. Everybody thinks the earth is going to . . . When is the end of the earth? Let me see now. That was supposed to be last week. [both laugh]

So we should be protecting the earth. But what does that mean?

Well, now with our space program we've been to the moon. And now we're shooting out further. What is our next objective? Mars? They've taken pictures of Mars and the other planets and everything. It seems pretty apparent so far that Earth is the only planet that has human beings on it. So therefore . . . I don't know. I guess you have to take care of your planet, or where are we going to go?

The uncertainty Louise Fredericks expressed in the passage above resurfaced again when it came time to generalize about our discussions:

Concerned, but not knowing what to do. Kind of at a loss. Kind of needing someone to give me direction. I've got a lot of ideas, but I don't know exactly what to do—not so much individually, but overall—about now society can deal with it, though no one really knows exactly where we're at and what's going to happen. I don't think there's anything exact. We could have some direction from some central agency like an environmental Federal Reserve Board. No one's in charge, and everyone's looking out for their own little piece of it. I don't know if that's the answer or not. A lot of people are putting out a lot of information, but I'm not sure anyone's coordinating anything.

We need a quarterback?

Yeah! Maybe that's what I'll do with my life. I'll be a quarterback . . .

How much environmental protection do you think is enough?

No, no, no. I can't make that decision. I don't feel like I know enough. I know *some*, but I don't think that I know enough to say how much is enough.

Carol Chapman, a young corporate lawyer and mother, resident of an affluent Milwaukee suburb, answered the same question this way:

I think of problems. I think of all things living, actually. So I think of the Earth as a whole; not beyond Earth. My general attitude is open, worried, and willing to try. Does that sound like a Boy Scout, or something? . . . On each little segregated resource or issue that you want to talk about, it seems like there are very far-reaching consequences and you're going to have a hard time getting people to stomach some of the changes, but I think an awareness of the problem and a movement toward solving them is what we need.

Michael Cerutti, the letter carrier, would probably have agreed:

When I think of the environment I think of my surroundings, whatever it may be—air, land, water, our roads, our parks. My general attitude is that, now that I'm being aware, I want to be aware of my own personal responsibilities to help with these problems, whether it's in the daily use of products like insecticides, or whatever. . . . How much environmental protection is enough? I think we should get an inroad into it and not go all out, 100 percent. We have to give time for people to digest all of this and form opinions. If we go all out, 100 percent, it will be difficult to get cooperation. [*mildly sarcastic*] Yeah, let's go back to the days of the Indians, OK. When everything was OK, everything was balanced, nobody was disturbing anything. Let's go back to the early days. [*more seriously*] The perfect environment? That's really hypothetical. We can't really go back. All we can do is put the brakes on and say, "Hey! Stop! Look what's happening!" and control it from there.

Erik Johannsen, a young engineering student nearing graduation, described his general attitude to environmental issues this way : "I like to think of myself as open-minded, pretty progressive but not . . . I don't mind seeing slower change if it means the right change. I don't believe in every time a problem comes up making a superradical change right on the spot. I don't think that works. I'm definitely not shutting it out, though. I *am* concerned."

Don Wilson is an affable, talkative man, still "learning how to be retired" after a varied career as a civil engineer, much of it spent in his local Department of Public Works. Despite his obvious expertise on such issues as solid waste disposal, insecticide use, and road maintenance, philosophically he is no technocrat. On the contrary, like his counterpart William Noone, the town planner, he repeatedly deferred to a higher authority, especially when the questions moved to the abstract plane:

> *How much environmental protection do you think is enough?*
> These are all relative issues and depend upon what the people will accept. There are always limits on what you can do—like budgetary limits—and there are always exceptions. I think we'll continue to make improvements.
> *How far should things be improved?*
> That'll be up to the people through their representatives. It almost gets to the point of what they can convince their representatives to spend. I mean, improvements are there.
> *And what people say goes? There's no ideal environment we should be aiming at?*
> I've given up on that. [*laughs*] I think we are. I think we are. Really I think we're trying to continue to achieve . . . I don't know the definition of ideals. I mean, I don't find any negatives. I'm saying, on a personal basis you have pluses and minuses, but the trend is plus, the curve is up. There'll be glitches. There's always glitches. God forbid, if we have a depression, you know, I mean, this might slow down improvements. I don't think it'll stop them. And I don't think it'll make anything so that you say, "We're going to use landfills again." That'll never come. I mean, it'll just be held in abeyance. It won't go up. But I don't think anyone's going to go back.

Joe Page, a self-described jack-of-all-trades who led a group of local property owners in a bitter and ultimately unsuccessful environmental fight, saw the interview at least partly as a way to tell his own tale of mushy-headed environmentalists, corrupt politicians, and arrogant bureaucrats. But for all his impassioned government-bashing and rough libertarianism, he ended up rejecting only 1 of the 19 policy reforms I suggested. And when I asked him how much environmental protection he thought was enough, he mused:

> I just wonder how many rules are already there. I really don't know that. I think there's a lot of rules but, as happens in a lot of cases, they're not enforced. You can make all the rules you want, but I'm just thinking that maybe we ought to look and see if they're there and if they're being enforced. I don't know. We've got an Environmental Protection Agency, right? I don't know what their budget is or anything, or *exactly* what their job is. I guess I could answer that question better if I knew a little more about that. I really don't know.

Val Gotti was without question my most enthusiastic participant. Frustrated at first with her own inability to answer my questions, she soon caught on to the idea that the interview offered her a chance to test out her ideas, try on new perspectives, and get answers to at least some of the seemingly endless questions she had. After actively thinking through the 19 different policy proposals I offered, she summed up her overall environmental perspective this way:

> It depends on each little thing that we're talking about. Some I would agree with; some things I may not. I guess it depends on each little issue. Otherwise, if I don't hear anything about it, I don't really think a whole lot about it.
> *Is there anything that is shared across all of the issues that sort of ties them together or that's common to them?*
> That I'm basically worried of what's going to happen in the future around us. And I'm worried . . . It all ties in with . . . Yeah, I'm worried about the animals because they're being extinct by other things that are making them, so it all ties in together, I think.
> *So the thread that ties all of them together is that you're worried about the future, or no?*
> In a way. I'm not worried about the future, but I guess I worry about it for my kids: I want them to be able to do things in the wilderness.

At age 94, Adela Hill, a "La Follette Democrat" with a history of activity in the farmers' cooperative movement of the early part of this century, frankly admitted that she found many of the individual policy questions we discussed unfathomable. At one point she asked me, "What if we knock down the rain forests? Will it still rain?" Little wonder she described her overall view of environmental problems in such plaintive terms: "Do what we can when we got a chance at it. But what can we do?"

Even those who approached the environment with a program for change in hand occasionally expressed uncertainty and sometimes confessed that their knowledge was simply too limited to answer the questions I posed. Paul Zalens, a young, third-generation dairy farmer active in the sustainable agriculture movement, provides the best illustration of how, even for the most committed, the environment remains a rich source of political puzzles. Zalens earned a degree from his state university in biology during the Vietnam era, has read many of the environmental gurus from Barry Commoner to Herman Daly, and has long been active in local politics. He told me that he loves farming, his land, his cows. But spend five minutes with him and you will also learn that he loves to philosophize. The second time I drove up to his farm I found him out in the barn, tending to his cows. He wanted to show me his manure storage system, an integral part of his efforts to recycle resources on the farm. Gazing down on this not inconsiderable mass of nutrient, it wasn't three minutes before Zalens had turned the conversation to Einstein, quantum mechanics, and chaos theory. Less distracted in his living room, he spontaneously spelled out his own answer to the environmental crisis. Among the elements of Zalens' program: progressive taxation within and between countries; future-oriented, increasingly democratic regulation of new technologies; environmental pricing for all resources (with the aim of equalizing per capita resource use on a global basis); and increased political participation. He concluded by arguing:

> I'm more convinced all the time. I think I've said this to you—
> that we find in sustainable agriculture that peer group pressure
> has as big an impact on why people farm the way they do as the
> economics. That is, that your social context is reinforcing. I think
> the same thing is going to be true for addressing the larger frame-
> work of environmental concerns, and especially the idea of over-
> consumption. I think we have to start developing almost a religion
> of environmentalism—a religion that's premised on the idea of
> that little phrase or that little idea I just articulated to you, and
> that is a more equitable distribution of the world's resources. To
> me, if we're going to win that battle, it's going to have to deal
> with the social context.
>
> *Yeah. And how does that come about?*
>
> We need a new religion in the world. Religions have always
> attempted to address fundamental basic needs that people have.
> It seems to me that increasingly the environmental context of the
> world becomes, is obviously growing in, people's concerns. . . .
>
> *Can it be legislated?*
>
> No, no. That's how it's distinctly different from the other
> approaches. We need a new religion predicated on environmen-
> talism or environmental limits. You know, really, if you look at
> other religions people have belonged to or are belonging to, are
> part of today, you know, they've always been predicated on, you
> know, things like treating your neighbor decently, respect for
> other people and other things. What I am thinking of is a sense
> of collective well-being, and so on. And it seems to me that
> some of those same ideas would be very relevant to a religion of
> environmental sustainability.

Zalens was a clear exception to the rule. He had lots of answers. But like many others, he wasn't particularly wed to those he offered. In a way not very different from those I quoted on the preceding pages, he was willing to settle for *movement*. When I asked him, finally, how much environmental protection is enough, he pondered for a while and then argued:

> You know, I don't know that that would be very difficult to do, I mean, you know. Look at lots of Europe. People have very good housing. They have a high quality of life, yet they don't have individual homes. So, maybe a minimal level is that people have decent housing but not necessarily individual homes. But even that's a huge undertaking in the world. Something with food also, it seems to me. Our goal should be to make every country's agriculture as sustainable as possible, and supplement that with imports from other countries. I think there's enough room to start working in those directions without rigidly defining the endpoints at this point in time. It's a big enough arena to start working on the project without knowing exactly where the end of the project is.

Awareness of Specific Dilemmas

To focus only on participants' general comments on environmental issues, as I have thus far, would still be to understate the degree to which uncertainty characterized their thinking. Only six participants were not hesitant, ambivalent, or confused on at least one issue (four of these were active environmentalists, one a generally progressive developer, and one a crop duster). It would be only a slight exaggeration to say that no one I talked to was perfectly sure of her or his responses on all 19 policy proposals.

The most straightforward indicator of this kind of issue-specific uncertainty was the number of participants (10) who declined to say yea or nay on all 19 of the policy dilemmas that constituted the first portion of each interview. Even after having a chance to work out solutions with me, only 10 individuals gave positive answers to all 19 questions, half of the 10 being environmental activists. Similarly, on only 1 of the 19 questions (regarding a tax increase to fund pollution abatement) did all 46 participants give a clear answer one way or the other. The greatest ambiguity surrounded the issue of expanding environmental education: 10 participants declined to declare themselves either in favor of or opposed to such a policy change.

Far more revealing than this crude measure of participants' indecision, however, was the manner in which they came to decisions they did make. To begin with, fully two-thirds of the group said at one time or another during the interview that they would need to know more in order to be able to judge the question at hand reasonably. Often this occurred repeatedly during the course of the same interview.

Carol Chapman was extreme only in the frequency with which drew attention to her own lack of knowledge. On virtually every policy issue she said at least once: "I don't know how prevalent the problem is"; "I don't know what existing regulations are"; "That's a tough issue"; or simply "I don't know enough about it." Don Wilson, too, felt many of my questions required knowledge he just didn't have. When I asked him about town planning, he expressed sympathy for the concept of greenbelts, but finally concluded: "I think some of these things . . . *You're* the professor!"

Even those who were most confident at the general level were often the most uncertain when it came to specifics. Donna Scheda in many ways fit the stereotype of the radical environmentalist: she was idealistic, impassioned, and thoroughgoing in her rejection of the status quo. And, yes, she thought tree-hugging is a great idea. But no one who listened to her talk could mistake her concern for hysteria. More so than any of my other participants, she looked at the interview as a chance to discuss environmental issues, not hold forth on her own views.

I started the interview by asking her age and ethnic background, which she told me. But then she quickly asked, "Is it OK if I ask you questions, too?" When I said yes, many other of her questions followed.

With or without reason, most participants were more confident in their own knowledge than Donna Scheda was. But in working out their positions most asked for clarifications, further information, or some other kind of help on at least a couple occasions. Other participants admitted they needed to know more about environmental issues in general. Betty Mikels, the real estate agent, was one. Interestingly, her admission comes in the midst of an argument against environmental technocracy. Note, too, that it leads her to a position broadly receptive to the kind of deliberative solution I defend in chapter 6.

> *Would it make sense to let those who know most about the environment, say, ecologists, policy experts, and administrators, have more power to deal with our environmental problems?*
>
> I don't know if we should give them more power or not, but I think since they are the quote experts unquote, they should be filtering more information back to the average person, you know, or what the average person can do to help the situation. And I think most people are pretty cooperative and everything, and I

think a lot of times people don't conserve energy or anything simply because they don't realize what a savings it would be— you know, I mean how if everybody turned their thermostat down one degree, for example.

So you mean like public service announcements on TV, newspaper things, whatever?

Sure. Educate the public. I think that's, you know, because most of us, we know just about enough about the environment according to what we read in the paper, or according to what we hear on the news. And other than that, we don't get that directly involved, you know. So I think educating the public on, you know, what the average person can do to help the environment . . . I think that's a start. That's where it has to start—right there.

Several other participants insisted that no one really had the final answers to environmental dilemmas. When I asked Fred Mechler, a sharp and assertive union officer, what he would be willing to give up to achieve an environmental utopia, he responded:

Well, I am willing to make the sacrifice to recycle everything that you know is recyclable. And you're definitely going to have to pay some of that cost. I personally don't think I damage the environment when I go out into it in most cases. I don't leave things laying in the woods. I don't pollute the river. I think those that do or whatever should be prosecuted to the extent that it has to be. Other than that, you know, it is a hard question to say what will you do. [If] somebody's going to say, "This is what needs to be done. Will you help?" then in most cases, yes, I would. It's hard to say *what* you are going to do because I don't think anyone knows what they have to do.

When I asked Erik Johannsen, the engineering student, for example, whether he thought centralization might be an antidote to our environmental ills, his initial reaction was to argue for strengthened local monitoring efforts within the context of a federal system. But then he quickly asked me for my own opinion. I replied with a précis of the debate described in the first chapter. His reaction:

That's interesting because, you know, it just seems that these groups . . . You know, there's a place for these groups. I mean, there definitely is; I am not against that at all. But it just seems like they've got an ideal world, you know, and it's ideal. And, OK, let's implement their changes right now. What are going to be the consequences of those changes right now? You know, you just don't do it; it just doesn't happen. And it seems like they want to change everything, you know. And they want to change *everything* now. And you know, it's just going to happen, and it's going to be a perfect world. Well, nothing is a perfect world. I mean, let's deal with what we have right now. Let's change what needs to be changed right now.

These passages really only begin to scratch the surface. The 240 hours of interview recordings are shot through with expressions of puzzlement over the environment, vague affirmations, and various combinations of the two. Only five individuals seemed sure of themselves throughout, three of them environmental activists. A few samples from the often equally vocal majority follow:

Frank Hauser, conservative dairy farmer, on whether government ever goes too far in protecting the environment:

Yeah. I think they are. They're going in the right direction. If I'd said that they weren't doing enough . . . I think there's more to be done, but they are working on it. And if you recognize that there's a problem, you've got half of it solved already. They have recognized that there's a problem. You can't do it overnight and if you try to do too much at one time you'll go way overboard. And then all of a sudden you got all of these people working on something and they've got, they've gone overboard, they're just going to go too far.

Summing up his perspective, Michael Cerutti, the letter carrier, closed the interview with this final statement:

I know some of these questions you're asking me are very confusing to me, and I'm answering on the left side and the right side. But there's no simple answer. All I know is that we have to conserve, right? Everybody knows that. But I think until we get away from the idea of . . . I think money is a big thing in this whole doggone issue. Making the money. Until we get away from the making of money, money the number one priority, and face the reality that there's other things more important. You know, when I was a kid, money was important, but believe me, we didn't have much and we were happier. That's why, I guess. . . . I just remember what it was. And I remember how happy we were. We didn't have as much, OK; we had the medical and all that other stuff. But we were happy. Nowadays I got much, much more (and I am speaking of my individual past) and I don't know if I am any happier.

Jay Little, a hard-working, self-employed auto mechanic who, in a suit, one might easily confuse with someone who had done stints at both the Heritage Foundation and the Brookings Institution, said:

> We've got to get the Congress, or a law would have to be instated. I don't know. It'd have to be . . . You'd need a law to be made. And if we're talking about, like I said, the first part not costing a lot but just looking for results, then that . . . that's a very feasible way to handle it. It wouldn't take a chunk out of anybody's pocket, really. Not for a while, anyway. You know, those things got to roll a long way. But to take the initial action, I think, is the biggest step. Because, you know, that'll go for any of these things we're talking about. But once you get going on it, you know, tend to stay with it, you know? The hardest part of the job is starting it.

Don Wilson, the recently retired civil engineer, closed our discussion with this summation:

> I think American government, by and large, is pretty responsive. With all of the pros and cons and what we have in the pushes and pulls, at least judging it from other areas that I read about (the Eastern Bloc countries, even Europe), I think that we certainly are not behind anybody with regard to the realistic approach to improve the environment. And, I think it's . . . What our challenge is is trying to bring this out to other areas. But, of course, there are other issues involved: economics and social, political. But, I think we're very . . . Government tends to be not only theoretical; I think that pressure has been exerted on government to do things, and I think government has responded—maybe reluctantly at first. Usually it's always an economic reluctance. You know, "We'd love to do it, but . . . " But once they have responded, they've not reneged, and I don't think we're in a position now of public approval. The public will not let the government renege anymore. It can only go up. I don't think . . . They may stand still, but never again will they go down. So I tend to be rather optimistic.

Judith Sanders, middle-aged accountant and administrator of a Milwaukee community center, on the importance of long-range thinking about solutions to solid waste problems, said:

> I'm willing to spend money on the future because it is going to affect me sooner than people think.
> *Yeah? What gives you that idea? I mean, why do you think that?*

I don't know. Just a thought. Nothing, no . . .
No concrete data?
No, no concrete data, just . . .
Can you think of anything that has especially impressed you, or started you thinking that that was the case?
On what?
On recycling—that it may affect you sooner than a lot of people would think.
I don't know. It's like there's just this little mouse or little something in me that says we just cannot continue throwing everything away.

When I asked her at the close of the interview if she'd changed her mind about anything we'd discussed, she replied: "I don't know if I've changed my mind in any way, but you've given me a lot of things to think about. You brought up a lot of things that I basically hadn't even thought about."

When asked if there were any conflicts between her social and environmental ideals, Betty Mikels responded:

I'm sure you're going to run into a conflict with that sometimes, like with the use of our lakes: people want to use the lakes but yet they abuse it, or . . . I don't know. So I think that sometimes there would be a conflict on that.
Can you think of any general solution to such conflicts?
I don't know. I don't know.

Jack Schmidt, a middle-aged dairy farmer whose greatest ambition in life was to render part of his farm forever untillable so that it could remain a haven for the "3–4–500 redwing blackbirds, 30–50 pheasants, 50–200 meadowlarks, 30–40 crows," and assorted other wildlife that now occupy it, wrote me these lines in response to a short follow-up questionnaire:

I think you were quite objective, and I would assume you took a particular view in some attempt to get me to think (not easy). It raised some tough questions on the environment. I remember it as a pleasant chat with many issues raised that I had no answer for. . . .

Why the Environment Is Viewed as Posing a Problem: A General Answer

In chapter 4 I will show that this cross-section of the American public was environmentally progressive, and solidly so. The above passages show rather clearly just how apt the term is, for it describes *how* these individuals held their environmental beliefs at least as well as it describes the content of their beliefs. This group believed strongly in a better environment and believed that collective action, through the government in particular, had a clear role in bringing it about. But the group was far from sure about just what, if anything, ought to be sacrificed to achieve that end. Nor was it very certain about what, precisely, government's environmental role ought to be. In other words, the uncertainty, confusion, and vagueness that characterized the vast majority of the interviews I conducted had two rather obvious cognitive sources: (1) the difficulty of the *value dilemmas* involved in most environmental issues, and (2) the difficulty many Americans find in thinking in explicitly *political* terms.

Value Dilemmas

Awareness of Value Conflict

When people told me, as they so often did, that environmental issues pose tough questions, often what they meant was not that these issues are complex or require trained expertise (as I note in the next chapter, almost three out of four participants argued *against* an environmental technocracy). They meant, rather, that environmental issues often pose choices between important values or complexes of values.[6] In chapter 5 I list the 38 different values this group found in nature, sometimes alone but far more often in combination. Most respondents were sensitive to the fact that protecting these values sometimes requires compromising other strongly held values: economic efficiency, economic security, personal freedom, or local autonomy. In fact, only 12 out of 46 consistently denied that this was so.[7] For this group, environmental and social ideals either posed no inherent conflict or could be reconciled through advances in technology. For the rest, however, the two ideals at least occasionally clashed. Some illustrations follow:

Fred Mechler, the union officer, said of wetlands protection:

> Personally, I'm against banning *all* use. I think it should be . . . Anytime they're going to use it, it should be looked over, but I don't think somebody should be able to just be able to tell somebody else what to do with their land. I've always resented that.
> *Well, what should they look for, then?*
> How it affects the rest of the area. If somebody says that I own a farm, or whatever, and I shouldn't be able to develop that farm because they want to come look at the birds and the bees and the whatever, it's none of their business, in my opinion. If it would

have an impact on where the floodwater goes, or whatever, then I think there should be.

So you don't see any sort of absolute kind of value in wetlands that would make them completely off-limits to development?

No, no. I'm an avid duck hunter, and I can't, you know . . . Wetlands in certain areas, yes, but wetlands that have a community impact—I'm willing to weigh that.

OK. How big does the community impact have to be before it's OK to develop it in some way?

Well, I wouldn't like to see the whole marsh developed, but I would like to see portions of it developed because of the lack of industrial land available. Jobs are important. Don't make much difference who's going to go out and look at this environmental land if you don't have any people around.

I have already quoted Betty Mikels' admission that she didn't have any general answer to the value conflicts posed by environmental issues. But she had no trouble identifying what for her was the central dilemma: "We want enough controls; but we don't want to become a Gestapo."

Tim Behringer, the duck hunter, cast the dilemma as one of economy versus environment in arguing for expanded environmental (policy) education in public schools:

Students get taught that nature is nice and that smokestacks belching black smoke are bad. But I don't think . . . I don't think that most people realize that they've got a big stake in that smokestack still running and in . . . in that muskrat swimming in the marsh. They've got a stake in both of them. It's real easy to say: "I like muskrats; I don't like smokestacks."

Frederick Lorenz declared that social and environmental ideals "absolutely conflict, of course they do." He argued, for example, that managing the Mississippi River is at root a matter of balancing commercial, recreational, and wildlife needs: "What we need to find is the via media"—a phrase that became a refrain over the course of our discussions. When I asked him if anything had especially influenced the way he thought about government's role in environmental protection, he replied:

Marx. Karl Marx. Sure, because at times I have this gut disgust about what I see, and feel that perhaps draconian steps were necessary to make things happen in an appropriate fashion. But thereafter, upon more learned and mature reflection, I see that we'd certainly be losing much more than we'd be gaining if we employed such tactics. . . . What these environmentalists have in mind is more on the order of shooting the tsar.

Louise Fredericks began the interview complaining about paper mills. I asked her if she thought the jobs they provided were unimportant: "I know, this is it. What are we going to do? We're in a Catch-22, I think. [*theatrically*] I think we're just doomed."

Even among the most ardent environmentalists there was a willingness to admit that the realization of their vision would entail certain sacrifices. In fact, this was clearly true of three of the six participants that I have classified as radicals. Carmen Wiley, a working mother who assists Hispanics looking for employment, exclaimed early in our first session that "we have to get hysterical" about environmental problems. She willingly acknowledged, in the case of recycling, that "it's work" and "we must make the sacrifice." Lynda Evans, active in a campus Greens group and now studying to be a public interest lawyer, argued that economic and environmental health can go hand-in-hand, that "we *can* have both." Yet she had begun the interview by observing that dealing with the environmental crisis "will take a lot of money." Even Paul Zalens, the most "ideological" of all my participants, who characterized the relationship between social and environmental ideals as "mutually supporting," said he could accept environmental trade-offs for products that are "really needed."

Avoidance of Value Trade-offs

In the opinion of the vast majority, environmental policy issues pose tough questions. This is thought to be so because people recognize that these issues often involve balancing opposing values, finding a way to minimize the conflicts between them, or a tragic choice in which something of value must be given up.

Balancing competing values was a relatively common strategy invoked by the participants to deal with value conflicts. But how this is to occur was never spelled out very clearly. Bob Kovalek, a dairy farmer who had been among the most active proponents of the preservation plan Joe Page had so strenuously resisted, called the meeting of social and environmental ideals a head-on collision. His solution:

It's like the scale they use to weigh cattle when you take them down to sell them. You have to balance both sides.
How?
The scales are *never* balanced. If one side is too low, you add weight to the other side.

Carol Chapman, the corporate lawyer and mother who had repeatedly pleaded lack of knowledge during the early portion of the interview, would have agreed with Kovalek:

I guess it comes down to deciding at any given point in time how high a priority certain environmental issues are going to have as opposed to . . . I mean, if 10 years from now we seem to have moved along further in our poverty problem, but our environmental issue is either not being addressed at all or we're not progressing as far as we can, we'll have to keep shifting emphasis. I think it's a gradual thing and a shifting of funds and a shifting of emphasis on various levels of decision-making. There might be, 20 years from now, other major issues that we have to, you know . . . They'll have to take a higher role. It's a good thing we have environmentalists, because they'll keep promoting environmental issues, and there are other people . . . And so we'll have . . . Everyone's being heard. . . . I mean, I would think that everyone you talk to says that, yeah, I want to see environmental concerns addressed, but there are so many other huge issues that go into a lot of the individual decisions that we're making that it's not a clear-cut case of "Well, here's the decision that needs to be made: let's favor the environment."
Which means that there is a lot of confusion surrounding the issue at all times.
Yeah. My feeling, I guess, is that better confusion to some extent now than apathy or lack of knowledge to create that confusion. I don't think that the confusion is ever necessarily going to be erased. I think we're always going to be doing something that's going to have some cost to the environment. I don't see any solution in sight. I see people maybe adapting a little bit better and companies maybe changing their priorities a little bit, but I don't see us solving the problem.

Elizabeth Naess, suburban homemaker, birdwatcher, and hiker, put it this way while discussing her view of land use planning:

We compromise on everything in life.
How should we make those trade-offs?
You weigh all sides of it and then compromise. I wouldn't say one's right and one's wrong until I looked at all sides of it. I'm just trying to be fair, that's all. You want what's best for the community, and you want what's best for the people who live there, and you want what's best for the environment.

Can that be done all at once?
Sure, sure.
We never have to inevitably trade off one thing against another?
No. Not completely.
So some trade-offs might be necessary?
Yeah, right.

Judith Sanders provided another typical example of this when I confronted her with the choice among jobs and tax revenues and increased pollution in her town:

We have Stephens' Graphics out there where I live, which added lots of jobs. . . . If it would add to the air and water pollution? I wouldn't want it.
Even if it increased the tax base?
Our taxes are atrocious and we do need help. So that's really a tough question. But I would imagine it would impose some kind of restrictions on the kind of pollution they could put out.
Sure.
I think they're pretty strict, pretty stringent.
So let them in; it won't be so bad?
I'm talking in circles. I'm not being consistent here.
In the end, would you be for or against it? I haven't specified all the parameters, but how would you go about making your decision?
If they cut the pollution down, I'd let them in.
How low would it have to be?
It would have to be below standards.
Then it would be OK?
Yeah—it would have to be below.
And how much would your town have to gain?
Jobs *are* important. If it could be brought within safe limits, OK.

Later I asked Sanders if she thought value conflicts underlay any other environmental issues, and she added:

. . . Of course, there's a lot of housing in the inner cities that could be totally redone and totally rebuilt. You've got to have the housing to put them into, and that, in turn, could affect the environment. It could take space, it could make pollution, it could have an adverse effect, yeah.
So how do we resolve those problems?
. . . See what you can do about coming to a happy medium, if that's possible.

> *Can you tell me how, in general terms, we ought to strike that balance?*
>
> No, I can't.

Even more frequent than such theories of balancing were attempts simply to delay making choices about value dilemmas. Over and over again, and by 29 of my 46 participants (including half of my environmental radicals), the hope was expressed that the future would bring better answers to our environmental problems. Sometimes hope was pinned on technological innovation or advances in environmental science. Far more often, though, it was a strong belief in a continuing attitudinal change that eased the cognitive pressure to arrive at definite answers. Perhaps the single most recurrent argument in the interviews as a whole was this one: I don't know how to resolve this dilemma, but I need not resolve it completely because, as a society, we are all getting wiser.

Elizabeth Naess rejected the proposed limit on economic growth. When I repeated the usual argument about the necessary link- between economic growth, resource depletion, and pollution, she replied:

> Well, I just don't go along with that.
> *Why not?*
> Why not, why not . . . No, but you know it's one of these . . . Well, I really feel that we live in a world that we . . . make adjustments. And we'll continue to make adjustments. We're evolving.
> *We're that smart?*
> Somebody is! Maybe I'm not, maybe you're not, but there will be somebody else who is. I'm an optimist.

I had this exchange with Karen Brunson, who was consistently conservative in her outlook on morals, politics, and the environment. She explained how we ought to resolve conflicts between economic and environmental ends:

> . . . I think the pendulum swings back and forth according to how . . . what the greatest need is perceived.
> *Well, is it appropriate for the pendulum to swing back and forth like that, or is there one mix that is best?*
> No, I think sometimes you do have to have those swings to . . . Yeah. Everybody has to have their day. And I think the pendulum swinging back and forth does give everybody an opportunity to get their licks in. It sort of balances out in the end.
> *Yeah. What if the pendulum started going all one way or all the other way?*

I don't think it would.

But what if it did?

Well, if it did then we'd darn well better get upset and tell the right people about it, and, you know, then we'll have to use the legislative process to do something about it. You can always elect new senators or representatives and state officials and so on if you don't like what's going on.

Personally, how do you think the mix should be made? I guess this goes back to the same old question, but . . .

Well, I think I told you before, it was like, I'd like not to see things get any worse. I'd like to see us maintain the status quo with regard to the quality of the environment around us. And I believe that we should try and maintain the status quo. And if something is going to drastically affect the environment negatively, then I think we'd better . . .

What if that starts costing us in terms of economic growth?

Well, there's that pendulum again. You can sacrifice a certain amount of growth until you've found a better way to do something, or a cleaner way to do something. And you may have to. You maybe aren't going to have so much money to spend on capital improvements or expansion or that kind of thing. But, sometimes, you know, those things gotta suffer, too.

What if it seems like that's happening for five years running? What if growth is all but completely stopped?

Well, then, if our economic health is not good, then we're going to have to start stimulating it somehow. I don't know. It just seems to even out. You know, when I see it, it just seems to even out that things get just so bad, and you do something about them and then you focus on something else and you do something about that, and in the meantime this is deteriorating a little bit, but not too much to get concerned about, and when it's deteriorating again, you go back and fix it again.

What if the choice was between preventing any deterioration in the environmental status quo or allowing economic growth? What if the only way to protect the environmental status quo was to stop growth? Would it be worth it?

Yeah. For a little while it would be. I don't think it could go on too long. We would have to find . . . Well, we have very imaginative people in this country, and I imagine we would pretty soon find a way to stimulate growth without hurting the environment, you know, in that particular case. We probably would, but we'd probably find another way to stimulate growth, or we'll be imaginative enough to find a way to do that. But yeah, I think we'd have to stop for a while.

Finally, participants sometimes chose to make light of the discomfort caused by the quandary they faced by relying on recourse to verbal sleights of hand or logical legerdemain or by simply ignoring the discomfort altogether. Val Gotti was obviously concerned with preserving open space and protecting wildlife. But she was also a strong believer in individual property rights. After going around and around on my wetlands preservation proposal, she arrived at this position: "Anything that's not built up, leave that alone." But when I asked if that included roads, the uncertainty returned:

> *What if the traffic is getting really congested?*
> Build another lane on the freeway.
> *What if that forces people who used to live there out of their houses?*
> I don't think that's right. I think that, if that's their property, they should be left there, and they'll just have to build it the other way, and if they can't, well, they're just going to have congested traffic, is how I look at it. Seriously, that's how I look at it. I do *not* think you should have to force somebody out of their home so you can build a freeway or a big building on top of your house!
> *OK, well maybe we'll leave those people in their houses, but we'll build a freeway through the marsh.*
> I personally think they shouldn't do it, but I think they'd do it. See, I don't know if I should be giving you answers like that, but I personally don't think they should, just because it's getting congested, they should figure something else out. I don't know what, but . . .
> *What if it's so congested that people start leaving the community in disgust, because they can't get around?*
> Well, then, it won't be congested anymore, true? [*laughs*]

I asked Louise Fredericks, who had characterized environmental protection as a Catch-22, if she saw any general conflict between full employment and adequate environmental protection: "How do you resolve it? That is *your* problem! I'll tell you what the problem is, and *you* guys figure out how to solve it. How's that? I don't have the answers; I just know there's problems."

Fred Mechler took a similar line. He suggested that there is no "long-term" conflict between environmental and social ideals, but then quickly added, "That's a philosopher's question."

All this is not to suggest that the members of this group, or Americans more broadly, are fundamentally irrational. Quite the opposite is true, in fact. Making tragic decisions is, of course, rational only if one is indeed confronted with tragic choices. Before admitting that, a rational person will look for less unpalatable solutions. And that is precisely how my participants tended to approach the value dilemmas with which I confronted them. Their first instinct was to look for an easy way out, such as postponing the issue to a more environmentally aware future. (What could be more reasonable?) When they saw the way blocked they did not deny the existence of the value dilemma; they freely admitted their cognitive dissonance (a sign not of confusion but of puzzlement). And many were at least able to suggest a general method by which such dilemmas could be addressed (which suggests inexperience, not some kind of cognitive deficiency). Still, the puzzlement and inexperience reflected in the above passages are undeniable. They sometimes existed alongside, and sometimes in combination with, the second factor which rendered environmental policy problematic for most of my participants: politics.

Political Quandaries

Environmental issues were problematic for most of the people I talked with, not only because these issues pose difficult value dilemmas, but also because they pose difficult political quandaries. But those quandaries would, I think, appear much less profound to many people were it not for the kind of individualism that will figure importantly in the analysis I present in chapter 5—an individualism which predisposes many people to look for individualistic solutions to social problems. Hence the political side of the environmental problem frustrates some individuals because of its perceived impenetrability, others because it is largely irrelevant given the promise of purely individual solutions, and still others because they hold both of these mutually reinforcing beliefs.

The Inscrutability of Political Solutions

The numbers here parallel those recounted above: only 12 participants out of 46, 3 of them dedicated environmentalists, offered a clear political solution or set of solutions during the course of the interview. Even late in the interview, when I asked point blank, "What do you think ought to be done to solve our worst environmental problems, if anything?" only 17 could present me with a concrete program. The rest expressed everything from hope and uncertainty to concern to frustration and, occasionally, despair, as the following passages illustrate. Don Wilson, the civil engineer, said: "I'm never too much for these blanket solutions. Thank God, in this country we've got a lot of people and a lot of exceptions."

Near the end of the interview I asked Betty Mikels, the real estate agent, the questions above. She sighed deeply and then said, "I'm just exhausted—all this thinking, all this brain power." After she repeated an earlier pitch for recycling and regulations on surface water pollution, I asked if the government should be involved in any way.

> *Obviously you don't see any systematic structural change is necessary in the way the economy works or the way the government works?*
> No.
> *The system can handle the problems?*
> I think so. I think we're going in the right direction as far as environmental projects and controls and everything is concerned.

Doreen Brill is in her 30s. She had recently moved to Wisconsin in order to obtain special medical care for one of her three rambunctious sons. Despite occasional expressions of interest, it was clear that environmental issues were not among her burning concerns. She was preoccupied with finding work and making sure that her son's treatment went smoothly. Most of our interview, frequently interrupted by sibling disputes and a garrulous neighbor, took place beside an outdoor pool with a radio blaring in the background. Ozone depletion seemed to worry this Hawaiian less than simply trying to relax for an hour or two. The environmental protection strategy she recommended was, like most of what she said, strongly worded, but it was neither concrete nor particularly well integrated:

> On any issue, the environment or whatever, people should have the right to vote: it's our country.
> *Do you mean in the marketplace, through supply and demand, or a political vote?*
> Vote. We're paying for everything. Why shouldn't we have the right?
> *But doesn't the market allow for freer decision-making?*
> It's OK, but after a point, they should intervene. Whenever it costs too much. And it's already that way with the environment.
> *So government should take over all of the environmental apparatus?*
> No. Darn, you got me again.
> *Is it a question of the government versus the market again?*
> Both sound all right. Vote on the important issues, when it's gotten out of hand (for example, on energy), on how we survive.

Brill wasn't alone in having other things on her mind. I asked Jill King, a young divorcee caring for her daughters and an ailing father, about whether the things we had talked about had ever influenced any decisions she'd had to make. She responded frankly: "I never thought about it before. *Never*. No one ever asked. I had other problems. It wasn't with the environment, I bet you—like Dad, the nursing home, doctors, my daughters . . . "

Adela Hill, my most elderly participant, at one point told me that my questions were "too complicated for [her] old brain." That was at best only partly true, however. During much of the interview she was quick to respond to probes and questions. Still, on this issue—what to do next—she ran out of steam, saying only, "It's going to take a lot of brains to figure it out."

Michael Cerutti, the letter carrier, responded to my general question about solutions with a certain frustration: "Number one is I still think we ought to keep a lot of land under conservation. I hate to see them sell off land like they've been doing. I want to see more parks so the future can be . . . You know, appreciate it. Not to sell all our mineral rights for the sake of a few dollars. You know, anything that can save our environment."

Louise Fredericks at one point told me that she differed from even the most radical brand of environmentalist only over the question of tactics. So I asked her if that meant she believed in more rigid environmental controls.

> OK, then the really radical comes along and says you gotta get rid of the car totally. Pollution control device isn't good enough.
> I think that's too radical.
> Why is that too radical?
> Well, nobody's going to do that, nobody's going to vote for that, nobody's going to put up with that. You know, you just can't get people to do that, so it's too radical. You have to use common sense.

As this passage suggests, Fredericks later would have little to recommend by way of a general strategy of environmental protection (except to plead for a "quarterback"). When I then asked her if centralization and expert planning were a good idea, she said: "Makes sense: increase local interest and at the same time have some overall guide. Yes, rebalance the power toward the local level as long as you tell me how to do it." So I did. I purposely chose an extreme localist solution: Murray Bookchin's clearly utopian vision of radical "municipalism." She responded only by saying, "Sounds good to me."

Even some of my most committed environmental radicals shared in the prevailing uncertainty about political solutions to environmental problems. Jack Schmidt, the dairy farmer I encountered while ice fishing on a gray February day, who was so pleased with the menagerie of birds and animals he had helped foster on his farm through his participation in the Conservation Reserve Program, despaired of any easy or obvious answers to population growth, acid rain, or the need for sustainable energy supplies. Later in the interview he observed wryly:

Government isn't always right.

But Exxon isn't, either.

That's right. They're not either.

So the question is . . ?

But maybe if the government had been hauling that load of oil out, maybe they'd probably screwed up two of them!

Why do you think that's true? Why does that happen to the government when it tries to run a big show?

Well, they're people. The government, they're humans, they screw up. They're no different than an industry. You know they're made up of a lot of people; there's a lot of politics. Government's larger, more people involved, more going in different directions.

Yeah, but Exxon's a big company, too, I mean . . . So it can't really be the number of people involved.

Only that as you're larger it's more difficult to control. You pass the buck a little simpler. It's like the service. You know, I was in the service—that's large, and that's not all perfect. Theoretically they're, you know, a well-disciplined organization. But they're not perfect. If I knew, which I don't, but if we could unconditionally say government, if by taking over problems they would solve them, it should be done.

May be we could try it.

I don't know if I've got that much faith that they could solve it. You know, I don't think Russia has solved a lot of their problems where the government has absolute say.

Where should we get the [money] that we need [for more environmental protection]?

I think we talked about that earlier. Taxes. I think it goes back to if we could solve x problem by being taxed x number of dollars, would I be willing? I'd say, "Sure, *IF*. If my taxes were to double, I wouldn't object if it solved problems. *IF*. But if my taxes were to double and the problem remained or got greater, then I would wish they were opposed. And this happens in some cases.

Do you think that happens very often in the environmental area?

Oh yes, I suspect it does. I don't know. I have no way of knowing. I think it does in everything.

So before you would vote for any increase in taxes, you would want to answer that?

I would want some assurance. I would want to see the game plan. What you going to get for what you spend?

Donna Scheda, who shortly after our interview left her job working for an environmental products firm for Wisconsin's north woods, had been talking about how urban sprawl was driven by a search for quick profits. "The whole system is set up wrong," she said. So I asked her if we ought to change capitalism. Her response:

> I don't know. And I don't think that we're about to do that. I'm not sure that I would say that that would be the best thing to do. I think that the way we have things set up isn't very good. I'm not sure that, I mean, that we should just get rid of capitalism, but maybe we should look at it a little bit and look at how things are done and why they're done because of money and what drives it and—I don't know. I'm not necessarily saying that we shouldn't do it, but maybe we should look at it a little more closely, a little more realistically. Because they do put up things very quickly and very fast, and they want to do it to make money.

The Attraction of Individually Oriented Solutions

Early in the interview Dr. James Burson, a young psychiatrist just finishing his residency, had exclaimed, "Gosh, I just have such a hard time thinking about economics." I later asked him whether leaving more environmental decisions to the market would be a good idea. The exchange that followed showed that the reason he had such difficulty with economics lay, not in the inherent difficulty of the questions it posed, but in the demanding nature of the standard he used to judge his answers:

> Well, the market hasn't done as well up until now.
> *Maybe that's because we haven't left the market well enough alone.*
> Yeah, I think it's . . . It's hard for me to answer that one. Other than to abstract it. To abstract in an abstracting which, I don't know how meaningful that would be. I mean, well, so is human nature basically going to be respectful of the environment or . . . You know, it almost seems as though when you ask that question, you're already in a place where you aren't in appropriate relationship to the environment. I don't want to sound too Eastern or corny or spiritual, but it sounds as though when you get to the point where you're asking these sorts of questions, it's a

clear signal that the relationship is already disturbed. These aren't the sort of questions that would come up if we were living in a correct relationship to the environment. And we wouldn't have to wonder about this. But, as to whether or not it was a generally free market and then if human impulse gets translated in a direct fashion in that marketplace . . . I don't know how to answer that one. It seems almost impossible to answer that question to me. I wish I knew why.

Is it because . . .

Because? Who knows? It's like, that's not known right now.

What isn't known?

The answer to that isn't known, I guess.

Why isn't it? What would we have to know in order to answer it? What kinds of things?

[*hesitates*] Well, I mean, you know, I could be pessimistic and say it could never work, but we don't *know* if it would never work or not. I don't think we *know* if it would never work or not.

What kinds of things would enable us to answer that question? I guess that's what I was asking.

[*hesitates*] God, I just can't answer that one. Can you help me out?

Well, yeah, I could try. Is it because we'd have to know more than we do about how people instinctively interact with the environment?

Well [*pauses*] I think it depends a lot on whether somebody . . . I don't think the question is whether or not people are basically environmentally sound, I think the question is whether people are basically content and without conflict.

Oh, I see. Yeah.

Course, you know, those sort of people would use a free market appropriately. You know, it always seems to me that, you know, those who are abusing resources are those who are using resources to try and make themselves happy.

Oh, I see what you're saying.

It seems like when you find some happiness apart from any resources, you start to see that resources aren't necessary for happiness. In fact, if you use them wrong they might often interfere with it.

So you're saying that in a society of essentially happy individuals the market might work environmentally because the people would be using the market in order to satisfy their needs in a way that doesn't damage the environment.

Yeah. I guess that's a tentative faith, but, you know, I think that if people basically feel secure (maybe "secure" is a better word than "happy") they feel good about themselves, they like who they are, they feel they have a right to be loved, and they don't fear they're going to lose that. You know, I think that those sorts of people naturally relate to the environment and thus the market in a much different way.

OK. So now we can get back to the question of, right now in our present society, would it be a good idea?

Well, I guess you'd have to ask, How is the market as you have it structured now affecting people's happiness and security, contentedness? Is it somehow adversely affecting those variables and somehow creating conditions where it is almost impossible to feel secure and happy! If that were the case, then maybe changing the market system to a genuinely free one would be just exactly the thing to do. That sounds like a pretty complicated analysis. I don't know how you'd determine . . . I guess my bias would be to say that those sorts of factors, those sorts of structural factors within the system, may be affecting people's security and happiness, but they're not going to be the dominating factors, and probably we're not at a place right now where we're ready to use a more genuinely free market in an appropriate way.

Yeah. No wonder you were thinking hard about this. Pretty complicated, huh?

You know, it's terribly dangerous though; these ideas are very much just my ideas. You know, I'm sure that very little of this is truth, I mean, in the sense that it's accurate. It's quite a leap to say that somebody that's secure and happy is going to use the free market in a right way, but that's *my* leap.

Yeah, well, you were still pretty confused, though, in making that leap in terms of the real-life, everyday world, though, because you said you weren't sure at all whether that was appropriate to do now.

Well, it's a hypothesis. I guess that's what the root of this whole point was, was that, given the position we have currently in relationship to the environment, all we can do is make hypotheses. Because there's something fundamentally disturbed about our relationship to the environment in this culture, and we don't know what else to do but make hypotheses, and they may be right and they may be wrong. It's like we've got to discover some other way to do this instead of make hypotheses. That would be some sort of metalogical leap that I can't quite make here today.

Later I asked Burson more directly about government's role vis-à-vis the environment. Given the above, his answer was predictable: "The government could structure . . . I mean . . . the government—we are the government! I mean, it's pretty hopeless at this point. I don't know how things will change, I guess, other than just doing what you can on an individual level."

Burson thought of himself as politically incompetent—or at least naive. Logically, that still left two paths open to him: squarely confront the mysteries of environmental political economy or search for a purely individually oriented explanation and solution to environmental problems. He consistently chose the latter route, not because he was unable to reason politically (in fact he once presented me with a textbook analysis of the free-rider problem—on city buses!), but because he was never satisfied with the results of his reasoning. It was a pattern that was repeated in at least 10 other interviews, between a quarter and a fifth of the total. (Another half dozen placed some hope in individual change.) Some were so politically "realistic" that all political solutions seemed utopian. Others were simply unable to envision collective solutions. For all these participants, the logically unassailable argument "If all individuals change their behavior, society will be transformed" was far more compelling than any necessarily nebulous political program.[8] Hence those who perceived themselves as hard-boiled realists and those who considered themselves politically inept were often driven to the same conclusion: political change presupposes individual change, whether in attitudes, awareness, or consciousness.

It is tempting to see in this pattern yet another reminder of this country's Protestant cultural heritage. Perhaps one could call it the Lutheran complex: a belief in individual renewal coupled with an extremely guarded attitude toward the larger society. But the label doesn't quite fit. True, there was agreement in this group that society is difficult to change, difficult to reform. And some did see society as little more than the regulated struggle of competing interests. But for many others, society is less corrupt than simply complex, less corrupting than simply difficult to grasp. It is also important to point out here (as I do again in greater detail in the following chapter) that no one in this highly individualistic group proposed a general rollback of environmental policy, and all endorsed at least half of the policy reforms I proposed—some many more than that.

And now, some illustrations. I asked Julie Binns, who was about to begin her medical training, about the ultimate aims of environmental policy. Her response was telling:

I think, you know, it's just a matter of everyone doing their part. And, I don't see a huge government action, you know, a national movement, as really a solution. I just think it should be on a personal level that things can get done if everyone just keeps track of their own. . . .

And do you have faith, or whatever you want to call it, that that's going to work that way?

Well, I would say maybe it should, but it's very ideal.

Is it so ideal that we gotta think about doing it a different way?

I think maybe we should educate and publicize it more, because there's just a lot of people who just aren't aware.

Is that something government should get involved in doing?

Maybe government. You know, like public service messages. You know, agencies, they do their part. I guess, you know, even as little as it may seem, just . . . You're out at a gathering . . . It's by your actions, or take after you, that's . . . You know, people will catch on, you know, they'll understand. Just on a real little level, things will start to roll, I think.

Several hours into the interview, Erik Johannsen, the young chemical engineering student, paused to say:

See, that's the whole thing. Our industry caters to the consumer, right? So you got your . . . If your attitude changes and your needs change, then they are not going to make stuff that has to sit in a warehouse, or whatever the case. They are going to only use as much as they need. So I think it's a feedback type process, not a "We'll give you this much; here, this is all the consumer gets," you know. I think it's attitude driven. I think that's the way this all should be—every question you've pretty much asked me should be, you know, fairly attitude driven.

Michael Cerutti, the letter carrier, said:

I think once people start getting aware of all these things that are happening in our society . . . I think they will be the determining factor in the future. Not going to happen overnight though, will it? But you got laws, yeah, you can put laws on the books, but how do you enforce these laws? You know, how many laws do we have on the books right now that you can't enforce? Come on, you know, I mean, I believe in rules and regulations and all that stuff, but sometimes people got to take it into their own hands, starting at the bottom.

Carol Chapman responded:

> On each little separate resource or issue that you want to talk about, it seems like there are very far-reaching consequences and you're going to have a hard time getting people to stomach some of the changes, but I think an awareness of the problem and a movement toward solving some of them is what we need.

Doreen Brill repeatedly said that "people should be more aware" of environmental problems. Late in the interview I asked her if government should also be working toward a better environment. "Not just government. Everyone should be working toward it," she replied.

Edward Hollister, an inner-city tutor of "problem" kids, was as thoroughgoing in his individualism as anyone I met, partly because he does see society as irremediably corrupt. Interestingly enough, that didn't keep him from endorsing more than four-fifths of the specific policy reforms I put to him.

> Politically, I think we have to evaluate the correct people that have this same idea that they going to do right for people and not right for what they're happy with, which is greed. And we don't have too many people today with integrity, that are into politics, government politics. Seems to attract the wrong type of people. You gotta lot of collusion and a lot of things going on around with politics. Well, they say, nothing corrupts any more than power, and power corrupts absolutely. So we have this power struggle, and that's what politics is about: power, power, power, power, power. How you get what you want—and that's greed again? Another solution I can see is people have to learn to say, "I have to evaluate me and appreciate myself enough that I treat you well, regardless of the way you treat me." And that calls for a strong constitution, a personal constitution.
>
> *So if we are going to deal with this thing of greed, the only way we are going to do that is if a bunch of people are willing to make a sacrifice?*
> I'm one of them, right?
> *How are we going to convince . . . Are we going to be able to convince any other people to make the sacrifice, too?*
> I can't force them to.
> *Is there some way to persuade a lot of other people to do that, too?*
> By acting good—what you think, what you do, what you consider.
> *So would you say that the best education is personal example, then? I mean is that the best way to go about it—to say, "This is how I'm*

*running my life''—and that's what's good, to show by the way you
are, what the right way is?*

Well, see, I am a product of my environment. I am a product
of what I have been taught. I see all of this is relative. And I
know what human beings do. And I've learned history, and people do things. But, it takes . . . Some people have to refuse to be
manipulated.

*I mean it's not an easy thing to solve, but if people are also . . . If
you are partially a product of your environment, then maybe we should
change the environment?*

Well, that's my endeavor. That's what I attempt to do. I have
to be me. You have to recognize [that] people with power have
power over me. That includes rent, that includes employment,
that includes endeavor. People manipulate people to do what
they want them to do for *them*.

How are we going to change that?

The only way I see of doing it—I am going to be me. I am trying to treat people as I want to be treated.

This retreat to individual solutions characterized some of my committed environmental activists as well. Here the dynamic was different:
the gravity of the problem was seen to render any political solutions
inadequate. I asked Carmen Wiley, for example, how we might avoid
conflicts between our environmental and social ideals. She answered:

Like I said, I guess that it would just be shifting the whole
structure of what this economy's based on. You know, I don't
think we can do it with what we have, and just pull out a couple
of old sticks without everything . . . You know, it just . . . I don't
think it would collapse anyway, but I don't think it can be done.
I think it has to be something very complete, and it has to start
with our thinking to restructuring things. I don't feel it can be
done with what we have right now; I think that's why we have
the problems. And until there's an entire way of seeing things
that includes global impact, too, Dow will be able to come in and
build those factories and people will feel like, "Oh, this is won-
derful, yeah, this is good for my life," until your children after
Dow closes, and they get the clusters of this and that, and then
it's too late. That's what's been happening all over the country.

*Why don't you think that the present system or the present way the
economy works is going to be able to cope with the whole situation?*

Because it wasn't meant to take into consideration human
beings. It was meant to take into consideration the basic needs of

all human beings outside of our county, extending to other areas, and that's why: it's a very closed way of thinking, about doing things.

And why does change have to start with the way people think about things?

Because then there's going to be a big resistance, and as long as there's big companies and lobbies and money, they're going to fight people that want to, that can see that if we don't change, you know, something catastrophic is starting to happen—is happening. That's why.

So then the next question obviously is, Where do we start or how do we start people thinking differently?

I guess we start with ourselves, and then we start with our immediate family, and that expands into our—the neighborhood, the community, the city, the county, and on and on and on.

Wiley concluded the interview with this summation:

Well, I think the EPA is a joke. I mean, you know, I was reading some people saying [that] I have to trust the government to protect me. I have to trust the . . . I guess, you know, here somebody would say they have to trust the Department of Natural Resources; I don't. Somebody would say, "Well, we have to trust the EPA"; I don't. I mean, they just don't do enough. There needs to be new watchdog agencies, you know; there need to be new things constructed that really have the heart of the matter, I mean, that really are watchdogs for the government. Not like the little watchdogs. I mean, they're nothing. And something apart from the whole machine that would, of course, be respected and that would have an impact on the government, you know, and what the government does and does not do in regulating and whatever. I think we need that. I think that's our hope with the government.

Ralph Thorisch, a college student about to quit school and his job as a cabby to work on an organic farm, would have agreed. He was at a loss for political solutions, partly because of strong libertarian leanings, partly because he simply couldn't imagine any that would really work. His summation echoed Wiley's: "I think when I said 'attitude' I think that would be the big thing because it's got to . . . I think people will only take so much regulation without really believing in it. And I really, you know . . . I think that's valid, too. I think the attitude has to change before the policy changes."

The Environment as Problem and Our Search
for a Solution

One way to read these passages is to see in them confirmation of the accuracy of the most consistent longitudinal data we have on the subject of environmental attitudes. In the next chapter I cite a series of opinion polls which show that Americans became concerned about the environment in the late 1960s and that they have, if anything, become more concerned since. Social scientists have long debated the significance of these data. But from all that I have said, one thing at least should be clear: that concern indicates a clear recognition of the existence of a *problem*.

As we have just seen, there are a number of reasons Americans view environmental policy as problematic, some of these reasons being mutually reinforcing. As unsurprising as this may be, it is of far more than academic interest. To see something as a problem is to search for a solution or, at a very minimum, to be open to the consideration of solutions. It is because the environment is viewed as problematic—often deeply so—that my participants agonized so un-self-consciously over the questions I posed to them. For deliberation to work as a political prescription, people must be both willing and able to deliberate. They will be willing to do so only to the extent that a subject is viewed as a problem, an open question. Clearly the environment is just such a subject. Precisely why that is so I take up in the next chapter.

4

Why Citizens Are Willing to Deliberate about Environmental Protection

> I think both political parties are very conscious of the environment.
> There's not really a big difference between them on the environment
> compared to other issues. The public would revolt if they said, "We're
> not for the environment."
>
> —real estate agent Betty Mikels

There are plenty of reasons to be interested in what Americans think about environmental protection. Since the late 1960s, the subject has drawn the attention of historians, sociologists, psychologists, and, of course, political scientists. Literally thousands of studies exist on the subject of what Americans think about nature, the environment, and environmental policy. Political scientists, for their part, tend to view the public's environmental beliefs as a constraint on the nature and extent of public policy in the environmental area (see, for example, Chubb 1983: 145). And they are no doubt correct in this view. While it is certainly not the case that, in real world democracies, "what demos wants—demos gets," it is generally true that "what demos rejects, usually doesn't last very long." And, of course, the better greased the wheels of democracy, the truer this is. But one needn't assume away the flaws in our democratic institutions to appreciate this fact. As one observer put it recently, "Some level of agreement between policy and perception is necessary for policy enforceability but also for long-term public identification with the purposes and rationales for policies" (Berberet 1988: 4; see also OECD 1988: 97; Vig and Kraft 1984b: 7; Mitchell 1984: 53; Porritt 1984: 168). Even in a largely undemocratic country, environmental policy change can been stymied by public resistance. In 1979 the People's Republic of China adopted virtually the entire corpus of American environmental statutes. A full decade later they

90

had made almost no headway, largely because of widespread citizen indifference (Flader 1989). There are simply some things that people will not stand, and this applies to the environmental realm as much as to any other.

Individual Beliefs and Citizen Deliberation

As important as the constraining function of citizens' beliefs might be, however, I had another, essentially theoretical, interest in what kind of environmental policy citizens are willing to endorse (or merely put up with). I wanted to know if the beliefs they brought to the interview situation tended to support my hypothesis that citizens are both willing and able to deliberate about environmental protection. In the last chapter I showed that the very way people approach environmental protection supports that hypothesis because to view the environment as representing a problem rather than a program is to be at least open to deliberating on environmental issues. As we saw from the interviews, few people appear to have preconceived environmental strategies, so most are willing to think about them. But the interviews reveal far more than that. They indicate that the actual content of people's environmental beliefs also supports deliberation, and rather strongly. First, the interviews showed that Americans clearly want, at a minimum, to preserve the integrity of the environment; many want to improve its present condition. They are also in favor of expanded environmental controls, even when those controls take the form of government policy rather than more informal group sanctions. The interviews focused almost exclusively on environmental policy, that is, on the realm of formal government action. Still, despite attitudes toward state action that ranged from ambivalence to outright hostility, these Americans made an exception of the environmental realm. One can only suppose that their attitudes toward nongovernmental collective efforts to preserve the environment were even more positive. Furthermore, like Betty Mikels, they believed most other citizens share their general orientation. Second, these citizens soundly rejected radical political restructuring as a means of promoting environmental ends. Taken together, these beliefs produced a strong willingness to deliberate on environmental policy questions—a willingness that other types of data suggest is as broadly distributed in the American population as a whole as it was strongly represented among the 46 citizens I interviewed.

Americans as Environmental Progressives

Environmental Policy Goals

That Americans are willing to deliberate on environmental questions seemed obvious from the very outset of my research. Approximately 90 percent of those I contacted about the interview happily agreed to participate. Of those that declined, all but one pleaded lack of time. In addition, only a handful of my participants complained about the length of the interview. And, most important, the interviews themselves usually proceeded in a deliberative, not interrogative, fashion. That is, once participants noticed that I was after their *thinking*, not their opinions, they were generally willing to work at piecing together more satisfying answers to my questions. But of that, there will be more in chapter 6. Here I want to continue the explanation I began in the last chapter in regard to just why this cross-section of Americans came to the interview situation in such a deliberative frame of mind.

We have just seen that this group of citizens tended to frame the environment as posing a problem. Viewed as problematic, the environment becomes a fitting candidate for deliberation. But that is really only half the story, for it is one thing to be puzzled, quite another to work at finding solutions. The raw material of deliberation is questions. But people must believe that those questions are worth answering—that the finished product will be valuable—if they are to have any motivation to deliberate in the first place. Why do people so avidly pursue their questions about environmental policy? They do because, quite simply, they are interested in, and have an interest in, answering them. That is, people are willing to deliberate about the environment because they strongly believe in improving, or at least protecting, it. The 46 individuals I talked with were evenly divided between those who clearly believed that we need to improve the present state of the environment and those for whom maintaining the environmental status quo was goal enough. Of the group interested in improving the environment, only three singled out one aspect of the environment (pollution) as requiring special attention. The other 20 spoke in much more systemic terms of "preserving and enhancing" the environment, "clamping down" on violators of environmental regulations, "helping the land grow," or restoring "all this wrecked land." One even equated "taking care of the environment" with the Good Life. But a more typical description of the kind of environment this group envisioned was that given me by Caroline Stowe, a retiree:

> Clean. Unassaulted. Free to prosper. We should be helpful
> and support it and more thoroughly understand the relation-

ships between this and that. We shouldn't be playing politics
with the environment.

Free to prosper? You mean all parts of it?

Well, we shouldn't cut down the rain forests, for example. We
shouldn't damage the ozone layer. We should help it along.

Others, like Carol Chapman, the young corporate lawyer and mother
we met earlier, suggested simply trying harder:

On each little segregated resource or issue that you want to
talk about, it seems like there are very far-reaching consequences,
and you're going to have a hard time getting people to stomach
some of the changes, but I think an awareness of the problem
and a movement toward solving them is what we need.

Suzette Schell, a registered nurse forced into early retirement by a medical disability, was more emphatic:

See, I don't think that using natural resources and pollution . . .
I don't think that this drive for using less and less resources
and the drive for diminishing pollution . . . I don't think any of
those things should ever stop. I think we should always strive to
[reduce them] more and more. We're never going to reach infinity. I mean, we're never going to reach the final end where everything's perfect. But there's nothing wrong with continuing to
strive for that, for the rest of time.

Carmen Wiley, whose household was a model of ecological correctness,
spoke of an ideal environment in terms of not only respecting nature
but also renewing it: "We would be re-creating what was natural. With
all the technological changes, couldn't we find a way to halt the decline
in the ozone layer? It would be ideal that the life that's there would be
respected." Fred Mechler, the hard-nosed union officer, said simply:
"Let's clean up the mess."

Only two participants went so far as to call for a return to something
like a preindustrial economy; three others flirted with the idea during
the course of the interview. I asked Jack Schmidt, the middle-aged dairy
farmer who had recently retired much of his land and thereby gained
plenty of extra fishing time (and a great deal of wildlife), if he would
seriously be willing to return to a preindustrial mode of existence. He
answered:

Of course I would. I would love to go back and see Lake
Koshkonong 40 years ago. I would love that. I might have to ride
a damn horse to get there! Or walk, you know, for five hours.
Sure I would do it. I would love it.

You would?
You bet.
I just wanted to make sure that I understood how radical you were being here.
Pretty radical, pretty [*pauses*] horrible actually.
And you called yourself a conservative!
I'm a minority, obviously.

Yet in all these cases, participants shied away from actually recommending that society pursue such a vision. When I asked Schmidt, for example, how much of the environment we ought to leave behind, he replied simply, "All we've got now, hey, and hopefully better than we've got." For all of these individuals, setting back the economic clock remained a healthy mental exercise or, at most, a personal project. Ralph Thorisch was one such participant. He had just dropped out of college in order to start work on an organic farm in eastern Minnesota. His was one of the most clearly radical visions of an ideal environment. After mentioning preservation of species and some of the other more typical goals of environmental protection, he seemed dissatisfied with his own response. So I asked him again what an ideal environment might look like. His answer was phrased in terms of an ideal interaction between humans and nature: "Our existence should not go any farther than not dominating. Always kind of on the edge, susceptible to uncontrollable forces, like a hurricane or avalanche or cold snap or, like, increases in the number of wolves, [so that we are] on our toes, *alive.*" This vision of a preindustrial, or even preagricultural, society was not, however, one Thorisch himself was willing to press on other people. He admitted that he felt insufficiently schooled in environmental issues to lecture (or "preach") to other people about them—hence his desire to learn about land from the ground up on a farm.

The other half of my participants generally believed in simply keeping the present environment intact, either over the long term or indefinitely. That view was expressed in many different ways. Four participants made specific references to the survival of their children, grandchildren, or the human species in general. Virtually all the others stated variations on the theme of sustainability—that is, the ability of the environment either to maintain us or to keep us healthy and prosperous. Carol Chapman spoke of a "maintenance level" of environmental protection, Dr. James Burson referred to a "sustainable, dependable, secure" environment, and even developer Joseph Palasota made sure I understood that he favored "enough environmental protection to keep us moving along in a healthy, prosperous way." What is most interesting in the following more-or-less typical examples of this view is less the difference in emphasis than the fact that all these participants considered their views to be simple, obvious—not just sensical, but *common*sensical. Recall Betty Mikels' rhetorical question: "Now with our space program we've been to the moon. . . . What is our next objective? Mars? . . . It seems pretty apparent so far that Earth is the only planet that has human beings on it. So therefore . . . I guess you have to take care of your planet, or where are we going to go?" Billy Franks, a young refugee from the industrial fallout of Flint, Michigan, argued:

> Life is precious, man. It's . . . It's . . . It's like . . . more precious than anything I can think of. But in order to preserve life, you got to be able to preserve the surroundings. And if you don't preserve the surroundings, life is going to die off, because this is what life's adapted to. This is how life survives, you know. And without that, man [*lowers voice*], you got nothing, you don't have nothing.

Bob Kovalek, the semiretired dairy farmer, put the point slightly differently, but the thrust of his remark is the same:

> We've got to breathe, we've got to have water, we've got to have food. We protect the environment up to that point without batting an eye, you know what I mean? Whatever it takes, we got to do it, because I mean we don't want to die. We don't want our society to disappear because we're a bunch of idiots, because we're not. . . . We're certainly too intelligent to hurt ourself. My God Almighty it . . . We've got to be better than that!

For Michelle Washington and Jill King, two young African-American mothers for whom household demands left little time for leisure, environmental policy was no great mystery. What is the proper state of the environment? "Kept up," said Washington. And the goal of environmental policy? "Just making the world go around," said King.

At the level of broad goals, then, even the least radical among this group were rather adamant about maintaining the environmental status quo. Many were more emphatic. All shared a strongly felt interest in the aims of environmental policy. As I noted in chapter 1, that shared interest is the bedrock upon which environmental deliberation can build.

Deliberation cannot proceed without both disagreement and agreement. Without disagreement, we engage in mutual affirmation but discuss or deliberate nothing. Yet if disagreement is absolute, discussion fails just as surely, for there is no shared starting point from which deliberation can depart. Deliberation requires two kinds of agreement:

mutual recognition that the subject presents certain problems worth deliberating about, and mutual recognition of the general direction in which solutions to those problems lie. Deliberation involves speaking and listening, challenging and responding. But we cannot speak or listen without a shared language, a common grammar that structures what is to count as intelligible speech. This grammar is constituted by the values, beliefs, and convictions that we share as we begin deliberating with one another. It may change, as grammatical rules do, when we converse with one another. Yet we cannot converse without it.

Deliberative democracy, unlike representative democracy, depends fundamentally on this underlying value agreement, not on agreement about specific outcomes or policy decisions. Like the deliberative democrat, the representative democrat sees political disagreement as inevitable. But whereas the deliberative democrat looks for (and often finds) agreement underlying political conflict and then seeks to build upon this agreement, the representative democrat sees most political conflict as irreconcilable. If this is true, all that can be hoped for is an equitable settlement between the opposing sides. In the end, the broader underlying values that support democracy are taken far more seriously by the deliberative democrat than by the representative democrat because these values are viewed as changeable rather than incorrigible. Far from imposing limits on the public sphere, people's fundamental beliefs are the very stuff that make deliberative change in a democracy possible. They are the shared ground upon which citizens can explore new ways of thinking and new ways of doing things. In the case of environmental protection, this shared ground is both wide and solid. Again we see that democratic deliberation on the environment holds no empty hope; it can be expected to rest solidly on the public's belief in the importance and basic goals of environmental protection.

And there are other supports as well. Although just half of this group called for improving the present state of the environment when talking in abstract terms, for large majorities this entailed not just a general call for more collective efforts to protect the environment but also arguments for an expansion in (governmental) environmental policy, including the implementation of 17 of the 19 policy reforms I suggested, some of which were quite radical by any standard.[1] The distinction here between governmental and nongovernmental forms of collective action is important. Because each interview began with a discussion of 19 specific policy reforms, as opposed to suggestions for broader "political reform" or "popular action" on behalf of the environment (see table 4.1, p. 102), one might object that participants were systematically cued to equate politics with policy or collective action with government programs and that, as a result, participants' belief in the necessity of formal political responses to environmental problems was ingenuous at best, artificial at worst. But although such an objection contains a grain of truth, we need to remember that the intent of the deliberative interview I conducted was precisely to produce "artificial" responses; the goal was to induce participants to alter their beliefs by deliberating about them. To say that participants arrived at artificial beliefs during the course of a deliberative exchange is to say that only unexamined beliefs are real, that citizens have no right to change their minds, or that social scientists ought to ignore them when they do. The deliberative democrat, of course, flatly rejects all these beliefs.

The assertion that the interview schedule (see Appendix, pp. 211-235) was biased in the direction of formal policy and against non-governmental forms of collective action, however, is true enough. The longest portion of the interview was dedicated to sorting out 19 specific policy dilemmas; shorter sections during this and later questioning dealt with more general, open-ended questions regarding what to do about the environment. Still, this hardly invalidates the results. In this first place, there can be no such thing as an unbiased interview, conversation, or deliberative exchange: all must start somewhere and proceed through a necessarily limited agenda. No one has the time to ask all the questions that one can logically ask on any subject. Even if one did ask all the questions, they are not equally important. This holds true for citizens as much as for social scientists, both of whom must make choices. I offered my participants numerous chances to direct our discussions by asking them open-ended questions—at the beginning of each policy section, in a general section on environmental protection, in a general section on their political beliefs, and again at the end of the interview. Nowhere did I confine them in any direct sense to the text of the interview schedule.

Still, the charge that the interview was heavy on policy questions and light on nongovernmental suggestions is true enough. Yet that "bias" actually reinforces my argument that citizens share an underlying belief in expanded collective action on behalf of the environment. Policy is, after all, only one form of collective behavior—and not an especially popular one in late twentieth-century America. Had I asked my participants about neighborhood recycling collectives, citizen campaigns against toxic waste, or business councils' efforts to reduce manufacturing waste, I have no doubt that their reactions would have been almost universally enthusiastic. But I chose not to. I chose not to ask them about nongovernmental forms of collective behavior, because even an enthusiastic response would not have told us very much. It would have told us only that, where collective efforts on behalf of the environment can proceed without the state, they will be welcomed. But that is not enough. In some cases the state may have to get involved (wilderness, energy, and global pollution to name but a few), and then we shall need to know more: we shall need to know if Americans' openness to collective action extends to the state, an object of historical distrust, frequent opprobrium, and occasional hostility. If we learn, as I did here, that Americans, for all of their hesitancy about state action, are actually willing to experiment in the environmental realm, we have learned a great deal. We have learned not only that they will consider environmental policy a proper subject for deliberation, but that they are even more likely to deliberate about other collective ways to achieve environmental aims as well. A better appreciation for the degree to which that was so can be seen even more clearly from the participants' reaction to the various specific policy proposals I put to them.

More Environmental Policy or Less?

My participants were even more progressive when it came to the policy norms that are logically the product of the goals just discussed. And it is this progressivism that best explains their deliberative disposition. The great majority of this varied group of Americans was in agreement not only that more must be done to preserve the environment but also that this might at least occasionally involve the government in some way—precisely the conclusion, it will be remembered, that I arrived at in chapter 2. In other words, collective thinking, an important component of what I call environmental rationality (see especially chapter 6), was not entirely absent in this group.

Even late in the interview, fully 36 out of 46 were unable to think of a single instance in which the government had "gone too far" in pursuit of environmental aims. And the few who could think of one or more instances also saw those instances either as unavoidable or as exceptions to the rule. Little wonder that nearly two-thirds (65 percent) of my participants called for increases in environmental spending. Even more impressive, when the interview began[2] not a single participant called for reining in environmental policy, and only 17 were satisfied with present regulatory efforts. Of the rest, 1 participant had no solid opinion one way or another, and 28 pointed to a need for policy expansion. And for a quarter of this latter group this clearly meant a significant or even radical departure from past efforts.

Categorizing each participant was a relatively straightforward task. I simply looked for their first spontaneous generalization as to the proper direction of environmental policy.[3] I categorized Frederick Lorenz, for example, as an environmental "conservative"—one who endorsed maintaining the environmental policy status quo. Lorenz's favorite evaluative phrase was "via media," and early on he noted his satisfaction with the general thrust of U.S. environmental policy: "I think we're headed in the right direction. We're not there yet; we have to keep working on it."

Karen Brunson largely agreed. When it came to describing the Mississippi River, even her choice of words was similar: "Now it's much cleaner than it was before. We're going in the right direction; it's being worked on." Note that even these environmental conservatives tended to phrase their conservatism in progressive terms; for both Lorenz and Brunson, environmental policy was not so much adequate or satisfactory as moving in the right direction.

It wasn't too difficult to separate the progressives from the conservatives. Consider Jack Schmidt, for example, the dairy farmer who's ice fishing I had interrupted to ask for an interview. He was none too sure exactly how the state's environmental problems ought to be handled. But the general thrust of his thinking was clear: "Of course, EPA or someone's got to set some restrictions, guidelines. That will probably increase prices, but we'll just have to live with it when it does."

His colleague to the north, Bob Kovalek, whom I also labeled a progressive, said it was time to "wake up and fly right before it's too damn late." When I asked him what he meant, he referred to his favorite political metaphor, a scale, and then said: "It's going to cost a lot of money. In the U.S. we go back and forth, searching for a balance. The time is here on this, though: we can't compromise on air, water, soil, and crops. We do need to make money, but . . . "

Suzette Schell, whose disability sapped her energy but who always seemed to have some in reserve when it came to discussing the environment, phrased her position in very similar terms:

> We have enough businesses, for Pete's sake!
> *What about progress?*
> People are too much into material things. Progress is also quality of life, not just quantity. And quality's more important.

Fred Mechler, the union officer, stated his general view of government early on while arguing for recycling: "Government usually screws up, but individuals won't recycle without government support because private individuals and companies won't do the bad parts."

Jay Little, young co-owner of an auto-repair shop, made this rather telling remark just after we began talking: "Face it; everything costs something one way or another. It's OK to pay as long as it's really accomplishing something. A lot of government is waste, but the environment isn't in that category."

My final example of an environmental progressive, Michael Cerutti, the mail carrier, made this remark a few minutes into the interview:

> How do you compare a thousand jobs today with what it's going to do in the future? I mean, look at Lake Erie. That's a great example. It was called a dead lake. They're making it come back, aren't they? But look at all the damage we've done. When you've got all these quick-fix schemes, you got to look at the long range, too. It's important. I mean, we like the quick fixes. I got nothing against that. But you look at the long-range, too. Because we're gonna pay for it sooner or later.

Compare the above passages with these drawn from the first exchanges with two of my "radical" environmentalists. Here is how Carmen Wiley responded to a question about acid rain (which she had cited as an important local problem):

> What can I do about acid rain? You know, as a community we could probably do a lot. But, you know, just . . . It has to be a very, very major, radical, very . . . I think we have to get hysterical. If we don't get hysterical about it, there isn't going to be any . . .

Mark Allen, who lives in a 400-square-foot boathouse on the Mississippi River, told me he had given up on mainstream society: "My life is kind of back channel." He was equally up-front about his environmental views. When he spoke of a natural "balance," I asked him to define the term. His response:

> An attitude and a plan that would last forever—a thousand years, 20,000 years. Rather than worry about next year's election, thinking about making sure that, as long as this planet is still around, that there will always be trees, always be wetlands, always be riverbanks for kids to play on. To me it's a shame that the water in the Mississippi isn't drinkable anymore, that we've destroyed that.

These passages are a fair sample of what I heard during the course of the interviews as a whole. Remember, too, that they indicate that, when the interviews began, this intentionally mixed demographic group consisted of roughly one-third environmental conservatives, one-half environmental progressives, and one-sixth environmental radicals. That finding clearly suggests that Americans are neither would-be environmental radicals, as is so often suggested, nor essentially ambivalent about their environmental progressivism. Instead, it indicates that Americans are solidly progressive in their environmental beliefs, and that both conservative and radical environmentalists are relatively uncommon. That conclusion was further supported by the positions these citizens took on a series of specific policy proposals I put to them early in the interview.

Progressive on All Types of Environmental Policy

Intensive interviews are perhaps uniquely suited to answer a question long ignored by scholars, namely: What *kind* of environmental policy do Americans endorse? This is so because interviews, unlike survey research, for example, are capable of revealing the complexity and texture of individual beliefs. At least half of each interview I conducted was devoted to Socratic questioning on 19 different environmental policy proposals. (The full text of the questionnaire is contained in the Appendix.) Some of these proposals were rather modest, others fairly radical. To my surprise, only 2 of the 19 specific policy reforms were rejected by a majority of the respondents; only 6 others were rejected by more than a quarter of the group (see table 4.1).

What is remarkable about these findings is less the large proportion endorsing the reforms than the *way* in which the reforms were endorsed. Respondents did not simply vote on the proposals; in virtually every case they had to explain why they voted as they did. And, in virtually every case, some kind of explanation was forthcoming. (These initial responses are tabulated in the first column of table 4.1.) But the very fact that explanations were given at all is a reasonable guarantee that the positions people took were more than mere whims, even more than personal preferences. That guarantee is further strengthened by the Socratic nature of the interviews. In every case, participants endorsed or rejected items from my reform agenda only after being reminded of the potential costs—environmental, or political, economic, and social—involved in holding to their chosen position. Their positions were not "opinions," at least in the usual sense. Instead, these "postdeliberation" positions (column 2 in table 4.1) were the expressions of some rather strongly held beliefs or convictions. These distinctions are worth underlining with a couple illustrations, both of them taken from among my most conservative participants.

Betty Mikels, the real estate agent and active Republican, had rejected 68 percent of the proposals I put to her, but not the one that called for stricter controls on the possible negative environmental consequences of new technologies. When I asked her if stricter controls were necessary in this area, she replied:

Table 4.1. Summary of group responses to individual environmental proposals

Proposed environmental limit	% respondents rejecting before deliberating	% respondents rejecting after deliberating
LOCAL		
Total ban on developing local wetlands (W)	43	43
Ecologically oriented county land use plan (S)	17	13
Halting construction of polluting factory in city/ town (P)	43	36
STATE		
Giving localities veto right over prospective mine sites (P)	21	5
State aid to community business (S)	20	5
State-mandated recycling; subsidies; product bans (NR)	9	7
Expanded environmental education in public schools (S)	7	5
NATIONAL		
Environmentally bening agricultural policy (S)	15	4
Ban on all economic activity in wilderness areas (W)	29	23
Large-scale federal tree-planting program (S)	22	18
5% pollution tax on all consumer goods (P)	26	24
Environmental regulation of new technologies (S)	23	16
Renewable energy and energy conservation (NR)	11	4
Limit on economic growth (S)	60[a]	45
Tax on families with more than two children (S)	71[a]	67[a]
National limit on annual use of all natural resources (NR)	23	16
INTERNATIONAL		
Joining with other nations in treaty to limit greenhouse gases (S)	14	10
Devoting 3% of GNP to international environmental aid (S)	34	25
A treaty to ban economic activity in Antarctica (W)	27	16

W = proposals dealing with wilderness use.
P = proposals dealing with pollution.
NR = proposals dealing with natural resource use.
S = structural proposals involving limits on a combination of the other three uses of and/or effect on the environment.
[a] Policy proposals rejected by a majority of participants.

Yes.

Why?

Because new technologies . . . We don't know the effect they'll have 20 years later, so we do need restrictions. It will cost money. For example, in Vietnam, the effects caused by Agent Orange. I don't want to get in that situation again. We need to make sure it's safe for the future.

What if that leads to a slowdown in economic growth?

It may, but it could end up costing more in the future.

Who will make these decisions?

Probably you and your classmates!

Not a big bureaucracy?

No. I don't know. The bigger the bureaucracy, the more complicated it becomes, and then it gets to be a political issue rather than an environmental issue. And that leads to problems, too, and nothing gets done.

So the idea is self-defeating, since there's no answer to the question of who will test, who will decide?

Well, the federal government should set the basic controls and allow the states to implement things because they have different environments, along with the locals. The federal government should make the final decisions—basic federal regulations.

So you're still for the idea, despite the costs involved and the bureaucracy?

Yes, yes, I am.

Why not just deal with the problems as they arise?

It's like I was saying: You can't find time to do a project right in the beginning. But you can always find time to go back and correct the mistakes. So it ends up taking twice the time and you end up paying twice the money.

Fred Springer is perhaps the closest that late twentieth-century Wisconsin can come to a cowboy: wiry and weathered, hard-working, and tough-talking. A conservative populist, he clearly adores his work: crop dusting. Like Betty Mikels, he rejected almost 70 percent of the proposals I put to him. But he clearly favored preserving Antarctica, for the time being at least:

I don't know what else is down there. We should leave it until we really need it; then it's a different program.

Why should we keep it? What's so important about penguins? No one's ever going to go there. What if we find cheap oil there?

But at *this* point . . . Depends on how it's taken out.

How cleanly would it have to be taken out—if it meant a 25 percent reduction in gasoline prices for two years? One more Exxon Valdez?

That's just bait for someone to get in there. Leave it alone as a reserve. It's like what Bush said on the West Coast: leave it sit until we find better ways to get at it.

How badly would we have to need it before you would be willing to say, "Go ahead"? Another oil crisis like 1973?

Sure.

If there were an oil crisis, and the environmentalists were arguing, "Keep it untouched because it's delicate," what would you say?

If you're short of oil, that means the whole economy's going to be in bad shape. You go. You have to. You're shut down.

Why not head off the conflict and attempt to develop alternative sources of energy, financed, say, with a 2 percent tax on oil?

Never happen; that's just talk.

If you were in the Senate, would you vote for such a proposal?

No.

So you're willing to wait for the next crisis.

We have our own reserves now: the north slope [in Alaska], the national parks.

This is not to say that the numbers alone are of no interest. Consider the difference between the percentage rejecting the rather abstract notion of a limit on economic growth (60) and the percentage rejecting national limits on all natural resource use (just 23). Or consider the fact that, with the exception of population controls (which were usually rejected as either unnecessary or too invasive) and the limit on economic growth, every other proposal garnered the support of a majority of the participants. That finding takes on added significance when we recall that this group was intentionally selected to mirror both the overall environmental disposition *and* the principal demographic characteristics of the population at large (i.e., age, gender, education, occupation, income, religion, and community size).[4]

Perhaps more important than its endorsement of individual policy proposals, this group was remarkably balanced in its endorsement of what can be identified as the four different basic types of environmental policy, that is, limits on natural resource use, pollution, wilderness use, and various combinations of these. Note that, of the proposals summarized in the table 4.1, three deal primarily with pollution, three with natural resource use, and three with wilderness. The remaining 10 clearly contemplate limits on a combination of these uses of the environment. (For convenience sake I term these structural proposals or limits.) The only proposals rejected by this group as a whole were both structural, but the group also endorsed eight other structural proposals, often by wide margins. And by an almost three-to-one margin, it called for overall limits on what is taken out of the nation's forests, ground, and water supplies—a proposal some economists have advocated as a crucial first step in achieving a steady-state economy (Daly 1976). So while they rejected a limit on economic growth in the abstract, this cross-section of the public seemed ready to accept practical proposals that would move our society in precisely that direction.

To sum up, then, the results presented in table 4.1 show a (sometimes wide) majority of participants endorsing a wide variety of reform proposals. In fact, of the 19 reforms I advanced, all but 2 (population control and limits on economic growth) were endorsed by a majority of my participants when the interview began; by interview's end, even economic limits had won majority assent. When we recall that this assent was never passive, but actively asserted and defended, these figures strongly suggest that Americans are solidly progressive in their environmental policy orientations—at least at the level of policy specifics.

Preferred Strategies

Over the course of each interview, I also repeatedly asked participants how they thought we ought to be attacking environmental problems. The constant reply: Whatever works. This came as no great surprise. For good or ill, Americans are suspicious of grand ideologies. This group likewise doubted the existence of any environmental policy cure-all. As we will see in the next chapter, for some this skepticism deepened into outright cynicism. But for the great majority, it meant that only a grab bag of policy instruments and other political changes was likely to get the job done. Typically this involved stricter regulation and/or better enforcement (never nationalization), incentives, education, spurring benign technologies, planning or coordination, recycling, and manipulation of the price mechanism.

Far more fascinating was the fact that nearly half of my participants spontaneously recommended, as part of their prescriptive mix, one or more political changes that, if enacted, would likely improve the quality of public deliberation on the environment. Out of the 46, 7 included education among their recommendations; 5 suggested public information, enlightenment, or attitude change; 3 called for greater public involvement or grassroots action; another 5 called for various combinations of these. (Four made no specific political recommendations.) One even recommended that everyone be "put through an interview like this." I had a variety of more specific questions touching more closely on the theme of participation and deliberation. But these recommendations, not all of them involving governmental policy per se, were all the more remarkable because they were made either in the context of explaining responses to more specific policy questions or in response to the open-ended question: How do you think we should go about deciding how to treat the environment? One especially memorable response came from Frederick Lorenz, a vigorous Republican long active in local and state politics:

> In the Old Testament, we read the words of God, where he said, "Come, let us reason together." Those were also favorite words of Lyndon Johnson. If one thing we have learned, I believe, in the last 100 years, which has taken us from dynastic empires to [*pauses*] absolutely brutal dictatorships of differing stripes, [*pauses*] it appears that the answer lies in the democratic will of the people. The democratic will of the people is something which evolves when people sit down and talk and reason together. If people can be made a part of the process through our governmental institutions, they are going to feel much more a part of what is taking place than if some autocrat from on high imposes his particular idea of what is good for you. And so, [*pauses*] I believe that we pursue this matter initially through education ("brainwashing," if you wish), sensitization of the people. And that, I say, on the national level. On the international level, the same has to take place: where the people actually come to the realization that they cannot forever dump upon this planet and expect it to have the type of resiliency that we would hope for. So I think, very simply put, it has to be a matter of educating, orienting, sensitizing the people on the face of this sphere, so that we can extend the life as long as possible.

That there appears to be so small a gap between the public's political theory of the environment and the one I am advancing here is certainly humbling. But it is also immensely encouraging. The old saw about leading a horse to water is nowhere more apt than here. Fortunately, Americans appear to need little encouragement to drink at this particular trough. Many are already looking for it. At the same time, they clearly reject the perennial alternatives: leaving things to the experts and doing it all yourself.

Radical Decentralization and Technocracy Rejected

My participants were as conservative about how environmental policy is made as they were progressive about policy specifics. Here they at least partly inspired the argument that I made in chapter 2. Although more than two-thirds endorsed improving local communities' ability to resist environmental threats (see the first two proposals at the state level in table 4.1), more than two-thirds suggested no basic change in the way the government goes about making and implementing environmental policy. Moreover, the group was evenly split on the question of the proper relationship between local, state, and federal units of government: Eighteen favored giving more power to local governments. Twelve thought the federal government ought to assume more responsibility. The rest thought the present mix was adequate. And it was clear that, with but one exception, those favoring change envisioned tilting the balance of power in one direction or the other, not a fundamental restructuring of environmental policy-making. At the same time, fully two-thirds of my participants rejected handing more power over to environmental administrators, ecologists, and policy analysts, even after being reminded of the complexity and technical nature of many environmental problems. Given the puzzlement that most participants experienced, this is a rather surprising—and encouraging—finding. Many of those who rejected a technocratic solution to environmental problems did so because they believed either that experts can't be trusted or that they aren't really needed. Several suggested that, given the breadth and geographical variability of environmental problems, environmental policy expertise is inherently limited. Most simply expressed their faith in democracy in one form or another: "Define 'expert,'" replied dairy farmer Frank Hauser rather curtly. "Anybody can be an expert," Karen Brunson reminded me. "People with common sense make *better* decisions than experts," insisted Deena Champney. An environmental expert himself, Don Wilson warned me: "Experts are like lawyers; they say what they're paid to say."

When Environmental Policy Expansion Is Resisted

In the end the relevant question about citizen beliefs, viewed as a constraint on public policy, is: What is the public likely to resist? When it comes to environmental policy, I think most scholars have missed what is perhaps this question's most important dimension, namely, the temporal one. And they have missed it because most of the measures they have used are static: they ask, "What do you believe in now?" But what a person can accept today is often very different from what she or he may accept in the future. Recall that 28 out of my 46 participants advocated environmental policy expansion. Of these, however, at least a quarter stressed that expansion should be "slow," "measured," or "ratcheted up." More deliberate expansion, it was frequently argued, allows for policy learning on the one hand and public learning on the other. Hence the crucial issue is not *which* environmental policies people are likely to resist, but *when*. Richard Johnson, a farmer, summed up his overall view of environmental policy with this admonition: "You can do so much over a time period. You can't turn the world around overnight. Every time we try to do it, we get in trouble." A neighbor, Frederick Lorenz (whose deliberative prescription I quoted above), put the point more strongly. Although he himself had a clearly progressive view of environmental protection, recall that he cautioned, "What these environmentalists have in mind is more on the order of shooting the tsar." Several other participants suggested that simple fairness requires changing the rules of the game slowly enough for players to stay in the game.

How fast is too fast? That, of course, is a question of degree, and even more of perception. But perhaps this is the practical lesson to be learned from the defeat of California's 1990 omnibus environmental referendum: Big Green wasn't too big for voters, just too fast.

Environmental reforms are not likely to gain public support if they are perceived as too great a departure from the status quo. But is there any substantive limit that present beliefs impose on an environmental agenda? If my participants were at all representative, their responses suggest that there are two such limits. The first is on population policy. The proposal I suggested was rather mild (a tax on families with more than two children), and yet 34 of my group of 46 rejected it. Participants regularly denied that our overall consumption, based on high per capita rates of resource usage, justifies such a policy. Twenty rejected the proposal at least partly because such a policy was felt to infringe on parents' freedom. Seven others cited other important values: equity, utility, family integrity, religious strictures, and the overall size of society's talent pool. But for only 3 of these 22 respondents did the value cited stand alone as the rationale for rejecting a tax on family size; in all other cases, the policy was also seen as unnecessary because the United States has no population problem, because milder policies are sufficient, because such a policy is impractical or unworkable, or because of some combination of these reasons. The dozen respondents who cited no important political value in justifying their rejection of the population proposal were evenly split among those who denied the existence of a population problem, those who believed that milder policies are sufficient, those who saw the tax as unworkable, and those who combined two of these reasons.

The first thing to notice about this welter of numbers is simply that most people's responses to environmental policy are not based on a single reason or value, much less on impulse or whim. They are, rather, the product of a rationale in which facts, values, and judgments all play a part. I will have much more to say about this process in the following chapter, whose principal theme is the complexity at the heart of citizens' environmental policy thinking. Here we see a clear example of this, even where thought is focused on a single issue. Logically, we can say that, to be complete, any environmental policy argument must contain four types of statements. It must include statements about political facts and political values and about environmental facts and environmental values. A fraction more than one in six participants made such a complete argument. But almost two-thirds, perhaps more, made claims covering two or three of the four bases. (The precise number is difficult to determine: is the statement "Population is not a problem" a factual statement, a value statement, or both?) Whatever the precise numbers or percentages, it is clear that, for most people, the answer to any given environmental problem will rarely turn on one consideration (whether factual or evaluative) alone.

And yet, certain considerations will weigh more heavily in some instances than in others. The population issue suggests that the value Americans place on privacy is crucial in explaining an anti-environmental stand, despite the fact that a belief in the value of privacy almost always operates in unison with other perceptions. Not so on the issue of economic growth. In fact, political values played no significant role in leading a majority to reject limiting growth. Only 8 of 25 cited values like civil peace, utility, freedom, and human potential in their responses. Instead, the dominant rationale for resisting such a cap was either that technology will solve the problems created by growth, or that "clean" growth is possible, or that limits are impossible to implement, or some combination of these.

A slim majority rejected any cap on economic growth, largely on the grounds that there are better ways of pursuing environmental ends. But there was some evidence of a more general resistance to outright bans. In the first place, none of my respondents suggested bans as a method, either to deal with specific problems or as a more general environmental protection strategy. And, although majorities endorsed banning both further development of local wetlands and the construction of a polluting factory in their community, those proposals garnered the least support among the 17 proposals that were supported. However, this resistance to bans does not appear to apply to wilderness areas: all but 12 respondents supported a general ban on economic activity in wilderness areas and only 6 opposed such a ban on developing Antarctica.

To sum up: this varied group of citizens was environmentally progressive across the board—in terms of its goals, in terms of the broad strategy it saw as best suited to advancing those goals, and in terms of both the specific and general levels of policy it saw as following from that strategy. Skeptics will no doubt object that this group, as mixed as it was, was simply expressing its adoration for the political fashion of the moment. To that objection, I offer these considerations. First, as I explain below, the environment is no fleeting fashion: its popularity in the polls has remained amazingly constant for some two decades or more. Second, natural processes do not give a hoot about the candor of *Homo sapiens*; it matters not a whit to these processes why people wish to preserve them, only that they wish to do so. I for one much prefer that my neighbors believe, however frivolously, in energy conservation than that they be genuinely and authentically committed to driving their Cadillac to the corner store three times a day. Third, to a person, these individuals were able to give political justifications for their environmental beliefs. As we shall see in the next chapter, the number and variety of values they found in nature were truly astounding. If environmental protection is just a fashion, why did virtually every one of my participants take it so seriously and defend it so eloquently? Fourth, and finally, I should emphasize that my primary aim throughout this study was to test two parallel propositions: (1) that citizens are willing to deliberate about environmental policy and (2) that they are capable of doing so. I consider these citizens' environmental progressivism to be one strong warrant (among many) for believing the first of these propositions to be true. But if am overestimating their progressivism, this would only reinforce the second half of my deliberative hypothesis, for it would underestimate the environmental gains made as a result of the interview. In other words, my interpretation in this sense is self-correcting: the less progressive my participants appear, the greater the resulting gains must appear; the more limited one judges them to be in their willingness to deliberate, the more one has to appreciate their ability to do so.

Interview Findings and Survey Data Compared

Intensive interviews cannot produce statistical generalizations; they are based on far too narrow a population sample. What they can do is suggest whether existing interpretations of more representative data are accurate or not (Hochschild 1981: 22–24; Reinarman 1987: 19). The result is not to "falsify" one or another interpretation, but to provide support for one interpretation and simultaneously to challenge its competitors. Not a crucial experiment, intensive interviews nevertheless provide great interpretive leverage. It is their depth, not their breadth, that allows intensive interviews to generate evidence that has direct significance in adjudicating empirical disputes. I interviewed people across the environmental spectrum. If these individuals all held true to form, the data would contribute nothing to sorting out competing interpretations of Americans' environmental policy beliefs. However, systematic deviations across the groups, or even a few significant deviations, might give cause to reject one or another of the conventional interpretations. But not necessarily sufficient cause. As one of the originators of the interview method noted, intensive interviews ultimately function "as illustrations, not as demonstrations" (Riesman 1965: 28).

Normally the direct comparison between competing interpretations afforded by interview data is highly illuminating. But in the present context it is likely to be especially revealing, since there is relatively little variation in environmental policy beliefs across most demographic categories. Innumerable studies have shown that environmental policy beliefs are relatively invariant by gender, race, class, age, residence, or any other simple category (Van Liere and Dunlap 1980). Beliefs do vary, of course. But not in any way that can be simply predicted on the basis of census data. Hence if a pattern were to emerge even in my small sample, it would be more generalizable to the population as a whole than, say, a pattern of attitudes toward distributive equality (Hochschild 1981), the state (Reinarman 1987), or community life (Bellah et al. 1985).

What light do the interviews I conducted shed on previous interpretations of Americans' environmental policy beliefs? In the first instance, they show that Americans are neither especially radical nor particularly conservative when it comes to environmental policy. While it is true that radical environmental groups have swollen in the past decade, that environmental philosophy is making inroads in academia, that American churches are beginning to take an interest in environmental problems, and that there are even some survey data that seem to suggest a kind of environmental awakening in America, most survey data tell a less exciting tale,[5] and radical environmental groups (not to mention churches) are a distinct rarity, representing perhaps 1 percent of the population.[6] My participants were relatively open-minded, willing to learn—and they did. But they gave no indication, as a group least of all, of being prime candidates for a conversion to a new environmental *Weltanschauung*. Many expected their thinking to change as the times change and hoped U.S. environmental policy will change along with it. But radicals they were not, emphasizing almost always the importance of timing, planning, and careful judgment.

But neither were they conservative, much less reactionary, in their environmental beliefs. We are often reminded that American culture contains within it the seeds of continued environmental despoliation in the form of individualism, consumerism, and a worldview hopelessly incompatible with long-range environmental stability.[7] As attractive as these cultural critiques occasionally seem, they often suffer from important conceptual flaws. Some are woefully short on evidence. And where positive evidence does exist, it is usually mixed. Similarly, it may be true that, as sociologist Riley Dunlap has argued, "the limited electoral impact of environmental issues (particularly relative to economic issues) indicates that support for environmental protection is not as strong as the tradeoff responses suggest" (summarized below in figure 4.6) (1987: 35).[8] But survey data (as well as popular resistance) show quite clearly that Americans rejected Reagan's environmental agenda, and we cannot simply assume that Americans' environmental beliefs are just the residue or distillate of a long (and toxic) philosophical-historical tradition. In fact, the evidence presented in this chapter suggests that these beliefs are anything but that, that Americans are not only pro-environment but generally pro-environmental *policy*.

Indeed, my participants were rather progressive. In one sense, at least, that should come as no surprise. After all, Americans like to think of themselves as progressives (Lipset 1986). But my own findings are hardly the only kind of data that point in the direction of environmental progressivism. In fact, most of the other evidence we have on Americans' environmental beliefs includes the best survey data available.

In the early 1980s Lester Milbrath conducted a series of careful and comprehensive surveys designed to gauge the public's willingness to endorse environmental policy. His published summary of the results argued that, despite a great deal of residual ambiguity, there had been "substantial movement away from the [materialistic] dominant social paradigm towards the New Environmental Paradigm, at least at the level of beliefs and values, even among some business leaders" (1984: 40, 80). Parallel studies by Stephen Cotgrove (1982) and Riley Dunlap and Kent Van Liere (1978, 1984) resulted in similar findings. The best longitudinal data on environmental policy likewise point to a solidly progressive orientation, as figures 4.1 through 4.5 indicate.

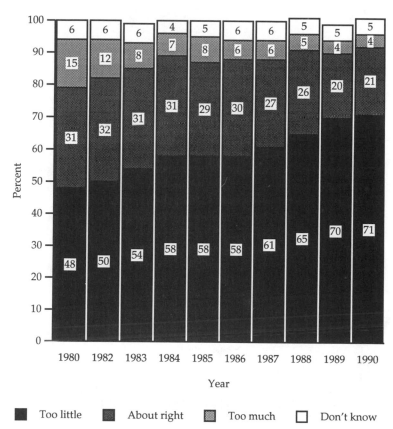

Figure 4.1. Views on U.S. government spending on the environment.
Source: National Opinion Research Center (in Dunlap 1991).

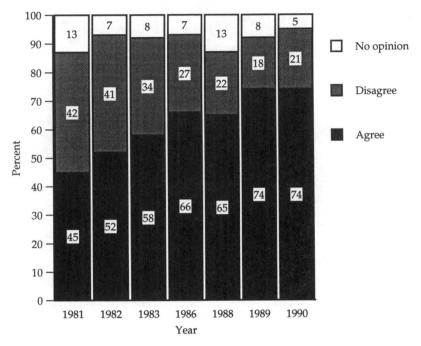

Figure 4.2. Views on protecting the environment regardless of cost.
Source: CBS News Poll in the *New York Times* (in Dunlap 1991).
Note: The 1982 survey was limited to voters only.

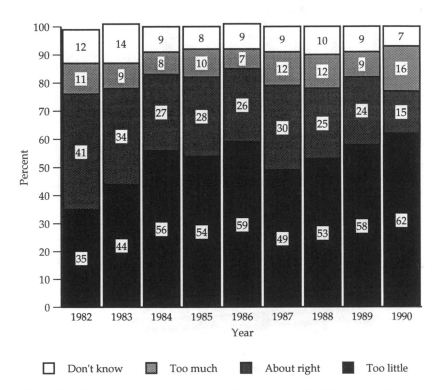

Figure 4.3. Views on environmental protection efforts by the U.S. government. *Source:* Cambridge Reports and Cambridge Reports/Research International (in Dunlap 1991).

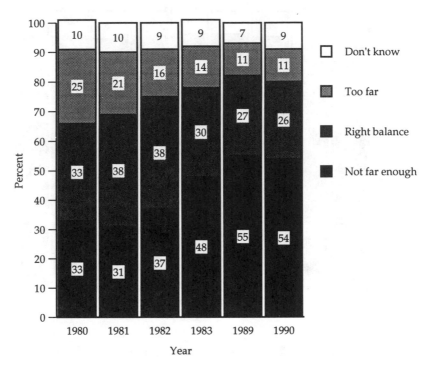

Figure 4.4. Views on environmental laws and regulations.
Source: Roper Organization (in Dunlap 1991).

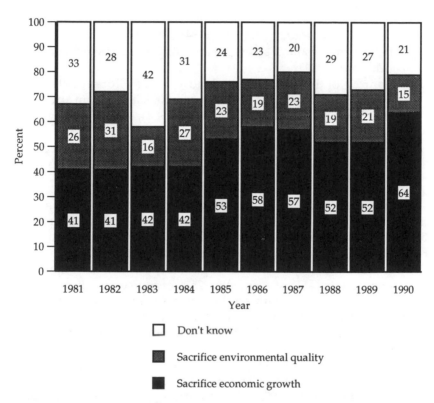

Figure 4.5. Views on environmental quality versus economic growth.
Source: Cambridge Reports and Cambridge Reports/Research International (in Dunlap 1991).

These polling data are really only the tip of the iceberg. Polls also show that (sometimes very substantial) majorities of Americans

- are concerned about the environment (OECD 1985: 19);
- believe that pollution is among the most important problems facing the nation (Petulla 1987: 59);
- believe environmental risks to be serious—and worsening (Hays 1987: 206);
- believe that we are losing ground in our efforts to preserve the environment intact (Milbrath 1984: 97);
- believe that resource shortages are likely in the absence of reform (Milbrath 1984);
- approve of the environmental movement (Milbrath 1990: 284);
- believe that nature is inherently valuable, apart from any use it may have for humankind (Milbrath 1984);
- endorse the broad concept of ecological limits, including the notion of a steady-state (Milbrath 1984: 22, 246–247; see also Dunlap and Van Liere 1978, 1984; Berberet 1988: 2; Dunlap 1985; Hays 1987: 125, 149).

It turns out that there is a great deal of overlap between my own findings and those of most survey researchers. In fact, my interviews differed from the results of national polls in only two significant respects: unlike the interviews I conducted, national studies show that the populace *is* ready to invoke population controls and limits on economic growth—at least eventually. This, of course, simply reinforces my overall conclusion that Americans are environmentally progressive. On the other hand, surveys generally show that the public is *not* willing, as my participants were, to sacrifice economic prosperity for energy conservation.[9] One series of polls shows that a consistent plurality of the populace has ranked having adequate energy above protecting the environment (see figure 4.6). The high tide in the environment-energy trade-off was reached in 1976, when 46 percent put environmental protection ahead of adequate energy sources (Dunlap 1987). And yet the evidence on the energy issue reveals a public not hostile to the environment but ambivalent about how to balance environmental and other aims. To begin with, only 2 percent of the public blamed environmental regulations for the energy crisis itself Kelley et al. 1976: 218). In addition, the evidence is at best mixed that Americans see increasing energy supplies as superior to conserving energy (Milbrath 1984: 34). Even before the Persian Gulf war confirmed it, there was also general agreement that maintaining adequate oil supplies through the year 2000

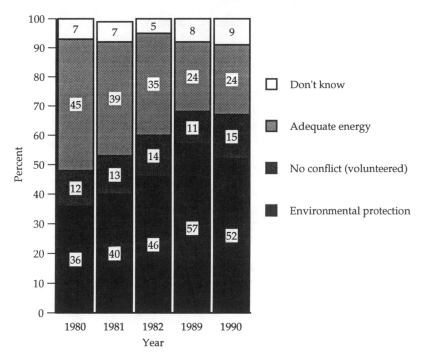

Figure 4.6. Views on environmental protection versus adequate energy.
Source: Roper Organization (in Dunlap 1991).

would be problematic (*New York Times*, July 1, 1990). Finally, the public as a whole has also expressed a desire for a solar future and is increasingly wary of nuclear energy (Milbrath 1984: 31–32).[10]

To the voluminous survey data on the subject, which, with the exception of the single graph shown in figure 4.6, all point in the direction of environmental progressivism, one can add data on everything from membership trends in both small and mainstream environmental groups[11] (see figure 4.7), and trends in consumer purchasing habits,[12] to recreational patterns,[13] trends in mass media coverage,[14] and even financial forecasts[15]—all of which, especially when placed in historical context[16]—point in the same direction: when it comes to environmental protection, Americans have in mind not a night watchman but a vigilant patrolman.

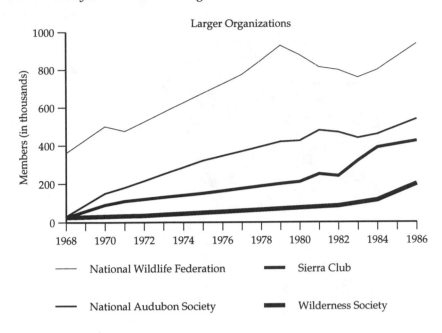

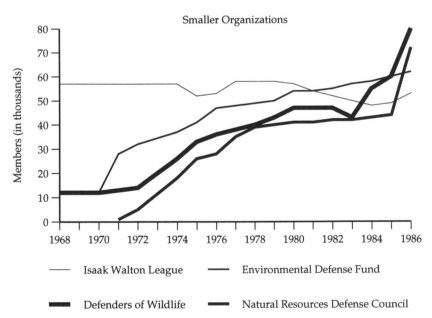

Figure 4.7. Membership in selected U.S. environmental organizations.
Sources: Susan B. Tyner, *The Christian Science Monitor,* January 13, 1987; Dunlap 1987; *USA Today,* April 20, 1990.

The Consensual Nature of American
Environmental Policy Norms

In chapter 6 I will argue that deliberative democracy holds the key to any longterm reconciliation between society and the environment. But deliberation cannot occur without a shared commitment both to deliberation itself and to the broader substantive goals deliberation is meant to address. From this normative perspective, it is crucial to gauge the extent to which environmental policy norms are shared. Unfortunately, much of the literature on the subject sorts people into apparently discrete categories. In so doing, it inevitably emphasizes (some would say "creates") divisions in the population under study. In the next chapter I will bring my own interview findings to bear on that issue. But even the above figures suggest that whatever cleavages exist in American society on the proper scope and direction of environmental policy are relatively shallow. This is borne out not only by the figures I have cited here but also by the overall tone of the many hours of interviews I conducted. The figures speak for themselves. In open-ended questions, *no one* suggested that the government do less to promote environmental ends. Even when challenged on normative and practical grounds, participants from a wide variety of backgrounds and circumstances endorsed 17 out of 19 policy reforms in the same interview. One of these proposals—expanding environmental education in public schools—deserves special comment. Only one in six of my participants rejected this proposal, even when it was pointed out that such a change might be seen by some as a pernicious injection of "politics" or "morals" into the curriculum. This finding was perhaps the best evidence of the existence of an environmental consensus among the American public, because it shows that the great majority of citizens themselves believe in the existence of such a consensus. And that, in the end, is what "consensus" means in the real world: a belief that others' views do not represent a threat.

The interviews likewise suggested consensual support for expanding public deliberation on environmental policy measures. Two-thirds of these citizens rejected handing environmental policy over to "the experts," and almost half spontaneously suggested expanding public deliberation in one way or another.

The overall tone of the interviews cemented this view of a broad and generally progressive environmental policy consensus. No one I spoke with had any great love for the government, but not a single participant challenged the basic legitimacy of government's role in promoting environmental goals. I suspect most would have agreed with college junior Lynda Evans, co-organizer of the local Greens chapter, who produced this off-the-cuff analysis:

> I think it's certainly the government's obligation to society. I mean, if you want to go to the Preamble, which hasn't always been serving for all people, but is meant to, you know, allow people to have domestic security and well-being, and liberty and life and happiness and all these fantastic things between our original documents, you know . . . That would be naturally the government's obligation—would be to promote the best possible environment for its people, you know, physical, economic, what-ever environment. So that would be part of the policy. You know, the government, with its tremendous power, has a variety of possible ways to do that at its fingertips, so to speak.

Everyone recognized the environment as posing a continuing problem for which solutions have to be found. At the same time, few insisted that their own answers were especially privileged. And very often the interview moved quickly from simply soliciting respondents' positions and justifications to mutual theorizing about how to improve the reform measures I had suggested. The responses summarized in table 4.1 thus belie an underlying willingness to invent new and better answers to environmental dilemmas. But this willingness contrasted sharply with the general absence of any more abstract theory of environmental protection. In the environmental realm, people are wary of government but not of individual policies.

I am not claiming that environmental protection has always commanded this kind of consensus. The first Earth Day, as the *New York Times* rightly pointed out, "was clearly on one side of the cultural schism that divided the country." Earth Day 1990, on the other hand, "was a mainstream event" (April 23, 1990). Environmentalism had become normal, expected, even American. And the content of Earth Day 1990 was less challenging than celebratory. Moreover, it was almost entirely apolitical. For all these reasons Earth Day 1990 was an inclusive event. But norms are designed to exclude, to limit, to separate the right from the less right and clearly wrong. Hence the best reading of the twentieth anniversary of the original Earth Day is that Americans' normative circle is clearly expanding, even if tentatively. From the standpoint of recommending a future course of action, it is the breadth and direction of the change since the first Earth Day that count, not the distance some few have taken the change.

This particular public's view of environmental policy can, I think, be summarized rather easily. It is neither radical, nor conservative, nor reactionary. All those labels suggest a kind of fixed commitment that simply does not exist except among a tiny handful of citizens. Instead, people are looking for plausible, concrete solutions to environmental dilemmas of whatever type, from whatever quarter. There is no innate ideological bias (much less a prejudice) against collective solutions. Given a reasonable environmental policy proposal, people will generally accept it, or at least give it a hearing. I recorded fewer than half a dozen occasions on which any of the 19 proposals I made were rejected out of hand. Even when participants ended up rejecting specific proposals, they wanted to know why in the world anyone might ever contemplate such a move. Americans are looking for a better environmental-protection mousetrap. It is in that rather specific sense that they can be called environmental progressives, and it is because of this orientation that expanded deliberation can be counted on to improve our collective environmental understanding, and hence our environmental policy.

5

Accelerating the Evolution of American Environmentalism

It's becoming obvious to everyone. People are aware. It's common sense that we have to cut down, slow down. *That's* how it should change—not government putting a cap here, a regulation there.
—college senior Erik Johannsen

From the normative perspective with which I approached this study, gauging precisely how progressive Americans' environmental beliefs are was far less important than learning how progressive they might become. My primary interest was in citizens' environmental potential. This led me to ask, first, What keeps people from being more environmentally progressive than they already are? In this chapter I let my participants themselves pinpoint the two key barriers. Although unaware of doing so, in the process they also be suggested a way around those barriers, a suggestion I take up in the remaining chapters.

At the same time, this chapter in one important sense completes our portrait of the public's environmental policy beliefs because the question of *what* people think about environmental policy is inseparable from the question of *how* they think about it. Knowing how people think about environmental policy—why they think about it the way they do—tells us a great deal about the kind of environmental protection the public endorses. But, despite oceans of empirical data, we still have only the dimmest understanding of how people think about environmental policy: about how the components of environmental policy beliefs are linked, about the kinds of reasons that lead people to one view or another, about what contextual factors are most important, and about the actual process of arriving at conclusions about environmental issues. Nor do we have any clearer understanding about what environmental policy means to people. Plausible theories do exist, and empirical studies of the issue are not wanting. Still, they leave many questions unanswered. Again the problem appears to be one of methodological distance: it is simply impossible to fill in the details of a map—in this case, the connections between individuals' various thoughts—unless one actually travels to the place being charted.

Thinking about Environmental Policy: The Need for In-depth Interviews

A full understanding of environmental policy thinking involves coming to terms with the origin, structure, and dynamics of individuals' environmental policy beliefs (see Dunlap and Van Liere 1978: 10). This is obviously a daunting task, because neither component (political thought, environmental thought) is very well understood at present (Hastie 1986: 30–31; Cook 1985; O'Riordan and Turner 1983). No single study can hope to resolve the many ambiguities and gaps I pointed out above. All the same, the interview method contributes greatly to our paltry understanding of this highly complex subject.

The interview method is important because, first, neither survey data nor historical explanations can ever fully specify the origins of individual beliefs (Reinarman 1987: 16). Moreover, those methods have a difficult time coming to terms with affect, with people's emotional responses to the world around them (O'Riordan and Turner 1983: 31–32). Although interviews are inherently biased toward the rational, they at least allow the interviewer to experience individuals' emotions directly (Converse and Schuman 1974). Since the argument between emotive and rationalist ethics is as alive and kicking in the field of environmental ethics as it is in traditional ethics, the in-depth interview's openness on this score is a distinct advantage.

A decade ago, Jennifer Hochschild argued that understanding how individuals' think about distributive justice requires "a research method that permits textured, idiosyncratic responses" (1981: 21). Certainly this is doubly true of understanding individuals' environmental policy thinking, which may involve the integration of the political, economic, and environmental domains, and in which the environmental domain may itself be further partitioned into discrete cognitive categories such as pollution, wilderness, and natural resource use (see Gill et al. 1986). In contrast, surveys by their very design are insensitive "to the *texture* of belief systems, to the nuance and complexity found in virtually every study that looks up close at the moving target of ideology as it exists in everyday life" (Reinarman 1987: 15, emphasis in original).

All too often environmental beliefs are treated by theorists, empirical researchers, and critics in an almost Manichean manner: either people are for environmental policy or they are against it. At most the observer offers four or five categories of environmental beliefs. As plausible as such categories sometimes seem, it is highly doubtful that people can (or should) be so neatly categorized. The practice is all the more troublesome given the widespread consensus that environmental beliefs are very important and the common finding (replicated again by my own fieldwork) that most people have a rather moderate view of environmental policy.

Interviews are at their best in revealing the microprocesses of individuals' thinking, at showing, in Reinarman's phrase, "how those living within [particular forms of consciousness] create their phenomenal 'truth' " and at the same time illuminate "how individual experience is informed by and comes to affect social structure" (Reinarman 1987: 14n10). Interviews, in short, can help uncover both the nature of individual thought processes and how these processes are related to individuals' social context.

The importance of social context in shaping or constraining human psychology and morality is perhaps the most fundamental axiom of political theory. This is true even of much of liberal theory, so often criticized as "individualistic" (see Gaus 1983; Billig 1976). The axiom is likewise either assumed or admitted by most schools within academic psychology (see Billig 1976) and much of political psychology as well (Stone 1987: 54). More specifically, there is a growing body of evidence to suggest that political reasoning is situationally variable (Hochschild 1981; Reinarman 1987: 161–162; see also Bennett 1980: 51–52, 56; Merelman 1969, 1971: 1047; Cook 1985: 1085; Barnes and Kaase 1979; Verba et al. 1978). At the same time, some environmental ethicists, most notably Christopher Stone, have argued that environmental norms must be situationally sensitive if they are to be fully rational (Stone 1987). And most empirical researchers, as we have seen, specifically argue that environmental thinking cannot be divorced from the larger socio-political milieu in which people find themselves (see also O'Riordan and Turner 1983: 10).

A second basic problem with much of existing research on environmental policy thinking is that it allows little insight as to how individuals link particular beliefs: How do people arrive at conclusions on environmental policy questions? How do they arrive at the standards they employ? And why do people seem to make an exception of the environment when considering the advantages and disadvantages of state activity? Surveys are generally unable to do more than identify correlations between different beliefs, and even then the beliefs are compressed into the surveyor's categories; thus, the elements, configuration, and significance or meaning of those complexes of individual beliefs are all lost (Hochschild 1981: 21; Sandbach 1980; Reinarman 1987: 212; O'Riordan 1976: 10). Researchers have unfortunately failed to heed Springer and Costantini's call, issued in the early 1970s, to focus on the "overarching concepts" linking environmental issues in people's minds (Springer and Costantini 1974). This failure has occurred despite early evidence that combinations of motives seem to be of central importance in individuals' environmental policy thinking (O'Riordan and Turner 1983; Bruvold 1973: 214–215), and that they seem to be central in other areas of political reasoning as well (Hochschild 1981; Gill et al. 1986).

It is no comfort that this deficiency extends beyond the area of environmental thinking. As Ward (1986: 141) pointed out not long ago, "Although many studies purport to address structure, most are little more than catalogues of belief content, employing passive collection measures, and are analytically limited to identifying 'what goes with what?' (Carmines and Stimson, 1982; Converse, 1964; Field and Anderson, 1969; Luttbeg, 1968; Nie and Anderson, 1974; Nie et al., 1976; Stimson, 1975)." She went on to point out that "the structural dimension of ideology" can only be revealed only "by engaging the subjects in *active*, *direct*, and *multiple* tests of cognitive processing, rather than relying solely on passive survey responses" (Ward 1986: 142, emphasis in original; see also Merelman 1969, 1971). In practice, this means that "what is important to ask is not *what* is believed, but *how* it is believed" (Ward 1986: 146, emphasis in original; see also Werner and Schoepfle 1987: 192; Gayin 1975). The interview format allows this question to be asked, and asked repeatedly. Interviews can thus offer real insight into the process of political thinking. Unlike surveys, for example, interviews are capable of revealing how individuals justify contradictions between principles and their application (Billig 1982: 221ff.)

In the last chapter I argued that in-depth interviews provide a crucial complement to historical and sociological data on Americans' environmental thinking. The considerations just presented add up to a second claim: interviews allow us to see how that thinking actually functions. Interviews are thus likely not only to help eliminate bad interpretations of existing survey data but also to pick up where surveys leave off, because they provide insight into the general contours and dynamics of individuals' environmental policy beliefs. For this reason, interviews offer more than interpretive guidance about what the mass of people think; they hold out the promise of revealing *how* people think (Hochschild 1981: 22–24). And it is a promise that has been amply and repeatedly fulfilled in a lengthening series of interview-based studies, focusing variously on political ideology (Lane 1964), judicial decision-making (Gayln 1975), distributive justice (Hochschild 1981), state-market relations (Reinarman 1987), welfare programs (Bumiller 1987), and race relations (Lukas 1988).

It would, of course, be impossible to investigate every facet of individuals' thinking in one sitting, or even in multiple sittings. I chose to focus on the relationship between individuals' political orientations and their environmental ethics for a number of reasons. The first reason has already been noted: theorists are virtually unanimous in arguing that the environment poses an inherently political problem (a representative sample would include Perrings 1987; Schrader-Frechette 1985; Kelley et al. 1976; Ophuls 1977; and Commoner 1976). The second is that social scientists of varying methodological persuasions have found at least some evidence of a linkage between individuals' social ideals and their view of environmental policy (Springer and Costantini 1974; Buttel and Flinn 1978, 1976; Dunlap and Van Liere 1984, 1978; Cotgrove 1982; Kenski and Kenski 1984). Most of my questioning consequently centered on this question: How do individuals formulate the relationship between policy and the environment?

The two essential dimensions of environmental policy are named in the term: environment and policy. All environmental policies specify environmental goals on the one hand and mandate action on the other (see White 1966: 125). To endorse a given environmental policy measure requires both that one believe in the environmental limit it prescribes, and that one deem state action the appropriate means of enforcement. (This in turn presupposes the belief that the given limit has been, or will soon be, exceeded.) Likewise, to oppose a given policy is either to oppose the limit it prescribes, or to oppose the use of governmental means to enforce it, or both. Indecision in judging an individual policy can result from ambivalence about the propriety of the limit it sets or about the rightness of state action as a means of securing the limit in question.

At the level of aggregate policy, the possibilities expand, at least in the middle range. To advocate a stronger overall environmental policy means that one endorses a stronger environmental ethic and governmental action to enforce the limit(s) prescribed by that ethic. Hostility to present environmental policy as a whole may result from the absence of even a moderately strong environmental ethic or from the combination of a moderate (or weak) environmental ethic and the belief that it requires, for whatever reason, a lesser degree of government enforcement. Belief in a middle-range environmental policy—a belief apparently shared by most Americans—might result from simple indecision about either the proper scope of environmental limits, or the efficacy of government action, or both. But it might also result from either of the following: (1) a belief in a wider range of environmental limits coupled with either a denial of the need for government action or a failure to consider its necessity; or (2) the positive endorsement of a limited number of specific policy measures.

The first goal of the interviews themselves was always to find out if any of these combinations led an individual to a given environmental policy orientation, or whether a more complicated explanation was required. Throughout the interviews, my basic strategy was thus to ask two basic questions repeatedly: What limits are necessary? Of those limits, which require state action? I then asked respondents to explain their answers: Why are some limits necessary and others not? If the limit is not to be enforced by government, how is enforcement to be secured—voluntarily or technologically? Is the limit widely abridged? Would it be abridged in the absence of government involvement? These theoretical questions, embodied in my questionnaire, were just that— questions. To return to the metaphor of discovery, the questions delineated an itinerary, but only loosely. They are not "hypotheses"; my first goal was not to test any of the explanations reviewed above, but to have explanations given to me (see Riesman 1965: 16). And, to repeat, the most crucial of these explanations was: "I am against that proposal because . . . "

General Orientations and Specific Positions: Consistency, Not Deduction

Despite all the advantages of in-depth interviews, I cannot lay claim to any new theory of how people, or even Americans, think about environmental policy. But the interviews did allow me to pinpoint why Americans aren't more environmentally progressive than they already are. Along the way, the interviews also showed that most of the going theories on the subject are plainly incorrect. To start with, take the hoary controversy over the degree to which Americans' political beliefs are "consistent." As formulated by Phillip Converse in a seminal article in the mid-1960s, "consistency" means there is a correlation between individuals' specific policy beliefs and their position on the left-right political spectrum. And Converse found that perhaps only one in five Americans' political thinking displayed this trait (1964). My

Table 5.1. Consistency between general and specific environmental policy positions

General oritentation toward environmental policy	Average percentage of policies endorsed
Need radical reforms (n = 7)	89.7
Need reforms (n = 21)	77.8
Status quo satisfactory (n = 17)	56.4
Unsure (n = 1)	53.0

respondents, on the other hand, were exceedingly consistent—at least within the more restricted realm of environmental policy (see table 5.1). That is, their overall orientation correlated rather well with the number and scope of specific policy proposals they were willing to endorse. (I should also add that if by "consistent" we mean simply "averse to contradiction," the typical participant was exceedingly consistent: despite the length of the interviews, outright contradictions were a real rarity; most participants succeeded in avoiding them entirely.[1] At the same time, however, this clearly does *not* mean that people *deduce* their views of specific policy proposals from their overall orientation to environmental policy (much less from any overarching political ideology or disposition or philosophy). If anything, quite the reverse seems closer to the truth: people arrive at a general view of environmental problems *inductively*. But that general view, as I will explain below, is cognitively inert: once in place it does not play any adjudicative role. In fact, its only role is to allow people to have a ready response when the pollster calls.

Balancing Multiple Values: Neither Deduction, nor Paradigms, nor Residue

Although I can offer no full-blown theory of environmental policy thinking, my participants made clear that their policy conclusions were the result of a highly complex cognitive operation, involving judgments of environmental fact and a constant balancing of multiple environmental values against competing political goals. This finding, as commonsensical as it appears, flies in the face of some of the more popular theories on the subject. I will mention but three of them here. The first holds that environmental policy views are deduced from more fundamental political orientations; the second, that they are embedded within larger worldviews, or "paradigms"; and the third, that they are the by-product or residue of important social or psychological conditions.

The Independence of Environmental Values

Anthropologist Mary Douglas and political scientist Aaron Wildavsky have advanced the most original and closely argued statement of the view that individuals' environmental orientations are the product of prior political commitments (Douglas and Wildavsky 1982). They argue that individuals' environmental views follow directly from their choice of social model (democracy, hierarchy, or market) because these models structure individuals' view of risk. Whatever the other problems with this view, it is woefully inadequate as a description of, much less as an explanation for, my participants' conclusions.

At first glance, table 5.2 appears to confirm Douglas and Wildavsky's view, at least in the sense that my radicals tended to be democrats and my conservatives more market-oriented. But we hardly need theory to tell us that, because such a result was logically guaranteed from the start: environmental policy is *policy* after all: it always means at least some government intervention in the marketplace. Devotees of the market are hardly likely to miss that implication. Beyond this, however, my findings run directly counter to Douglas and Wildavsky's theory in several ways. The most important is simply that participants in all three main groups, including the extremes, found a *variety* of social ideals to be compatible with their environmental views. The only model no one endorsed was hierarchy. Even allowing room for the reduced size

Table 5.2. Environmental and social orientation

Overall environmental policy orientation	Social orientation	Number of participants
Radical change	Democracy	4
	Enlightened democracy	2
	Social democracy	1
Expand present policy	Enlightened democracy	3
	Democracy	3
	Social democracy	3
	Regulated market	4
	Market	5
	Mixed or pragmatic	2
	None	1
Maintain present policy	Democracy	2
	Social Democracy	1
	Market	6
	None	2
	Regulated market	3
	Mixed	3
Unsure	Democracy	1

of this sample, it seems highly unlikely (to put it mildly) that social ideals control environmental beliefs to the degree that Douglas and Wildavsky claim. Moreover, despite the rough correspondence between belief in the market and environmental conservativism, all but one of those who fitted the environmentally conservative–market oriented pattern argued on at least one occasion that the environment must be exempted from market control. Fred Mechler, the politically savvy union officer, was typical of this group. Skeptical in regard to how much environmental restraint could be brought about through legislation alone, I asked him if perhaps we ought not to rely more on market forces. His response was, as usual, brusque: "Is the market stopping anything now?" As committed as he was to his social ideal—a market economy offering true equality of opportunity—this social ideal in no way controlled his environmental policy norm. He was genuinely surprised that anyone would confuse the two realms. Clearly his view of society no more controlled his view of environmental policy than his view of that realm controlled his social ideal.

In addition, table 5.2 conceals a large degree of variation *among* those in each of the three principal policy orientation groups. Even among the seven respondents who advocated major or radical environmental reform, for example, none supported precisely the same mix of policy proposals. And while one participant supported all 19 of my suggestions, all the other participants found fault with at least 1 of them, and one participant rejected 4. The other groups were even more mixed. The 21 who advocated more moderate policy expansion rejected anywhere from 2 to 8 of my proposals, whereas among just 17 supporting the status quo the range of rejected proposals extended from 2 all the way to 14.

Moreover, among the 46 interviews I conducted, there was abundant direct evidence that the kind of almost subconscious deduction Douglas and Wildavsky posit is a distinct rarity. Far more frequent is a fully conscious, if always ultimately ineffable, environmental balancing act. The question (and it is always a question, not a given) is where to place environmental policy on the spectrum or how to weigh environmental values against other social values. The following are among the innumerable examples I could cite from even this reduced sample:

> It's a case of "something had to happen," but maybe we swung a little too far. (environmentally conservative farmer Richard Johnson)

> We got to find the middle ground between the ecologists and the "bad guys." . . . I'm an environmentalist—not a pure environ-

mentalist, kind of a hermaphrodite. (environmentally progressive farmer Bob Kovalek)

It's a gradual thing, and a shifting of funds and shifting of emphasis. There might be other major issues that will have to take a higher role. It's a good thing we have environmentalists because they'll keep promoting the environmental issues, and these other people . . . And so we'll have . . . And everyone's being heard. (environmentally progressive corporate lawyer Carol Chapman)

I still think capitalism is the way to go. But, just like anything else, how far do you go along any lines? You know, eating is great, but how much can you eat? Drinking is good, but how much can you drink? Capitalism is good, but how much capitalists can you have? The thing is, money can't give you Almighty God and everything. I mean, there's got to be a concern about our individuals. (environmentally progressive letter carrier Michael Cerutti)

These are all relative issues and [depend upon] what the people will accept. (environmentally conservative engineer Don Wilson)

Finally, it is a virtual certainty that social ideals are not controlling in the *way* that Douglas and Wildavsky would have us believe. Their view is that what is central to explaining environmental beliefs is the differing attitudes people have toward risk. But if this cross-section of American society is at all representative, that view is patently false, or at least woefully incomplete. The historical record shows that American environmentalists have been motivated by a wide variety of motives: spiritual in John Muir's case, utilitarian in Gifford Pinchot's, and ecological in Aldo Leopold's. The average citizen is different only in that she or he tends to be motivated by some or all of these at once. This was true of all my participants, sometimes even in the context of judging individual policy proposals. Risk is only one of many value considerations that enter into individuals' environmental policy thinking. More generally, not one of my participants had anything remotely resembling an environmental ethic. Or, to put the point another way, their ethics were in every case decidedly pluralistic: they all invoked a wide range of values during our discussions, often in the course of dealing with one topic. The minimum number of discrete values any one participant invoked was 2, the maximum 16. Most participants cited at least half a dozen different environmental values, including those participants who were least progressive in their outlook. Likewise, almost all my participants combined various values at one time or another in defending individual proposals such as wilderness preservation or energy conservation. Moreover, people endorsed the same policy measures for a wide variety of reasons. For example, I had participants argue for a countywide, ecologically designed land use plan because (1) it would prevent conflicts of interest, (2) it would make for a more prosperous community, (3) it was good for the ecosystem as a whole; for some participants all of these at once seemed pertinent. For these Americans the environment represents truly a cornucopia of values, not just a source of risk (see table 5.3).[2] And this was just as true for environmental conservatives as for environmental progressives and radicals, which the following examples illustrate.

Gary Chauncy, a young man active in various cultural and environmental projects, was among the most radical of my participants. He is also a Native American who spends much of his time learning, practicing, and teaching "the old ways." One might have expected his environmental ethic to be thoroughly infused with the traditional Indian view of an animate Nature. And it was. But notice how he blends that view with other justifications for recycling, among them health, a concern for future generations, the integrity of what Leopold called the biota, the value of what contemporary environmental philosopher Holmes Rolston III has called stored achievement, and even democracy:

> Our landfills are getting used up. We're being "penny-wise, pound foolish." And our groundwater—it's not drinkable any more. A lot *more* are caring about Mother Earth, about the water, air, trees. Things are changing. Exxon is thinking twice now. But it's kind of scary, this polluted groundwater. We have to take care of these landfills and everything so that we can prevent disease. And the fish, too. The fish are vital because they go way back to prehistoric times. They're neat. I'm not too familiar with recycling, but I think it's good because our landfills are filling up.
> *Why don't we just build more of them?*
> Why would you want more of them? We have too many already. We should be planning for the future, a hundred years.
> *Why a hundred years, why should we care about future generations?*
> Because they might be your grandchildren.
> *What if I have no children?*
> Then you should care for your brothers and sisters.
> *Why not just leave this solid waste problem up to the free market to solve?*

Because recyclers are looking toward the future, because the space is already gone, because of the toxics.

All right, but why care about the future?

Because we owe it to the Earth that has sustained us and can sustain us in the future. If we take care of it, it'll take care of you.

Table 5.3. Variety and frequency of values cited in defense of environmental policy proposals

Values cited	Number of participants citing
System preservation (for humans)	39
Health	27
Future generations	26
Risk avoidance	25
Utility	23
Inherent value of ecosystem	16
Harm principle	16
Beauty	15
Recreation	14
Prevent free-riders/externalities	11
Community autonomy	11
Democracy	10
Individual autonomy	9
Inherent value of other organisms	9
Equality	7
Self-interest	6
More important than other social values	5
Education	5
History	4
Basic human needs	4
Employment	4
Community integrity	4
National (economic) autonomy	3
Charity	2
Inherent value of species	2
Family	2
Meaning	2
National security	1
U.S. role as moral leader	1
Spirituality	1
Personal growth	1
Human life	1
Equality of all parts of nature	1
Anticipation of scarcities	1
Inadequate information	1
Legitimate expectation due to past promises	1
Order	1

The next example of multiple values entering into participants' environmental policy calculations is from Deena Champney, a progressive. Here she is responding to my proposal to spend billions of federal dollars on a massive tree-planting program. Note that her positive response rests on no fewer than five distinct value commitments: future generations, the importance of allowing nature its own room to evolve, health, recreation, and utility or economic productivity:

> I would like to see, you know, the forest, like I said last time, those . . . What's that place in Brazil—that forest that they want to tear down?
>
> *The rain forest?*
>
> Yeah. Let that stay like it is, you know what I'm saying? Leave that. That's, you know . . . We don't have very many places like that left in the world. They're building up everything: condos, this, you know . . . Everybody want's to make a buck. So if we can change it,—you know, individual people—I'm all for it.
>
> *What about this building condos, building everywhere? Are we just going to . . . Where do we draw the line?*
>
> No, that I don't know. I wish we could draw the line. That's like part of Lake Michigan here, on the lakefront. Well, they put a lot of rocks there and they're building. So that's a resource they're taking, you know what I'm saying? *Down here.* Clean up the lake; don't build on it!
>
> *Yeah, right. What does it hurt to build on it?*
>
> Because you're taking away . . . You know these . . . OK, I say 30 or 40 years from now, if we won't have dolphins and birds, you know, things that are free . . .
>
> *Why does that bother you so much? I mean, what's so important about keeping those things wild?*
>
> Because it's part of nature. And to me, man has messed too much with nature. Because every time that damn shuttle goes up, this weather gets cracked all over the world, you know. It gets messed up. I'm all for change, but I'm kind of an old-fashioned girl. You know, I like to skip a rock on the lake, you know, and go fishing. See, we've never known what it was really like to live out of a polluted city. You know, when our grandparents were coming up, we didn't have all of that. You know, the kids were healthier, there were no pesticides on food or anything.
>
> *One thing's interesting, though, because you're . . . You've never seen a shark, have you?*
>
> No, except on TV.

But you still care about the sharks. So it's not just that you want to be able to see them, because you've never seen them. So why do you care?

Yeah. That's part of God's creatures. You know, he made those things.

So we should respect everything that God made. But what does that respecting mean? Does that mean we can't touch any sharks? That we can't . . . Because we got to eat; we got to touch some parts of stuff. So how do we decide what parts we're going to touch and what parts we're not?

That's a good question. I never thought of that, because I like fish and shrimp like hell! I don't know. I think we're just doing too much.

It's the overall amount?

Yeah.

OK. Then try to tell me how we know when we go . . . Like we're using it, we're touching it, we're messing around, and then all of a sudden we go over this thing and now it's too much. How do we know that we're doing that? Or, what tells you that we're going too far?

Like the oil spills. We're becoming careless; like I said, it's always about the dollar. You know, look at the people in Alaska; they lost a lot of money, you know; that was their livelihood—fishing. But here was enough fish, you know, I mean the fish were reproducing. But now, they won't reproduce anything because the ocean is messed up, and then . . .

Yeah. We're wrecking the whole thing.

Right. To me, they shouldn't go up there [speaking of the shuttle] because for what? I mean, you got problems here. Why do you want to go see where there's some other people on another planet, and you can't take care of home? Take care of here first. Like, they were talking about the ozone layer, you know, with the chemicals people use in their hair, and then they were talking like the chlorine in swimming pools, and then they say the water you drink isn't any good.

But maybe these are all just little sicknesses and they'll all get better.

Well, it won't get better, Adolf, if we don't stop it.

But it wasn't only dedicated environmental types that found multiple values in nature. Glen Thorne, environmental officer for a power company, argued against a complete ban on developing local wetlands. But here, and throughout the interview, his environmental conservatism was based on the conviction that the present environmental regime works rather well. In what follows, he cites three distinct values that are served by wetlands protection policy:

In the end, though, what is your decision based on?
Well, you'd need a lot of biological information on the area, and I think some of it's being gathered right now, the inventory. And then some sort of a consensus by the group that's looking at it.
There are some things that you're going to say, "OK, we're going to leave those alone." What kind of things are those usually? Is it the biological richness or the number of species in them?
It's the . . . Everyone is dependent on what's there. You still want to maintain diversity, so . . . That seems to be the interest from an environmental standpoint, is to continue to have the diversity you have.
And how do you decide whether you're going to have to create that diversity or whether that diversity's already there?
Well, you just have to look and see what's there now. And if something you're doing . . . The project can improve what's there now, and that's desirable. In the Ojibway situation, you know, one of the things that's desirable from the standpoint of the local public is good fishing. And spawning habitat is important, so if you can create more spawning habitat for the fishing, then, hey, that improves the local situation. So, it kind of depends on what people want.
So it's not as if you had some kind of scientific catalog and you try to make sure that that exists there. Say it's some list of species, and if that's not there then you try to re-create that. It's partly decided at least by what the people want in the local area. So are you then trying to create a balance between what the people want in that particular area and these other, more environmental concerns?
And economic, yeah.
So you're really trying to keep three balls in the air all at once.
"Yeah, trying to come up with balance, and say, OK, we can agree, this is going to be better for everybody.

The Absence of Integrated Paradigms

Environmental policy thinking is thus far more complex than suggested by the structural view. But it is also far less organized than another influential view would have us believe. A series of studies published in the late 1970s and early 1980s purported to show that Americans' environmental thinking is paradigmatic, that is, that people's beliefs tend to coalesce into identifiable structures containing numerous individual elements. The more people share the emerging postindustrial worldview, which these sociologists dubbed the New Environmental Paradigm (NEP), the more likely they are to be strong environmentalists (Dunlap and Van Liere 1978, 1984; Cotgrove 1982; Milbrath 1984). The studies generally showed significant correlations at the individual level between both the NEP and environmentalism and between the various elements of the NEP. The problem, of course, is that correlations indicate associations, not the tight connections suggested, or even guaranteed, by theory (see Norton 1991: 68). Everything that I heard during more than 200 hours of interviewing indicates that those connections simply do not exist for most people.

If paradigmatic thinking is characteristic of Americans in general, it should have been all the more evident among those participants at either end of the environmental policy spectrum. But two of the seven individuals who advocated major policy changes (my "radicals") failed to connect their various positions to a larger and more coherent critique of industrialism, and all seven clearly rejected two or more of the key elements of the NEP (limits on population and economic growth). Teresa Hirschler, a social worker focusing on adolescents, for example, was insistent that growth and development are "of no value at all." But she later rejected the proposed limit on growth as "unrealistic" because "employment requires growth." She likewise argued against my proposal that we tax couples with more than two children because, she said, it is unrealistic and "would impoverish those least likely to be able to afford it." On the other side were my environmental conservatives. Of the 17 who were satisfied with the environmental policy status quo, only 5 had anything resembling an industrial mind-set. The others either balanced environmental values against other (not always material) concerns, or lacked faith in the present system's ability to address environmental problems, or had so much faith in that system that they saw little need for any deviation from business as usual. And all 17 supported at least some of the individual elements of the NEP. In the middle were my 21 environmental progressives, only 1 of whom stood out as operating with a coherent environmental or ecological paradigm. More than most of my participants, Joe Page was a likely candidate for paradigmatic thinking. Strongly individualistic in both lifestyle and political convictions, astride his all-terrain vehicle he struck me as a modern version of Davy Crockett, defending his beloved homestead not against the Mexicans but against big-city developers and the Department of Natural Resources. Yet he dismissed my reference to James Watt's approach to resource management with an abrupt "I don't believe in that shit." And of the 19 policy reforms I proposed, he rejected only 2: increased environmental education in public schools and a ban on economic activity in Antarctica.[3]

Perhaps the authors of the paradigm studies simply misjudged the nature of the dominant paradigms. That is of course possible, but rather unlikely. In the next section I show that there is indeed much agreement on environmental policy—enough, as it turns out, to underwrite a more deliberative approach to the problem. But that agreement, as we have seen, does not necessarily extend to policy specifics, much less to metaphysics. Moreover, and this is the relevant point here, the vast majority of people simply do *not* link their policy beliefs together to the degree suggested by the term "paradigm."

This should really come as no surprise. That people structure their beliefs, but do so in multiple ways that do not always conform to the demands of logic, objective consistency, or synoptic rationality, has long been the dominant view among cognitive psychologists. It is an increasingly influential view among political psychologists as well (Lau and Sears 1986b; Simon 1985; Steinbrunner 1974). As consistency theories have become discredited, theories emphasizing information processing and decision-making heuristics have come to the fore (Stone 1987: 50; Reinarman 1987: 161–162, 212; Hochschild 1981: 230; Lau and Sears 1986a). And, as we have just seen, the link between ideology per se and environmental ethics is rather weak. Milbrath, for example, takes special pains to point out that his data indicate a lack of integration between the two axes (1984). He also found that environmentalists were also the most likely to doubt the efficacy of static solutions to environmental problems. Other surveys show that, precisely as cognitive theory predicts, people very often resist making trade-offs between political and environmental desiderata (Gilroy and Shapiro 1986; Allen and Popkin 1988; Cotgrove 1982; see also Dahl 1989: 305). Furthermore, as various scholars have pointed out, to label all environmentalists "pro-state" does violence to the manifest heterogeneity within the environmental movement (Schnaiberg 1973; Fox 1985; Sandbrook 1986). Indeed, environmental writers over the past several decades have in fact occupied "almost every position on the traditional right-to-left ideological spectrum" (Paehlke 1989: 94).

Active Environmental Thinking and Learning

There are any number of theories about the origins of people's environmental policy beliefs. Unfortunately, most fare no better than the two theories just discussed.[4] On this question my interviews simply added further coal to an already hot fire. Some of my participants provided some clues to the origins of specific beliefs when they explained their positions on various issues. And I later asked all my participants what they felt had most influenced their environmental thinking. Again, what stood out most clearly was variety. As I noted earlier, existing literature clearly shows that demographic characteristics (age, race, gender, class, occupation) are of limited value in predicting people's environmental positions.[5] That proved true of this group as well. I had a crop duster tell me groundwater pollution is the most important environmental problem in the state, a 94-year-old "La Follette Democrat" agree to limits on economic growth, a disabled inner-city black woman defend the right of all people to skip stones on a clean lake, a man with no education beyond high school rival Aldo Leopold's poetic genius in describing ecological relationships, and a politically conservative developer argue for ecological land use planning. True, there are exceptions to every statistical generalization, but that list could be extended almost indefinitely (and in the anti-environmental direction, as well). A couple of illustrations follow:

Betsy Schon is a Seventh-day Adventist. True to the millennial teachings of her church, she believes environmental degradation to be yet another sign that the Second Coming is nigh: "All this what's happening is just signs, and it's right in the Bible, that he is coming soon. And I don't believe the environment is *ever* going to get any better. Everything is going to keep getting worse and worse, up until he comes." But that fatalism did not keep her from adopting a strongly environmental stance or from endorsing 13 of the 19 reforms I suggested. Apostasy? Hardly. At two separate points during the interview I posed the obvious question: Given the imminence of Christ's return, what's the point in trying to solve any of these problems? She shrugged the question off the first time. The second time she said matter of factly: "We are admonished to plan as though we'll be here a lifetime, but live as though we might die tomorrow." Having also repeatedly cited the biblical injunction against greed, it is little wonder that, for Schon, Christianity's main environmental message is not dominion but stewardship.

By the time the interviewing process was nearly completed, Erik Johannsen had graduated and was about to take his first job, with the Dow Chemical Company. He was not only about to start working for one of the environmental movement's betes noires; he is a chemical engineer to boot. He argued a lot with his roommate, a member of the local Greens. At times he resembled the stereotype of the reflexive technology-lover, but not always. Certainly he didn't when it came to wilderness or wetlands.

Why not develop wetlands?
I don't know why not.
To protect the birds?
Yeah, the nature part.
Why is that important? Because they're pretty?
No. They *are* important, but it's not the beauty. It's a matter of destroying what God gave us. It is. You can't put it back.
But didn't God put it here for us to use it?
But wisely, though. What's wise? That's the question. I don't know. The problem is, once it's gone, we can't put it back.
That presumes we want to.
We are . . .
We should keep our options open?
No, it's just to keep it. To keep it.
What if we need part of it for industry? It's easy to keep if there aren't any conflicts.
Right. There's a choice there. If industry will make Wisconsin strong . . . I don't think the people of Wisconsin want to do that.
It's a difficult question.
My vote is no.
Not even to develop 10 acres?
For industry, huh? That depends on how much is bad. I don't know how big this marsh is, but I would say no; if it's marked off as a preserve, let it be a preserve. I don't know why though.
Let's figure that out. You said God gave us the Earth for us to use wisely. Does that include a preserve?
Yes, in my mind it does.
So we should save part of everything in nature?
Yeah . . . No, I . . . You *do* want part of everything, or why would he have put it here? We are supposed to use . . . Like the Indian philosophy: use what you need, leave the rest. Now it's a matter of how much do we need? It's a matter of American self-ishness is what it is. We want more material things. I like to think I use what I need, but I waste. Americans are wasteful.
Back to the marsh.
Say this marsh is gone and my grandkids want to know where it is and I can't tell them. For no good reason.
Do you know your grandkids will want to see it?
Yeah.
Where did you get the idea that God gave us the Earth to use wisely?
It's like when God created the Earth. It's been taught to me forever. It's part of the Christian belief, I think.

Any specific teaching?
It makes good sense to me. I can't say I'm a strong Christian, but it makes good sense. It's common sense. Why waste?

Not only did this engineer invoke an even stronger sense of Christian stewardship of nature than Betsy Schon did, he took the opportunity to slam American consumerism on the way. And this exemplar of technological expertise reached out to Native American pantheism for ethical guidance and felt psychologically buoyed by democratic sentiment. People are amazing.

It has long been known that demographic variables explain little variation in people's environmental policy thinking, that environmental protection has broad appeal among Americans (see Van Liere and Dunlap 1980). The findings presented in the previous section (to be elaborated upon below) suggest an explanation: that appeal is as broad as it is because the spectrum of values people find in the environment is also very broad.

Because people's environmental policy views also rest on these widely varied values, we might reasonably guess that a wide spectrum of things influences those views. And, indeed, that was quite obviously the case among my participants. Only three participants failed to cite more than one important influence on their thinking; the average of influences cited was between three and four; six people cited more than four. And there was variety in great abundance, as can be seen from table 5.4.

No wonder demographic variables fail to explain much variance in individuals' environmental thinking. And not only is the population in general influenced by a wide variety of factors; individuals clearly are as well. As I noted, virtually all my participants cited several types of influences (one recounted nine). And not even the most frequently cited influences were mentioned by a majority of this group. Furthermore, the mass media were almost always way down on people's lists. Clearly the media are no environmental wellspring. If anything, they are more like an irrigation system which people turn on or off according to the dictates of beliefs they already have. Nor is occupation one of the more powerful influences—at least its impact can vary tremendously. I talked with four farmers. All were quite obviously part of the land they farmed. But their environmental views spanned the environmental policy spectrum, and the two who had moved furthest in the direction of sustainable agriculture were of political breeds as distinct as one is likely to encounter anywhere in the United States. The two developers I interviewed shared an enthusiasm for planning

Table 5.4. Variety and frequency of influences cited

Type of influence	Number of participants citing
Mass media	21
Occupation	16
Outdoor activity	12
Direct experience of degraded environment	10
Books, films, lectures	10
Family member	9
Education/training	9
Specific life experience	8
Organizational activity	8
Friends	7
Religion	7
Local environment	7
Personality trait	5
Poverty	5
Family dynamics	4
Specific historical period	3
Local political scene	2
Specific political issue	2
Contacts by environmental groups	2
Teacher	2
Personal health problem	2
Having children	1

(itself an anomaly), but little else. One strongly resisted any general expansion in environmental policy and virtually every policy proposal I suggested, and the other's sometimes strident attacks on environmental obstructionists belied a firmly progressive view of environmental policy in general and a willingness to endorse numerous specific reforms.

The number and complexity of the pathways by which people arrive at their conclusions on environmental policy certainly stand as a challenge to the empirical theorist. But from a normative perspective, the implication is quite clear: because no single influence appears to dominate people's environmental policy thinking, whatever remedy one prescribes must likewise be very general: it must be capable of reaching different people in different ways and the same person in multiple ways. Deliberation is just such a remedy. In the next section I finish explaining why deliberation can be expected to work: ethical variety underwrites a widespread consensus on the need, as one of my participants put it, to get busy about environmental cleanup. The final section explains just what deliberation is meant to cure. There I focus on difference, on why some people endorse stricter environmental limits than others. Rather than presenting a full-blown explanatory theory of environmental policy thinking, I limit myself to answering the narrower question: Why aren't Americans more environmentally progressive than they already are? The answer is absolutely crucial if we are to discover how to accelerate the evolution of American environmentalism.

Ethical Disensus, Policy Consensus

Given all this variety, how can the progressive consensus described in the previous chapter possibly exist? The answer is as simple as it is significant: the more ways there are to value something, the more likely people will *disagree* about *why* to value it and the more likely they will *agree* that it *ought* to be valued. The cornucopia of values described above simultaneously ensures ethical (as well as metaethical) disensus and policy consensus. In short, citizens can (and do) agree about what needs to be done without necessarily agreeing about the reasons. And they can agree about the general level of effort that is called for, because all can find numerous reasons for protecting the environment.[6] To put the point another way, the consensus exists not *despite* but *because of* the multiplicity of reasons people have for believing in environmental restraint.

The same is true, incidentally, of professional environmental ethicists. Despite their very lively and sometimes acrimonious disputes, one has to look hard for signs that they disagree about the imperatives that follow from their distinctive metaethical frameworks. To take but one example, both Kristen Schrader-Frechette (who has added an intergenerational component to Rawlsian egalitarianism) and J. Baird Callicott (foremost contemporary advocate of biocentric holism) would clearly agree with my proposal banning economic development in wilderness areas, though for very different reasons. Shrader-Frechette's position would follow from the view that we are obliged to leave future generations at least as well off as the present generation and, since we cannot predict their preferences in advance, we need to allow them a full range of choices, including the use or nonuse of wilderness areas. Callicott, on the other hand, would likely argue that wilderness is generally acknowledged to play a significant role in preserving the integrity, stability, and beauty of the entire ecosystem and that we therefore have an overriding obligation to preserve it. These are two theories—one individualistic and anthropocentric, the other holistic and biocentric—that share one conclusion.

To preserve the environment, it is necessary that we act collectively. In order to do so, it is enough that we move together. We need not all explain our movement in the same way. And if we spend too much time arguing about explanations, we won't be moving. The contemporary environmental challenge is thus analogous in some ways to the seventeenth-century religious strife that so concerned philosopher John Locke. His formula for peace—"many sects, shared duties"—likewise applies here (see Galston 1986). Besides remembering the fact that it would be dismal to live in a society in which everyone thinks like everyone else, it is worth reminding ourselves that the point is environmental purity, not doctrinal purity.

What Is Blocking the Evolution of American Environmentalism?

Why then do people disagree about environmental policy? More to the point, why do people resist certain policies and not others? One obvious possibility is that, despite the shared belief in the value of the environment, some simply value it more than others: they either find more to value or value what they do find more strongly. No doubt that is part of the explanation. But it is by no means the largest part. Instead, the central barriers to the continued progress of American environmentalism are primarily *conceptual*: an inability to see the deeply political nature of environmental problems and their solutions and the predominance of single-issue thinking.[7] What stands out with complete clarity in table 5.5 is that, in a group of 46 very different individuals, resistance to specific environmental policy proposals was based primarily on a competing value in fewer than 1 in 10 instances. Neither materialism nor resistance to government intrusion per se con-

Table 5.5. Primary justifications for rejecting environmental reforms

Primary objection	Conservatives (n = 17)	Progressives (n = 21)	Radicals (n = 6)
I. Political solution unnecessary or unworkable	1	2	2
II. Environmental status quo acceptable	2	2	0
III. Clear mix of I and II	7	6	3
IV. No predominant objection	4	8	1
V. Freedom and rights	2	3	0
VI. Utility	1	0	0

Note: Table excludes one ambivalent participant and one radical who endorsed all 19 policy proposals.

stitutes the principal barrier to environmental progress. (Hence any thesis that those are the causes of our present environmental malaise are likewise placed in serious doubt.)[8]

The single most important fact contained in table 5.5 is that, for a majority of environmental progressives (who we have ample reason to believe make up the majority of the American public), resistance to environmental reforms is rooted either wholly or in large part in the belief that those reforms are unnecessary, unworkable, or both. Some people see the present system as so corrupt or inequitable or under the thumb of large economic interests that they simply give up on the whole idea of collective action. Consider this analysis by Edward Hollister, a tutor in one of Milwaukee's inner-city "catch up" schools:

> I think that we have to evaluate and get the correct people that have the same idea that they going to do right for people and not right for what greed tells them to do. We don't have integrity in people. Instead, there's a lot of collusion in politics. Power corrupts absolutely. So a power struggle—that's what politics is about: that's greed again. Only solution I can see is I have to evaluate *me* and appreciate myself enough that I treat you well, regardless of how you treat me. And that calls for a strong constitution, a *personal* constitution.

Hollister is no longer is a practicing Baptist, but his stern Protestantism (reinforced by a life spent in one of the most troubled black communities in America) could not be more pronounced: the community is irremediably corrupt; the only solution is "the correct people" and, finally, correcting oneself. Carmen Wiley, a placement counselor with an organization working on behalf of Hispanics, shared Hollister's basic view. Much of her life is devoted to purifying her own environmental behaviors, but recall that in her closing remarks she showed that she resists monkeying with the policy machinery, preferring instead a policy *deus ex machina*:

> I think the EPA is a joke. I mean, you know, . . . I have to trust the government to protect me. . . . I don't. I mean, they just don't do enough. There needs to be new watchdog agencies . . . that really are watchdogs for the government. . . . And something apart from the whole machine that would, of course, be respected and that would have an impact on the government, you know, and what the government does and does not do in regulating and whatever.

For many of the most progressive of my participants, the real is irrational, but only the individual can make the rational real.

Many combined a more moderate version of this view with the belief that technology alone can solve many of our environmental problems. College senior Erik Johannsen was one such person. Another was town planner William Noone, whose support for a new road through an important local wetland hinged crucially on the likelihood of successful mitigation efforts. Frank Hauser, the conservative dairy farmer I quoted earlier, often combined a belief in technology ("they're really making strides with the new chemicals") with a concern that environmental cleanup should not consume too large a share of the social pie, all while insisting that the government force at least some environmentally benign behaviors.

In rejecting various reforms, another portion of the progressive group alternated between the view that "government is no answer" and the view that government's present answer is good enough: the problem is well under control. When asked about a 5 percent pollution tax, for example, farmer Frank Hauser stated flat out that the problem isn't that bad, nor does it require that much money. Interestingly, such conclusions were inferred at least as often from knowledge of recent policy *changes* as they were from any concrete or in-depth knowledge of the problem or the policy measures in place to meet it. Hence even here, where individuals' empirical knowledge of and value orientation toward the environment appear closest to the surface, what one finds is that people's eyes are fixed firmly on the government. How well off is the environment? If the government has acted on it lately, it must be OK.

Note, finally, that table 5.5 lists participants' *primary* justifications for rejecting reform proposals. All but one participant included other considerations in their arguments against specific policies. Still, whereas there are multiple reasons that lead people to support the same environmental policies (and often multiple reasons that lead one individual to support a given policy), the reverse is not always true. People find lots of reasons to be in favor of environmental protection. But when they object to it, it is often for a single reason or for a narrow range of reasons. The difference may in the end be one of degree, but the difference is crucial, nonetheless. Fortunately, it turns out to be much easier to explain why people are against environmental policy than why they are for it. Such a conclusion may disappoint some, but from the standpoint of political theory, it is all we need. Accelerating the evolution of American environmentalism can happen in one of two ways: either Americans come to value nature more, or they come to recognize that their present values imply greater collective limits on our uses of the environment. There are three reasons to believe that our best hope lies along the second path. First, as we have already seen, Americans already value nature a great deal and in a huge variety of ways. Second, only a tiny minority appears to reject environmental policy expansion because they value other things more than the environment. Third, asking a populace to change its basic value commitments is not likely to work, at least in the short and medium terms. I had some near conversion experiences during my interviews (see chapter 6), but they were conceptual, never normative. And not a single participant could foresee changing his or her basic environmental values in the future. Most, on the other hand, suggested that their view of environmental policy was closely linked to "how things are going."

Conclusion

The central obstacle to the further evolution of American environmentalism, then, is to be found, not in what Americans value, but in how they think society and the environment operate.[9] Environmental policy orientations are not deduced in any straightforward manner from prior political orientations. They involve the integration of an almost bewildering array of environmental values and a more restricted set of judgments about how the world actually works. Yet those elements are not so well integrated that we are justified in calling them different paradigms or worldviews. Similarly, there are a great number and many kinds of things that exert important influences on individuals' thinking in this realm. Although these empirical findings do not readily translate into an explanatory theory of environmental policy thinking, together they furnish solid support for the deliberative theory of environmental policy, to which I now turn.

6

Deliberation, Environmental
Rationality, and Environmental
Commitment

> I just don't know what the answer is. I guess nobody really knows
> what the answer is. That's why we're all kind of supposed to work
> together to figure out the answer.
> —office manager Louise Fredericks

In chapter 2, I argued that the environmental challenge requires no constitutional change. In fact, the existing constitutional structure is about the best we are likely to come up with. Neither centralization nor decentralization alone is likely to get anyone to "think globally." In fact, quite the reverse is likely to happen if we pursue those paths too far. Consequently, we need to look all the harder for ways to improve the environmental performance of representative democracy. Radical structural change must give way to accelerated evolutionary change. Precisely how rapidly we need to evolve, no one can say. But this much seems clear: because no structural fix exists, the chief danger is in moving too tentatively.

In the previous two chapters I let my respondents argue that they are willing, even eager, to evolve in the direction of environmentalism. At the close of the last chapter I suggested how we can take them up on that promise: expand citizens' opportunities to deliberate about environmental issues. The interviews I conducted constitute a kind of test of that prescription. In this chapter, I let my respondents show that they did make good use of such opportunities, that deliberation does accelerate the evolution of environmentalism. At the same time, my participants show that deliberation need not be restricted to a town meeting or even to a strictly public place. Nor, as we shall see, does deliberation depend on a direct confrontation with one's neighbors or fellow citizens. It need not even decide anything. As Socrates demonstrated long ago, deliberation requires only an interlocutor.[1] And it's a good thing: is there anything more incongruous than a global public meeting?[2]

Deliberation and Environmental Commitment

The argument that deliberation is good for environmental protection generally or environmental policy in particular, of course, assumes that people become more environmentally committed when they deliberate. Given the results of the 46 interviews I conducted, I believe that we can now upgrade that assumption to a confident assertion: deliberation *does* encourage environmentalism. Asked at the close of the interview if the experience had changed their mind in any way, at least a quarter of my participants said that they had become more aware or that their environmental conscience had been heightened. And those self-analyses were right on target: awareness did go up and conscience was heightened. For these individuals, the interviews clearly served to enliven what J. S. Mill called dead dogma. But far more than that had happened: participants had positively altered their environmental policy norms: they had become more willing to endorse state action on behalf of the environment. And it was not only those who had felt environmentally uplifted that responded in this way. In fact, 30 of 46 participants made some kind of gain in environmental commitment. (Sixteen maintained their original views; no one became less environmentally committed.) How large were the gains? Each of the eight sections in this chapter contributes part of the answer to that question, which only *seems* simple. However, a few figures and illustrations suggest the overall magnitude of the gains.

First, however, it bears repeating that the gains I am speaking of relate to policy commitment, not participants' general willingness to endorse collective action on behalf of the environment. Recall from chapter 1 that my view of democratic deliberation flatly rejects the popular equation between the public and public places, politics and government. Instead, I argued that we need to broaden our definition of politics radically to include political, or public, thinking as well as political, or collective, action, and we need to admit that political thinking occurs virtually everywhere. My emphasis on government, or policy, here is thus not meant to imply that either public action or public deliberation needs to depend on government. But, as I explained in chapter 3, the fact that my participants were so sympathetic to policy (i.e., governmental measures) suggests only that their sympathies were even

Table 6.1. Change in position on individual reform proposals

Change in number of reforms originally endorsed by the participant	Percentage of participants
Fewer reforms endorsed by end of interview (median = 1.8)	11
No change during interview	35
1–3 additional reforms endorsed by end of interview	44
> 3 additional reforms endorsed by end of interview (median = 5.4)	11

broader and deeper in regard to collective action more generally. To the extent that American political culture favors nongovernmental over governmental forms of collective behavior, my participants faced the dilemma of the environment versus collective action in its starkest form, namely, environmental *policy* versus a worsened environment. Moreover, they did so in a way which showed a willingness to admit and confront the value conflicts thrown up by that dilemma, as we shall see below. If deliberation pays off so handsomely when the dice are loaded against it in this way, it can be expected to yield even better results in other, nonstatist, realms of citizen activity.

Now for the figures. My measure for environmental commitment was two parts objective, one part subjective. The first objective element involved simply counting explicit instances in which people changed their minds on one or more of the 19 individual policy reform questions. As table 6.1 shows, deliberation encouraged reform in more than half the cases (occasionally strongly so), and discouraged reform in only about 1 in 10.

For example, we saw that Teresa Hirschler, one of a handful of social democrats I talked to (and clearly among my seven environmental "radicals"), at first resisted a cap on economic growth because she believed that full employment requires an expanding economy. But she went on to invent her own theoretical answer to that dilemma, and came to endorsing what amounts to a functional equivalent of a limit to growth:

> I just don't know if [full employment and a limit on growth] can go hand in hand. I just don't know if that's realistic, you know. And I . . . It's not that I don't favor economic growth, but it's just looking at what is lost or what is the trade-off, and if it affects the land or the environment, then that's too big a trade-off. But I think a program like that would be wonderful if you could limit it and still do something to guarantee employment in some way. But it's just simply not realistic.

Why isn't it realistic?

Because I don't think we could come up with enough other avenues of employment for all those individuals.

So employment requires growth?

Right. But it simply can't occur in a community if there's limited land available; the trade-off can't be that land.

So what do you do when there's . . .

. . . No land left? But that won't happen because I decided we would even increase our wilderness area by one-half, so there will always be land! [*laughs*] People have to leave the country—it's as simple as that! [*laughs*] I think we need to learn to use our resources better, that we have to use our existing industries far better than we have already. I'm not sure what that all means. We just don't explore enough other options; we don't problem-solve thoroughly enough as a society.

So I'm still not exactly sure . . .

. . . What in the *hell* you are saying!

What it is you're saying. So you're saying growth does *have to be stopped—or not?*

Well, no, I don't think so. Growth is not . . . Economic development, which would come with growth, does not have to be stopped. But we need to change our value system so that we do not allow our environment to suffer at that cost of economic development and economic growth. And I'm not convinced that it does have to suffer or it does have to be altered. And maybe, if I was instructed differently, I would say, "Oh, it's impossible, it's a . . . It just has to happen in that way." But I'm not convinced of that yet.

Well, so it can go on forever, economic growth can?

It *could* go on, if it didn't have a negative impact on us as human beings, or on the land around us.

Is that possible, though?

Well, see, it's a Catch-22; I don't think it is possible. But that needs to be our end goal. And maybe if we keep thinking and developing programs, and policy, and strategy based on that general principle, I think we'd be so far better off in the long run. But we don't operate under any semblance of that kind of principle now and . . .

OK. There are a lot of people that reject that as being the worst thing we could ever do because so much depends on economic growth: it makes us all better off, provides jobs, and so on and so forth. So how do you respond to those kinds of arguments—that it's way too much to give up because we depend on it for so much? It's the American way.

Yeah, exactly. Probably half of this town would say the same thing, I suspect. Again, it just comes down to looking at our distribution of goods, our distribution of housing and food and that which we have. If we take it down to that level, and try to satisfy that argument, my feeling would be that we could cover all bases and we could meet people's needs because of, you know, how so much of the wealth is based in hands of the few. So if we researched it in that way, we could meet everyone's needs and thus if, indeed, growth and development were for the purpose of feeding, clothing, and housing all people, we could accomplish that by overhauling many things. But if we continue to operate under our current mentality, you know, then, probably we'd never get around this constant development, change, and use of our resources.

My second objective measure of gain in environmental commitment was behavioral. On at least 13 different occasions, participants told me that the interview had moved them to act on their environmental beliefs. These behavioral changes ranged from paying closer attention to candidates' environmental views to writing a letter to a local newspaper, from inquiring more about environmental issues to beginning a household recycling program and searching out ways to get more involved. Tim Behringer, a quality control chemist and the very image of a concerned young father, explained the interview's impact this way:

I feel like these discussions have radicalized me.
Why?
Because I . . . I guess I realize . . . I guess I was expecting to find a lot of my opinions to be off-the-cuff opinions. They're not. They're actually examples of an ethic that I do have, that does exist. And I end up sitting here questioning myself: "Are you really gonna keep your mouth shut about that one?" It makes me realize how much I see going on around me that I keep my mouth shut about, for a variety of reasons: not wanting to make waves in a town in which I'm a very little fish, not having the time to spend out of my busy life tilting at windmills, perhaps. But, in the end, to do this . . . This has prompted a certain self-examination. I look at myself and I say, "Well, there are some things here that you really care about, and some issues that are fairly cut-and-dried." Not that they've been *decided* yet. But, on the other hand . . . And foul water coming down is a fine example of it. Everyday you let it go on without saying something

you're . . . you're letting someone piss on your own back. I don't appreciate that.

The third measure of strengthened environmental policy commitment was admittedly more subjective than the first two. It involved tabulating instances of a more general policy reorientation. Yet such cases were included in table 6.2 only if they were *specifically* and *spontaneously* acknowledged during the interview.

Louise Fredericks' commentary on the interview was one such case:

> *Have you changed your mind about government regulation of the environment in any way since we started this interview?*
> [*Chuckles*]
> *Have you?*
> Thirty times, back and forth!
> *No, I mean, you know, in a lasting kind of way.*
> Well, I guess I didn't really have any opinion—true opinion—before we started. But I guess in a lasting way I've kind of made up my mind that, yes, we need some . . . We need regulation. So I guess, as far as that . . . I've probably changed . . . thought about it a little bit.
> *I would say that's a change.*
> Yeah, because I don't really like regulation, but I think I've come to decide that we should have some more . . .

Roughly two-thirds of those who underwent an overall change in perspective simply strengthened their preexisting commitment to environmental policy. In four cases, however, participants who began the interview with a clearly conservative perspective ended up advocating an overall expansion of environmental policy. For example, just after finishing our discussion of my menu of environmental reforms, farmer

Table 6.2. Gains in overall commitment to environmental policy

Type of policy reorientation	Percentage experiencing (n = 46)
From conservative to progressive	9
From "no opinion" to progressive	2
Substantially strengthened progressive orientation	13
Movement toward more progressive orientation	4
Mildly strengthened progressive orientation	4
Mildly strengthened radical orientation	4
No reorientation	65
Weakened commitment	0

Richard Johnson stated that we already have "almost more government control" than we need. But after examining his political and environmental ideals, he had changed his view a great deal. Largely ignoring my next question (Do environmental and social ideals ever clash?), he said: "I think that we're going to have to make drastic changes. If you got to change somebody from what they've been doing—there you got it." By the end of the interview he had pretty well integrated these two views. Again ignoring the thrust of one of my closing questions, he admitted that government's involvement in the environmental arena in the future will be "unfortunately more, but it will probably have to be more, to get the job done."

The three indicators I have just discussed did overlap, but not always. For example, several participants changed their overall orientation without changing their positions on any of the specific reform proposals I put to them. Likewise, many people changed their positions on specific reforms without generalizing to environmental policy as a whole. And some of those who were motivated to act as a result of the interview remained almost fixed in their views throughout the interview. As a result, the changes I discussed (in policy positions, general orientations, and behaviors) were spread broadly among my participants. Thirty out of 46, in fact, manifested at least one of the three types (and more than half of that group experienced more than one). To me, the psychological puzzle of explaining the difference between those who change issue positions and those who change more overall orientations was far less interesting than the breadth of the interview's impact: By at least one measure, a series of three or four serious conversations was deliberation enough to strengthen environmental policy commitment in almost two out of three cases. And this was true of my 17 environmental conservatives no less than of my environmental progressives. Of that group, four reoriented themselves in a progressive direction, and only six showed no sign of strengthened commitment.

Taken as a whole these changes were modest enough, but only if we forget just how modest was the measure of deliberation that produced them. Almost two out of three participants became more environmentally committed; almost a quarter of the conservatives began arguing for reform. This is rather stunning support for the deliberative hypothesis. But how reliable is it? Very. In the first place, I am reporting participants' conclusions, not their opinions. My participants "owned up" to their views in a way that is simply impossible except in a dialogical situation. We can be relatively sure of their beliefs because, first, I continually asked them to anchor those beliefs in deeper or broader considerations, judgments, and values. Here is how those who responded to my postinterview questionnaire described my approach themselves:

> In the landowner-environmentalist battle I think you leaned heavily toward the environmentals but I guess I was heavily in favor of landowner rights. (farmer and landowner-rights activist Joe Page)

> It seemed that regardless of what side of the issue I favored you would find a point or two on the other side. I think this is fine as long as all participants get the same treatment! (college senior Erik Johannsen)

> I thought you were very objective, asking questions from both points of view. However, it seemed your personal point of view was made known because you were playing devil's advocate when speaking from the polluter's point of view. (actor and boat-house dweller Mark Allen)

> No, I didn't think you were biased. You asked the questions and let me ramble on with lots of "why" questions in between. (office manager Louise Fredericks)

> Good, stimulating discussion with argumentation, which I enjoyed. (dairy farmer Paul Zalens)

> No, you were not biased—you played devil's advocate quite well and always argued your point with enough "proof" so as not to have all your burden of proof rely on opinion alone. (premed student Julie Binns)

> You argued a good point, each and every time, being very objective to my negative thought of mind on certain situations. (young mother Jill King)

> It was very probing. There were times when it was uncomfortable because I had to put my beliefs or opinions into words, which forced me through a mental analysis before I could give my opinion. (legal secretary–accountant Karen Brunson)

> In the two interview sessions we had, I detected no biases coming forth. I distinctly remember feeling encouraged to further

support my views as you took a probing, at times opposing,
view in order to elicit elaborations. (social worker Teresa Hirschler)

A second reason we can be reasonably confident about these results
is that induction often led participants to gauge their own shifts in
thinking and then comment on the change out loud. More often than
not, there was no need to guess whether participants had changed their
views: they remarked on the fact themselves. Third, my coding procedure, as I noted in chapter 4, had a built-in corrective mechanism. The
deliberative hypothesis I tested was really made up of two conjectures.
The first was that citizens are willing to engage in environmental deliberation (at least in part because they endorse environmental policy
expansion); the second, that they actually benefit from doing so. As it
turns out, to favor either conjecture in interpreting the interview results
would be to slight the other. If, for example, I have overrepresented the
number who deepened their environmental policy commitment, then
I have underrepresented the number whose commitment was already
strong at the beginning of the interview—and have thus underestimated
the group's willingness to deliberate on environmental issues. Conversely, if I have been overly optimistic about the group's environmental policy norms and their consequent disposition to deliberate, then
I have been overly pessimistic about the overall impact of the interview
because, naturally, change would have been less dramatic. Fourth, and
most important, we must remember that the results I have reported
here are the product of a brief experiment, not of a sustained, wide-
ranging move toward deliberative democracy. However modest or
short-lived, those results are real enough. They foreshadow what we
might expect from a citizenry given greater opportunities to deliberate about public issues—the environment in particular. Although social
scientists may quibble about how much change took place as a result
of these deliberative interviews, change there was, indeed. And change
we can expect from a more deliberative public. How much change we
can expect not even the most rigorous methodologist can say.

The Excess Demands of Environmental Rationality

Deliberation clearly encouraged environmentalism in this
very mixed bag of citizens. It thus appears safe to say that thinking
about the environment tends to strengthen individuals' environmental commitments. More precisely, deliberation leads people (or, rather,
allows people to lead themselves) to endorse a wider range of collective environmental limits. My research also suggests an explanation for

this finding: political deliberation tends to strengthen individuals' environmental commitments because it heightens individuals' *environmental rationality*. Given the present state of the environment and environmental policy, enhanced environmental rationality will usually lead to a widening of individuals' environmental policy commitments. If this is so, it constitutes a powerful environmental argument for expanding citizens' opportunities to deliberate on environmental issues. But, because the requirements of environmental rationality are more stringent than those typically attributed to political rationality, there is an even more powerful argument for expanding deliberative opportunities in general. That is, if deliberation works in the environmental arena, it is even more likely to work in other areas.

Contrary to the views of most environmental ethicists and environmental radicals, there is nothing especially new about environmental or ecological rationality, at least at the formal level. Still, its demands are clearly more stringent than those that follow from the more familiar accounts of practical reason.

I do not intend here to defend a full-blown definition of environmental policy rationality, replete with metaphysical trappings. To do so would take me too far afield. It would also subordinate practice to theory in a way I find to be utterly objectionable. The point of this study is to offer a solution, not create more grist for intellectual mills. And, in any case, an entirely workable (if not unimpeachable) standard of environmental rationality is close at hand. Its mirror image is reflected all too clearly in the various institutional failings described in chapter 2. That mirror image provides us with a familiar and well-tested version of what environmental rationality requires: *collective, holistic,* and *long-term* thinking. Such an immanent definition has an enormous advantage over competing deductive accounts in that it is grounded in human experience (though not in any idealized golden age of environmental harmony). Moreover, it covers a great deal of the common ground that already exists among environmental philosophers (Norton 1991).

Environmental rationality is a general standard that can be used to judge competing policy prescriptions. As can be seen from either Table 4.1 or the interview schedule itself (see Appendix, pp. 211–235), all the reforms I suggested during the interview process qualified as "environmentally rational," though not, perhaps, in equal degree. In any case, my goal here is less to defend particular environmental policies than to recommend how we might improve our chances of arriving at better ones. To do so, we need know only what "better" means, namely, "more environmentally rational."

The question I now want to ask is: Are the requirements of environmental rationality (defined in this way) substantially different from those that philosophers have traditionally attributed to rationality? As will be seen, they are not, although they do differ in degree.

Environmental rationality requires, first of all, that thinking be political, or collective (Dryzek 1990: 10; Capra and Spretnak 1984: 124; Porritt 1984: xiv, 165; Bookchin 1991: 306). Thinking about the environment almost always entails thinking about a collective entity. Environmental rationality demands that thinking be as expansive as the environmental issue at hand. Although never susceptible to precise measurement, most often this will require that one think at least as far as one's community, very often further. At least occasionally it will even demand the global thinking so often advocated by environmentalists. What is clear is that environmental rationality's demands are neither so universal as Kant's categorical imperative nor so parochial as that which Aristotle might have condoned. At the same time, environmental rationality follows both philosophers in arguing that practical reason entails thinking beyond oneself.

Second, environmental rationality entails holistic thinking. This requirement, like the first, follows from the very nature of the environment. Even from a purely human, or anthropocentric, point of view, the environment cannot reasonably be viewed as a collection of separate parts because human beings are ultimately dependent upon it, because its parts are highly interrelated, and because it displays certain "emergent properties" which cannot be reduced to those of its constituent parts (Bartlett 1986: 228; Dryzek 1990: 9–10; Norton 1991: 146; Botkin 1990: 155; Brion 1991: xiv; Naess 1989: 78–80, 187, 195). That we think of the environment as a whole might seem overly demanding, and would even strike some as irrational. Human reason is not so capable, nor is our knowledge sufficiently well-developed, it might be objected. The best we can do is tinker around the edges, correcting our behaviors in light of past mistakes.

Of course, even those most opposed to granting reason any regulative role in politics might agree that clear factual evidence sometimes rules out policy options. But, they might argue, few systemwide facts are available in the environmental arena: witness the debate over the "facticity" of global warming. But the holism required by environmental rationality need not be so demanding. On the one hand, the point is not to establish systemic trends or facts but to consider their possibility. We may not know whether global warming is really occurring, but it would be irrational not to consider that possibility. On the other hand, we very often can predict the environmental impact of social and economic policies (as a reading of any environmental impact statement will attest). No one seriously suggests anymore that reason can fully know the world. All we have is a spotlight; its beam can be narrow or wide. Holism means keeping the aperture wide open so as to illuminate as wide a swath as possible. Environmental rationality may be a more demanding form of rationality than we are used to, but it does not presume omniscience. Instead, it demands that whatever science is available be focused on the larger whole and on the way various parts of the whole interact. Holism is a cognitive ideal. Like all ideals, it can never be fully realized in practice. And, like all ideals, it will also require occasional sacrifices for higher aims. It willingly sacrifices precision for breadth, accuracy for comprehensiveness. Perhaps most crucially, the very limitations we face in meeting the demand for holism have an important humbling effect. A synoptic view is required by the nature of the environment, but is ultimately rendered impossible by the limitations nature, time, and society place on reason itself. The proper course is, not to jettison the synoptic view, but to respect those limitations by limiting our actions accordingly.

Finally, environmental rationality means taking a long view. Precisely how long a view is called for is again largely a matter of empirical evaluation, though it is certain to be longer than what we have been accustomed to in making public policy: "The time horizons for ecological rationality are set by dynamic system processes and may be quite long, especially by comparison with economic, social, legal, or political rationality" (Bartlett 1986: 228–229; see also Naess 1989: 137; Norton 1991: 146; Botkin 1990: 65).[3] This requirement again differs, primarily in degree, from that entailed by more traditional modes of rationality. No form of practical reason I am aware of completely dispenses with a consideration of consequences. Even Kant would have us judge the rightness of a maxim by considering the result of universalizing that maxim. And even Hobbes must postulate a limited capacity to foresee the consequences of our actions in order to explain how individuals in the state of nature are led to seek respite under the sword of Leviathan. Likewise, few democratic theorists would object to Robert Dahl's claim that "an essential element in the meaning of the common good among the members of a group is what the members would choose if they possessed the *fullest attainable understanding* of the experience that would result from their choice and its most relevant alternatives" (my emphasis; Dahl 1989: 308).

However, it is one thing to say that nature works according to a clock marked in millennia, quite another to suggest that humans think that way. True, we cannot exhaustively predict the consequences of our actions for a future that is hundreds, much less thousands, of years away. But this is not what environmental rationality requires. It demands instead only that we do nothing that would clearly threaten the coming into being of that future on the one hand, and that we consider the obvious interrelationship between ecological and human systems on the other. "No society wisely decides whether to use nuclear energy sources for the production of electric power without considering questions about utilizing its own coal or petroleum, about threats to health and safety, about foreign exchanges and trade, about the state's regulatory role in markets, or about the physical location of electric generating facilities and of energy-using industrial enterprises" (Lindblom 1990: 239).

At the same time, like holism, a long-term perspective functions as a prudential limit on our actions. The very impossibility of knowing the distant future with any certainty renders irrational a whole range of environmental interventions. The centrality of both holism and a long-term perspective means that environmental rationality is as much a special kind of skepticism as it is a unique way of knowing.

Environmental rationality as I conceive it is also evolutionary: although it embodies a substantive norm (specifically, the collective pursuit of the long-term viability of the ecosystem as a whole), it cannot specify *a priori* either the ultimate nature of that norm or which of our immediate environmental ends are in conformity with it and which are not. Our reasoned view of what we are trying to accomplish can, and must, change over time. In that respect, environmental rationality is both open-ended and flexible. But that flexibility carries with it an additional obligation: that we continue to reason about ends.

To sum up: Environmental rationality embodies a form of means-ends rationality, for it insists on collective answers to environmental problems. It insists on taking systemwide facts into account (or on acknowledging that we cannot). And it demands that we judge the consequences of our actions far into the future (or acknowledge that we cannot). Finally, environmental rationality insists that the goals which fuel it be subject themselves to reasoned criticism. None of these criteria is wholly new. Yet each, in its own way, is more demanding than other available standards (especially the individualism and relativism of economic rationality). Environmental rationality demands a fit between means and ends, but adds the requirement that such a fit account for the public nature of environmental ends. It has a profound respect for facts, but is unsatisfied unless those facts tell us something about the state of entire systems and the relationships which they comprise. It asks about consequences, but not just those that will result tomorrow or next year. And because these criteria are so demanding, the process of reflecting about our original ends is itself made more difficult. In the end, then, environmental politics requires, not a new kind of reason, but more of the old. From this it follows that various long-standing prescriptions for enhancing the role of reason in politics ought to apply to improving environmental rationality as well—as long as they are administered in suitably strong doses.

Deliberation and Rationality

I argued in the last chapter that environmental rationality is hostage less to our present constitutional machinery than to the way that machinery is operated. Our institutions present no insuperable barriers to the evolution of environmental reason. The way is, in this important sense, relatively open. But few would deny that that evolution can and should be accelerated. The surest way to do so is to expand citizens' opportunities to deliberate on environmental issues. That central contention is supported by two complementary propositions. The first is that my research (supported by a growing body of theoretical literature) shows that deliberation works, and works quite rapidly. The second is that no other solution or set of solutions is likely to be very successful, except in the very long term. The very urgency of our myriad environmental problems, however, does not allow us the luxury of a piecemeal or gradual strategy.

Before laying out the evidence for those propositions, I want to specify exactly what I mean by "deliberation," and how my own conception differs from that found so often in contemporary theoretical discussions. Doing so will establish the limits on my claim that what might be called deliberative democratic theory and my own empirical research are mutually supporting.

Certainly no single definition of democratic deliberation is going to satisfy everyone. Yet most definitions, whether Habermas' "ideal speech situation" or Spragen's "rational republic," agree on certain essentials. They all require (or presuppose) that participants begin from a shared commitment to some conception of the good (however broadly conceived). They further insist that deliberation requires participants both to speak and to listen (Barber 1984: 175). Participants must be prepared to justify their positions and at least respect the views of others. Deliberation is also assumed to require a public setting—an agora, or some functional equivalent. Finally, *democratic* deliberation is seen to entail what might be called a principle of deliberative equality. The greatest disputes among theorists of democratic deliberation involve interpreting this last prerequisite. For some it involves no more than an absence of obvious economic or political coercion. For others it implies a kind of equal opportunity to deliberate (that is, to speak, to listen, or to do both). One might also logically construe the principle of deliberative equality as entailing strictly equal contributions to deliberation.

The interviews I conducted embodied a deliberative model differing from this definition in only one significant respect. Although it could not be assumed at the outset, the results indicate that, as I explained in previous chapters, a solid consensus exists not only about the nature of the environmental good but also about the need to pursue that good more actively. Although my participants did most of the talking, they were continually put in the position of listening to challenges to their views. Very often they asked me factual questions, and not infrequently abandoned the standard question-answer format to solicit my views of a given issue or philosophical problem.

I cannot say that the interviews met the requirement of strict deliberative equality or even of equal deliberative opportunity, but they came rather close. The interviews were strictly voluntary. Neither party forced his or her view on the other in any very obvious way. At the same time, two imbalances ran through all the interviews, one of which was unavoidable. Even if it had been desirable, there was, of course, no way I could achieve anything approaching equality between my participants' deliberative capacities and my own. Someone also had to arrange the deliberative situation. And, although I gave my participants every chance to define the issues, I was generally the one posing questions. The second systematic imbalance favored the other side of the conversation: my participants spoke much more and listened far less than I did. This, too, was partly inevitable, because I had difficulty explaining to people ahead of time how my project differed from a simple survey or poll. This imbalance was also aggravated by my interpretive interest in my participants' views. Understanding meant listening, not talking, and a "bias" in their favor.

The interview situation differed in one obvious sense from recent conceptions of democratic deliberation: it occurred outside the public realm. I suggest that public thinking can (and in fact usually *does*) occur in private. Democratic theory generally assumes that deliberation takes place in public, or is at least the product of public encounters. But my interviews were one-on-one (with an occasional spouse or friend circling around in the kitchen kibbitzing). And yet they produced most of the benefits typically associated with public deliberation. This is not to deny the putative advantages of the agora, of deliberation that takes place in public. On the contrary, it suggests that deliberation is simply indifferent to architecture. Intuitively this makes good sense. The key element in all deliberation, after all, is talk. What counts is not the number of speakers, but the quality of the speech (see Spragens 1990: 210ff.). We would hardly call a Super Bowl crowd a deliberative assembly. Why make the opposite mistake and assume that two people arguing over politics in the neighborhood cafe aren't deliberating?

Citizens as Students of Environmental Politics

My interview results show quite clearly that deliberation improves individuals' ability to meet all four criteria of environmental rationality. By posing political alternatives, deliberation encourages collective thinking. It allows issues to be linked together and systemic facts to come to light, thus spurring a holistic view. By forcing a consideration of environmental consequences, it promotes a long-term view. All of these, meanwhile, together with the very act of justifying one's beliefs, help to clarify environmental ends. If deliberation produces all these benefits in the environmental realm, the payoff is likely to be even larger in other areas of public policy where the demands of rationality are less stringent. Deliberation nowhere faces a more challenging cognitive test than it does in regard to the environment. At least among the public involved in my interview, it passed that test rather easily. Hence it is likely to score even more highly in other areas. Robert Dahl was no doubt right to call democracy "a gamble on the possibility that a people, in acting autonomously, will learn how to act rightly" (1989: 192). My findings suggest, however, that our odds are much better and the payoff far greater than even optimistic democratic theorists have assumed.

Collective Thinking

Recall that by "collective thinking" I mean something distinct from the "moral point of view" that is so often held to result from deliberation (Spragens 1990: 135). To think collectively is to think politically—to move beyond stating what I desire or think desirable to a consideration of what *we* can accomplish. It need not involve ethical justification; it invokes no universal or even general principles of right, justice, or goodness. Less exalted than a moral point of view, and less cognitively demanding, it ought to be easier. But in chapter 4 we saw that (in the environmental realm at least) just the opposite is the case. That is, most people are fully capable of invoking principle in defense of their environmental positions. In fact, they do so almost universally and almost reflexively. But, as we saw earlier, many individuals have difficulty thinking about environmental issues in collective terms. In this sense individualism remains the central barrier to the continued evolution of Americans' environmental thinking. But this is not the fabled individualism of classical liberal theory. Nor is it the privatization of desire we are so often warned is consuming America bit by bit (Bellah et al. 1985). Of my 46 respondents, perhaps 3 were philosophical individualists. And not one solitary individual justified all or even most of their beliefs by saying that they were simply individual tastes or preferences. I found precious little evidence that Americans are opposed to collective action in the environmental sphere and a wealth of evidence to the contrary. Still, the lack of collective thinking often prevents people both from envisioning an environmental future very different from the present and from considering how such a future might be brought about.

Do people think any more collectively after deliberating? Not everyone does, and no one does all the time. But some participants did begin to think more collectively—far more often about means than about ends. Only about one in four participants ended up thinking more *publicly* (primarily because three out of four people started the interview that way), but three in four began to think more *collectively*, if grudgingly. It was this heightened awareness of the political nature of environmental problems, not a deepened appreciation for values in nature, that was primarily responsible for the gains in environmental commitment I discussed above.[4] Jay Little, the hard-working young entrepreneur who is part owner of an automobile business, was typical of this group, if somewhat more self-reflective:

> *Have you changed your mind about government regulation of the environment in any way since we started the interview?*
> I think you'll probably find that I have, if you go back and check the tape from the first time.
> *What's your sense of it?*
> Yeah, a little bit. I'd be a little more tolerant of sanctions imposed.
> *Yeah? Why do you think you would be?*
> I don't know. Probably just because I've been thinking about it recently. If you asked me that after I paid my taxes I'm not going to probably say the same thing: let somebody else pay for it. [*chuckles*]

About a half hour into the interview, Dr. James Burson, the liberal young psychiatrist, had this realization:

You know, what I find disturbing is that . . . You know, a lot of what I'm saying seems very directive and controlling. But the way I reconcile that is that we are parts of a system and the system is always going to make decisions that affect us. I mean . . . and vice versa. There's got to be a balance there. It just seems like the balance has gone too far one way in this culture towards individuals making . . . or, from my perspective . . . individuals making the decisions that affect the system. And I don't know how something can turn back into a balance without first going through a phase of, you know, turning into its opposite for a time.

For a half a dozen participants, like Louise Fredericks, whom I quoted earlier, the gains were even more impressive. Val Gotti is 28 and planning a family. In the meantime she keeps the books for a real estate developer on the edge of a large city. She is energetic and open-minded, but her instincts are conservative. She confessed early on that she "never thought about these things." Well, she made up for it, enthusiastically, in the five hours I spent with her. The response I present here was to the question: Do you favor stricter controls on the possible negative consequences of new technologies? It followed 11 other specific policy proposals to which Gotti had reluctantly acceded, but without being especially happy about her conclusions. Her reasoning here is clearly fueled by the inductive momentum provided by the previous set of questions:

Yeah, I think they should be stricter. It just . . . It all comes down to, we're going to do without shit (excuse me)—we're going to do without stuff that we're just going to have to deal with. I mean, that's all it comes down to. You got to deal with it. You're not going to have stuff because it messes up things. That's how I look at it. You're going to have to do without. I mean I've done without a lot of things, and it's like, I don't know, what else am I going to have to do without that's going to really bother me? And that's how I look at it. Now, you see, somebody that has everything in the world—it may be harder for them.
But isn't this going to require a lot of governmental regulation and bureaucracy and intrusion and . . .
Yeah, it's probably not going to be a free country anymore.
But that's the price we have to pay?
I am starting to wonder if it's a free country anymore. That goes back to . . . I had this huge debate yesterday. It's like I start thinking about it, and it's like I shouldn't have had it yesterday. It was like with my husband, too, and it's like we were sitting here yelling at each other going, "Well, it's not free country if

you have to do that," and it's like "Yeah, you're right, but I rather live here than somewhere else."

So this is something we need, but it means we're not going to have a free country anymore?

Well, they're just regulating it more. Don't other countries have these problems besides us? I mean, it's the whole world. Maybe they do need to regulate it more. Because we're being too free, maybe. (I forgot what the question was.)

So do we need this control of new technologies?

I think so.

Even if it means that our country is less free?

Not necessarily less free. I just think that they should be in control of what is going on. I think they should keep it in control. If it's going to pollute more, then I don't think they should do it. And yeah, that's lessening your freedom to do something, but that's for the right of everybody. So, I think that way it would be OK.

What if it also slowed down our economic progress, since, you know, we were going slow on new technologies?

I think that's OK, too. I mean, what's the world going to be if everything's gone? You're not going to be able to progress from there on afterwards anyway. If you ruin the world . . .

What if we fall behind the Japanese, though?

Well, so what? I personally don't care what the Japanese know. I mean, that's my opinion. I don't care, I don't buy . . . I don't believe in buying Japanese products, so I don't buy Toshiba or any of those.

Erik Johannsen, the young chemical engineering student, experienced an even more stunning epiphany regarding the importance of collective considerations in reasoning about the environment. Perhaps it's no surprise that it came at about the same place in the interview. The question was simply what he considered the most important environmental issues at the international or global level. But he quickly brought the discussion back to the general question of environmental policy limits, which he had repeatedly deemphasized in favor of attitude change. After Johannsen cited global warming as the world's number one environmental problem, I asked him what causes it:

It's just industry, consumers putting their CO_2 into the sky, and, you know, scientifically knowing what's going on.

So if consumers didn't consume so much, the problem would be dealt with?

Yeah, it could. Sure.
Well, how do you think it should be dealt with?
Right there. Consumers shouldn't consume as much. We should, you know, conserve, whatever the case. I know I've kind of taken the attitude of, you know, we're going to just change. All by ourselves, we're going to change. Our attitudes are going to change as soon as we see what's happening. And, you know, I've really not taken a stand on any one side of, say—you know, we were talking about limiting industry—how much they can use. Just our attitude change probably won't do it. I mean, that's human nature, you know: my neighbor's going to do it. You know, it's got to be a team effort, and there's got to be some sanctions imposed, but which ones I don't know, and to what extent, I don't know, either. To cap our economy completely—I don't know if that's the answer. What I want to say is that I am not talking this "Man is just a good being, and it's . . . We're going to just change it all with our attitude change." It's not going to happen like that, and you're idealistic to think that way. But radical— I don't know about the radical change, either. You know, and radical change is just one portion. Anyway, I am way off the question.

Before moving on, it's important to underline the fact that larger gains were made in this sphere than in any of the others I discuss below. In fact, my best reading of the interview transcripts shows that approximately 80 percent of those who strengthened their environmental policy norm did so because of a revised view, not of the *environment*, but of *policy*. That is, people came to endorse more environmental policy, not because they had deepened their love or respect or understanding of nature, but because they had upgraded their view of collective action. That finding, of course, strongly reinforces the analysis I presented in the last chapter, which concluded that a lack of collective thinking was perhaps the single biggest barrier to the continued evolution of American environmentalism. Even more crucially, it shows that deliberation compensates rather well for that lack, and does so even when people are encouraged, as they so often are in American society, to equate collective thinking with policy thinking. (Here, as elsewhere, had I employed a more ecumenical definition of the "political" or "collective," one less hampered by the negative connotations associated with "policy" and "government," the gains would likely have been greater still.) From one perspective, this ought not to surprise us: deliberation tends to move thought in a public direction: if one agrees to deliberate at all (as all my participants obviously did), one is committed to considering things from another person's point of view. From there it is but a small step to considering them from a collective point of view. What astounded me is just how well it works once people make that initial commitment, and how well it works for many different kinds of people.

Holism

Holistic thinking means thinking of the big picture. That means seeing relationships between various problems and potential solutions, but it can also mean simply taking more empirical information into account in arriving at judgments about public aims and projects. The dialogues in which I engaged these citizens encouraged just under half of them to make gains in one or another of these two aspects of holistic thinking; an even 50 percent made gains in both. Only 4 out of the 46 resisted expanding their view of environmental policy in either aspect over the course of the interview.

The formal study of psychology began as an attempt by a group of eighteenth-century French rationalists to explain why people resist inconvenient facts; psychology is still preoccupied with that problem. Whatever the answer, it wasn't a huge problem for my participants. In the first place, many stated that what separated their point of view from that of "the environmentalists" or "the radicals" was simply a lack of knowledge. I then asked if that meant that they shared the values of these groups. The answer was almost invariably affirmative. Often I was told that the participant couldn't imagine anyone having stronger environmental values than he or she had. Clearly this indicated a lack of imagination as often as strong environmental values. But the critical point is that this belief is often felt to be true. And the strength of that belief then underwrites an openness to new factual information. Third, people had a difficult time imagining what might change their mind about environmental policy. However, almost all of those who could imagine a change of mind suggested that it would occur if the environment got better or if things got a lot worse. Participants obviously viewed their own position as hinging directly on the state of the world or, rather, on their knowledge of it.

Given all of this it is hardly surprising that queries for facts were rather frequent, and that over half suggested that more information might affect their answers on particular policy proposals, or that, if things got bad enough they might answer differently. Moreover, about a quarter of the group clearly reacted to new factual knowledge. The following illustration shows that even an offhand comment is sometimes enough. This is Betsy Schon, the environmentally progressive fundamentalist. On the subject of wilderness, her sympathies were clearly pro-environmental but, noting the hesitancy in her voice, I repeated the original question:

>*Should we double the size of U.S. wilderness areas?*
>I think there's a, well . . . I'm not even really . . . I'm not informed even how much existing wilderness there is, but . . .
>*No one I've talked to knows, so you're not alone.*
>I know, and so I wouldn't be in favor of . . . How could you double it? I'm sure that's just . . . That would be impossible—to double it. But I would say, What's there, leave it alone. You know?
>*If it was just hypothetically possible?*
>I don't think it . . . I don't think it would be possible. The population is too great, don't you think? I don't know. [*laughs*]
>*Well, let's just say, in theory, it* was *possible.*
>Oh, yes. Oh, that would be great.
>*OK. Well, we went around and around on that one.*
>I'm sorry.
>*That's OK. I wasn't quite sure what you meant. Now, at the end, I got it. By the way, about 2 percent of the United States' land mass (below Alaska) is wilderness.*
>Ohhh.
>*And there's about another percent and a half that's sort of under study. So it* is *possible. It is possible.*
>Oh yes.
>*A lot of people wouldn't like it. But it's definitely possible. And, if you include Alaska (huge pieces of Alaska are also wilderness), that boosts it up to about 4 percent of the total country is wilderness.*
>Uh huh.
>*So, you know, sort of 1 in every 25 . . .*
>I would definitely be in favor of doubling it! [*both laugh*]
>*See, most people don't know that, and they think there's a lot more.*
>Yeah, I thought there was more.

Thinking more holistically can also mean seeing new interrelationships: between problems, between solutions, or between different values, or between some combination of these. Fully half of my participants saw at least one such connection they hadn't perceived before, and 19 of those 23 obviously had a clearer overall view of environmental politics than before the interview began. Sometimes these realizations seem rather pedestrian—to the participant, at least. Consider the following exchange, which came during my second meeting with Caroline Stowe, a recently retired administrative assistant:

> *Should the U.S. provide, say, 3 percent of our GNP in financial aid to less-developed countries to help them protect especially sensitive environmental areas like the rain forests?*
> Yes. [*hesitatingly*]
> *It's not their problem? Some people would say it's, you know, it's . . . There is a problem with the rain forests, and the rainforests ought to be preserved, but that's their responsibility, since the rain forests lie within their boundaries—so let them deal with it.*
> Yes, I can see that, but they might be more willing to deal with it if we help them financially.
> *Well, why should we help them financially?*
> Because the greenhouse [effect] affects everybody, not just Brazil.
> *Yeah. OK. Three percent of our gross national product—you'd be willing to devote that much of our overall output to that?*
> Seems like I . . . The last time you were here I spent 20 percent of our gross national product! [*both laugh*] Well, I don't want to be committed to numbers. I don't know what it specifically is, but I do think it would be a good idea to see some of it—and to have a whole bunch of treaties, but of course how can you enforce them?
> *Well, that's a good question. If they can't be enforced, then they're kind of useless, aren't they?*
> Oh, yeah.
> *Well, then there's no reason to do them?*
> We'd have to get agreement. Either that or have environmental police chasing around the world.
> *Yeah, as a matter of fact I was going to ask you about environmental police chasing around the world.*

This episode was repeated 15 or 20 times in varying forms during my many hours of interviewing. This particular instance is important because the participant began to come to terms with the financial costs and the implementation of her chosen policy path. Moreover, notice that Stowe's comments were clearly spontaneous. I did not ask her: How much are you willing to spend on environmental protection? Nor did I ask: How will we enforce international agreements? She asked *herself* those questions, and arrived at answers to them largely on her own (through the process of induction on the one hand and deduction on the other).

Still, such examples are far less impressive than some of the more thoroughgoing moves toward holism that occurred during the interviews. About the interview, several echoed the first-year medical student who commented: "It raised my consciousness, though it didn't change my opinions." Tim Behringer, for example, commented: "It's pushed the problem to the forefront of my consciousness. So, in that sense, [it has involved] consciousness raising. I think I'm not worrying about the trees so much as the forest at this point." But it was Billy Franks, the young, black, economic refugee from Flint, Michigan, who gave me the most memorable example. He greeted me at his apartment door for our second meeting, visibly excited. Then, with some ceremony, he presented me with a small slip of paper, on which he'd summed up his (admittedly apolitical) theory of environmental politics:

S	Selfishness	L	Living
I	Ignorance	I	Independence
N	Neglect	F	Friendship
		E	Experience

That pretty much covers the waterfront.

As impressive as all these numbers and examples seem, they are less striking than those presented in the previous section. Wholesale changes in outlook were almost never based on a participant's having come to think more holistically. If anything, thinking more holistically tends to reinforce existing beliefs—rounding them out, not changing them. On the other hand, there is a good possibility that I am underestimating the gains made in this area, since my bias in conducting the interviews was toward probing the *value* component of the fact-value mix. That is, I cited environmental facts only where they were both plain and obviously relevant to the participant's point of view. As a result, I simply gave my respondents fewer opportunities to expand their empirical horizons.

Holistic thinking requires not just knowledge but breadth of knowledge. If deliberation can at least occasionally encourage holistic thinking, then it ought to improve people's knowledge on narrower issues all the more frequently. If deliberation stimulates the acquisition of environmental policy knowledge, it ought to stimulate the acquisition of political knowledge more generally. The result can be only good, both for policy and for democracy. Democracy can tolerate a "gap between the knowledge of the policy elites and the knowledge of ordinary citizens" (Dahl 1989: 338). But if the gap becomes too wide, citizens cease being citizens, and democracy withers away. If democracy is to thrive (or survive, some might say), one of three things must happen: either knowledge is rendered less important by a radical simplification of society, or limits are placed on the knowledge decision-makers are allowed to possess, or citizens must become more knowledgeable. However attractive the Thoreauvian option, it seems hopelessly utopian. The second option is neither attractive nor workable. Hence democracy's hopes rest on an increasingly knowledgeable citizenry.

Taking a Long-term View

Yes, there were some gains in regard to the long-term view, too. But they were clearly more modest than the gains made in the areas of collective and holistic thinking. Given what I said in the previous chapter about participants' environmental ethics, the limitation of gains in the long-term view could almost have been predicted. Most participants already integrated some long-term consideration, such as the survival of the life-support system or concern for future generations, into their environmental policy reasoning. Still, about a quarter of the group (12/46) clearly stretched their temporal horizon at least once during the interview. For a handful of individuals the interview may have produced a noticeable reorientation in this respect. (For example, one participant moved from thinking of regulation in terms of *controlling* negative effects to thinking of it in terms of *preventing* them.) But for most, the changes were far less substantial, involving primarily a reminder or recognition of long-term values already held dear. One such change took place during this exchange with Doreen Brill, who had recently moved to Wisconsin to get specialized medical care for one of her three young boys and was looking for a new job as secretary-receptionist.

> *Do you think it would make sense to put a ban—a total ban—on developing wetlands in Smith County? Put a stop to developing any wetlands?*
> I don't see what that would make any difference.
> *It would save the wetlands.*
> Save the wetlands? Why would they want to do that?
> *Well, some people think the wetlands are worth saving, and I suppose there are a lot of different reasons people would give you: they're pretty, they like the birds, they like the plants.*
> Why would they want to ban it?
> *Not ban the wetlands. Ban developing the wetlands. They would want to ban it just to keep them.*
> That's a new one to me.

Well, most of the people I've been talking to have said they want to keep these wetlands. But they have different reasons. I mean, different people have different reasons.

I don't really know too much about that.

Well, do you have any feeling one way or another? I mean, what if someone said, "OK, you know there's this big wetland in the north part of the lake, close to where we are now." And someone said, OK, we're going to develop it; we're going to just totally, you know, pave it over, drain it out, build condos there." Would that upset you?

Not at all.

Why not?

I'm used to seeing progress; I'm from Hawaii. It doesn't bother me one bit. I think it's good.

Even if there were some rare birds that were in there, say?

Well, get the birds to go somewhere else.

What if the birds like it there, though?

Then let them stay. That's a problem, huh—the birds, the wildlife?

OK, put them somewhere else, then. Then at some point we're going to be running out of places for the birds to go, right? And so then at what point do we decide that we gotta stop developing wetlands because we gotta leave some for the birds?

Ummmm . . . I'm used to having federal reserves for wildlife and all that on Hawaii, I mean . . .

Well, there's a lot of federal stuff up in northern Wisconsin—or some federal stuff—national forests, and so on. But for some people maybe that wouldn't be enough. I mean, right around here there's not any federal property that I know of, really. There's state parks.

But there's *lots* of land over here. Why is everybody so worried about just that one area?

Because they like wetlands. They'll say things like: Wetlands are important because they filter water (they filter groundwater out, they're places for recharging water); they're important because they're where the fish lay their eggs and we want the fish; or they're impor-tant because we need a place for all those different kind of things that live in there that don't have anyplace else to live; they're important because they're part of the big picture; they're important because we don't have very many of them. I mean, there's all kinds of different rea-sons you would get.

That's true. I can understand that. I could. I feel sorry for the birds, I mean . . .

So then what if I came back to you with this proposal?

What can one person do, though?
Before you said, "Build the condos." Now would you say the same thing?
No. If . . . if . . . I mean if it's *that*, you know, you make it sound so permanent.

Although I found less to rejoice over in this area than in the previous two, I think it would be a mistake to dismiss these findings as unimportant. It is remarkable in one sense that deliberation encouraged such foresight at all in the environmental realm. As I have said, many of my participants began the interview with a long-term perspective on environmental issues. Everything I heard suggests that deliberation enforces more than just "some degree of foresight" (Spragens 1990: 135).

Clarity of Ends

Although all these findings are encouraging, I am perhaps most heartened by the way the great majority of my participants were able to probe their own minds and, even more important, become conscious of the results. With very few exceptions, they knew more about environmental policy at the end of the interview than they did at the beginning. But what was surprising was how much better they knew themselves. Near the end of the interview I asked: Have you changed your mind in any way since we started the interview? Barely 1 in 10 said yes. But almost half of those who said they hadn't changed their mind were wrong, at least in one sense: they had come to know their own minds better than they had when they started. To use chapter 1's metaphor, their deliberative travel had led them to appreciate better their environmental home. Eight participants saw the ends of environmental policy with greater clarity; six understood their own reasons for endorsing those ends more clearly; and seven became more conscious of both ends and justifications. Fully 21 out of 46, then, were better environmental dialecticians at the close of the interview than when they started. I want to begin illustrating this finding with Deena Champney, who fits the sociologist's stereotype of the beleaguered, black, inner-city matriarch—but who ruptured it as soon as we started talking. She is a powerful woman, deeply concerned about her family and large circle of friends, but often overwhelmed by the problems they bring to her. And she is also quite obviously concerned about the environment, including the wilderness areas she confesses she will never see. Here, about a third of the way through the interview, she (re)discovers why:

Wilderness? Like in certain parts of Arizona where you have, like, yeah . . . No, they shouldn't, cause what's there?

Well, let's say that there's some oil in there. Why not go in there and take it out? We need oil.

Should we let them drill for oil? Yeah.

We should?

Because it might be a corporation that might drill and really hit it, and might help us in how we feel about certain things. I'm dreaming, because that would never happen, you know, but I think maybe . . . I don't know. Should you? Yeah, you should, maybe. Somebody has to start somewhere.

. . .

Well, OK then, let's say off the coast of California, or in Texas, or . . .

But see, there's not too much oil in Texas anymore; something happened.

Yeah, OK. So we got to look other places. What if it's cheapest to go into a wilderness area for oil right now?

Maybe, yes.

You don't seem too sure, though.

No, no I don't, because I really don't know.

Well, let me give you the other side of the story, because maybe that will help you make up your mind. Some people would say that you shouldn't let them go in there for oil because, for any number of different reasons, we got to keep those wilderness areas totally pure.

Oh, like the forests in South America?''

Right, or like, I think, I'm not sure, but I think the nearest wilderness area here is in northern Minnesota, where it's like a canoeing area—you know what I mean? Where it's just canoes can go in there, nothing else. And so they don't want boats in there, or snowmobiles, or . . .

Should they go up there and drill? No, no. Let that be like God had it.

Yeah, that's kind of what I thought you were going to say.

Yeah. Seriously. Let that just be like it is. No, they shouldn't. Yes, and they should drill, like, back out here. If it means me uprooting here and going somewhere else if they find oil, the government will put me somewhere.

Well, now, why should we have it like God created it up there? And in those other areas?

Why? Oh, because he must've put it there for a reason. But see, we're talking about religion too now, not just environmental issues. It says in the Bible that God created the Heaven and the Earth, and on the seventh day he rested. And he put things where they were supposed to be for reasons. And man, by Eve giving Adam a bite of the apple, opened up his eyes to a lot of things. You understand what I'm saying? And this is how we're living now. And he wants certain things left alone. Why did they make those national parks? Why did they do that? For man to leave alone. Let things be like they are. And I think man's going a little bit too far in certain aspects. I mean, like, we have diseases like cancer, Alzheimer's disease. We have acids now, you know. You have a lot of diseases, I don't think . . . I think that if man had left certain things alone, we wouldn't have these problems. I mean, you know, I don't have all them answers, but I think maybe I don't have the right words or terminology, but they should just leave certain things the hell *alone*.

I take my second example from a modern-day Thoreauvian. Mark Allen is an unusual person. Long a member of a Catholic religious order and rising in its educational hierarchy, in his mid-40s he dropped out of what he refers to as the mainstream. It's an apt expression: he now supports himself by working perhaps two months out of the year, promoting rationality at Renaissance fairs in theatrical reproductions of the conflict between Galileo and the Catholic church, and lives the rest of the year in a one-room boathouse on a back channel of the Mississippi River. His was among my longest interviews. Allen liked to think long and hard about each question, and his answers were always forceful but carefully constructed. Yet for some five or six hours I was unable to get him to explain the real foundations of his very clearly enunciated environmental ethic: the Long Term. "Why is that so important?" I had repeated over and over. He had made a number of stabs at it, all unsatisfying to himself. Then, on my third visit, when I asked him directly about what he would be willing to sacrifice for his version of an ideal environment, he came up with this:

I guess it really goes back to your basic idea of, you know, these real fundamental issues about: What's life about? What's morality about? What's the purpose of what you want to do with your life? What . . . When your life has ended and you look back and you say, "This is what I did that was positive and made my life worthwhile." To me, all the answers to all those heavy philosophical questions are connected with the long term. Both the long-term past (looking at what we evolved out of) and the long-term future (looking at what life is about here on Earth—what is

life about?). And so it's . . . Let me put it this way: What if . . .
When you look at the past . . . When you look at the past, when
you step back and look at where we are now in terms of the
past, we are . . . where we are right now is a product of all our
past history. And, you know, the future will be a product of
what we are doing now, plus all the past.

In this final illustration, Dr. James Burson, in his last year of a residency
in psychiatry, made a personal realization that he ended up applying
to society as whole.

*There is one more point I'd like to touch on. At a couple of points
you admitted that, like most people, you don't always act on your environmental ideals. Why is that?*
That seems like the crux of today's interview. Well, you know,
I think a lot of it comes down to time, convenience. Part of it
comes down to money; part of it comes down to compulsiveness.
Is this sort of in order of importance?
You know, this is really interesting. This is really interesting
for me, but I'd have to say compulsiveness. You know, when I
really think about it from the perspective of this last question, I'd
have to say that was a big part of it. Bigger than I had realized
before I'd thought about it in this way. More of a kind of a resistance to different ways of being in the world. That's probably
what it comes down to. I wonder what that resistance is based
upon, because that would seem to be the core of it all. [*pauses*] I
would have to say that a lot of it comes down to a lack of faith—
that it's even possible to be in the world in different ways. Part of
me would say it has something to do with a lack of courage, but
I don't think that that's accurate. Boy, this seems *really* important. I'm trying to figure out what it is that drives my own compulsiveness. I mean, this is a religious question as I look at it.
Religious because . . . ?
Because I think if you've answered it, you've answered the big
question. What is it that drives the sort of compulsive identification
to a certain way of thinking about oneself? This is like a koan.
Are you familiar with that word, "zen koan"? This is for me a koan.
*I don't want to interrupt the train of your thought, but it seems to
me, to be attached so strongly that one is compulsively attached to that
one [thing] means that it either must be painful to break out of that, in
some sense, or it must be satisfying in some sense, or both, right?*
Well, that's the traditional answer within the Western culture.
But it might be . . . Another possibility is that it's frightening,

painful to leave it, frightening would be a form of pain. Or it might just be habit. [*pauses*] There's another answer to this one as well. . . . You know what I think the answer is? There is no answer. I mean, it's true! There is no answer. There's no reason. I really think that that's the answer for me: that there is no reason. You know, I work through that riddle again and again in different ways, and I come back to that same point. You know, the more I realize that, the freer I get. [*pauses*] You don't have to spend your free time compulsively trying to solve it. You're free for a time, for a temporary period, and then the riddle's going to confront you in a different way, and you're going to work some more. But in the meantime, you're going to be productive. . . . That series of questions induced a small enlightenment!

These examples illustrate the dual connections between deliberation and rationality, especially environmental rationality. On the one hand, an individual's interests become known only by being challenged or "probed" (Lindblom 1990: 22, 27; Flanagan 1984: 195–196; Spragens 1990: 108; Majone 1990: 158; Gorham 1992: 254). For that very reason, Edward Hollister, who sometimes sounded like a Baptist preacher in our interview, explicitly encouraged me to join him in the pulpit early in our second meeting:

> *See where we got? And that was about . . . That was one question!*
> I'm trying to figure out where you're coming from.
> *Well, I just want to . . . I'll tell you all about where I'm coming from after this is over. I'll be happy to do that. If you're interested, I'll be happy to tell you what I think. But . . .*
> I'm interested.
> *I'm trying to stay out of this just because I think, well, I don't want to influence what you're thinking now before you tell me what you're thinking, you know?*
> Well, that's the influence. Sometimes it's necessary for you to influence *me* to get me to collect my acts so I can *do* what *you're* thinking. [*laughs*]
> *It's getting too complicated.* [*both laugh*]

On the other hand, deliberative discourse encourages individuals to become more principled, or at least better at justifying their principles (Spragens 1990: 135, 138). Betsy Schon, the fundamentalist I quoted earlier, had no trouble recognizing this. In response to my short follow-up questionnaire, she wrote: "The part I appreciated most about the interview was your helpfulness in *directing* my thoughts in various directions, presenting alternatives that I would not have thought of, thus helping me come to a rational [!] decision."

Why Some Students Learn More Than Others

If deliberation is important, understanding why some people benefit from it more than others is crucial (Lindblom 1990: 278). Unfortunately, I am able to offer only the most tentative explanations of such differences. And most of these explanations differ only slightly from those that philosophers and social scientists have been advancing since Plato's time.

I have already argued that two of the reasons deliberation works so well in the environmental realm is that almost everyone will find some reason (or complex of reasons) to work at environmental deliberation and that the environment is seen as a largely empirical issue. I also noted in chapter 5 that most people view their environmental values as more or less fixed. These observations are enough to adduce at least a crude theoretical explanation about when deliberation is likely to work and when not. It is most likely to increase environmental commitment when environmental values are already strong and least likely to have that effect when they are weak. Individuals whose values are strong have an interest in learning new environmental facts; they seek them out and actively work to integrate them into their view. And we have already seen that most individuals presume that more facts mean more commitment. Individuals with weaker environmental values, on the other hand, lack this interest in acquiring new knowledge. Moreover, the weight of new facts, which they generally recognize, must always overcome the resistance of prior values. And since values change slowly and are perceived to be invariant, any gains in environmental commitment will likely be small.

This theory fits many of my participants, but not all. There are three important, if infrequent, additional barriers to deliberation. The first involves individual identity, the second environmental values, the third individuals' views of collective action. The first is most complex and never easy to predict. Some people find their identity threatened by environmental policy. One of the developers I talked to, for example, was very obviously more concerned with his role as a community-builder than with profits. He was intensely upset with the local greenies, as he called them, not because they threatened his legitimate business interests but because they threatened his vision for the city and surrounding area. He was offended, not because of what he had lost financially to such opponents, but because of who he was: a growing pillar of a growing community.

Strong environmental values can also overwhelm deliberation by inducing an attitude of fatalism. Characteristically, that occurred with the two participants who most seriously recommended a return to a hunting-gathering existence: both found it hard to think of solutions to any of the problems I discussed. Although both ended up acknowledging most of the policy proposals I suggested, in the end they stayed true to their own beliefs that only individual or spontaneous neighborhood action might achieve any real results. At the time I was interviewing them, one was learning to make himself independent from store-bought bread, the other was reading Joanna Rogers Macy's *Despair and Personal Power in the Nuclear Age*.

Third, to return to a familiar theme, deliberation can be frustrated by the view that government is hopeless. The difference between this and the second barrier is that this one need not arise from intense environmental values. Not surprisingly, this barrier was rather more frequent than the first two, occurring in perhaps half a dozen cases. Its effect, however, was identical: the individual ended up asking: Why talk or think about the impossible?

In the end, whatever individual differences existed were far less important than the fact that most participants derived *some* benefit from deliberation.[5] If democracy, as Robert Dahl has written, "is a gamble on the possibilities that a people, in acting autonomously, will learn how to act rightly," then expanding people's deliberative opportunities in the environmental realm will certainly help slant the odds in the environment's favor (1989: 192). Nor is that all. As I explained earlier, environmental rationality does not displace individual rationality, but supplements it. Hence to encourage environmental rationality is simultaneously to encourage individual rationality. Deliberation thus heightens individuals' awareness of their own interests and how those interests are served or frustrated by the existing policy regime. Deliberation thus offers individuals an opportunity to keep pace with the increasingly complex nature of environmental policy. It can help narrow the gap between the average citizen and policy elites (see Dahl 1989: 335). It can, in short, help us not only to "act rightly" but also to preserve democracy in the process.

The Preconditions of Political Deliberation

As I argued in the preceding two chapters, we can be reasonably sure that there is a public consensus on the need to expand environmental policy. That consensus is not only wide, as is shown by a vast body of survey research, but relatively durable as well. In the interviews I conducted, it held up to varied and repeated attacks. Public opinion may be a moving target, I said, but the public's convictions are not. And my public was clearly behind an activist environmental agenda. That fact alone is significant. At a minimum, it means that we ought not be overly hasty in closing the door on democratic environmental change. But it also means that one of the two essential conditions for successful democratic deliberation, broadly shared goals, has been met. There is no deep value conflict over environmental ends, no unbridgeable schism or cleavage separating citizens on environmental policy. Human communication can further mutual understanding. But it must have some shared understanding to build upon (Pierce 1972: 36; Spragens 1990: 108, 116; Lindblom 1990: 291). Fortunately that does exist here. Not only is there an ethical consensus, there is a broad political consensus as well: people endorse not just the environment but also environmental protection. Incidentally, this finding flies in the face of the argument that any kind of fundamental consensus on basic policy questions is impossible in large, heterogeneous polities (Dahl 1989: 301). Size need not imply unending or wrenching conflict, even on an issue of such basic importance as preservation of the environment.

By definition, a more deliberative public would argue more about the environment. But citizens would be starting from a shared commitment to a greener world. Improving the environment really *is* as American as baseball and apple pie, which suggests that arguing about it is likely to come naturally. It also means that debates are likely to focus, not on metaphysics or the disputants' personalities, but on strategy and tactics—that is, on relative priorities and how to realize them. Disputants' credentials can be acknowledged, but they will seldom preempt debate. Results will be accorded respect, but won't be automatically extrapolated into the future. Most crucial of all, it means that disputants have agreed not only on how the game is to be played but also on what counts as a win, what counts as a loss. There is admittedly a great deal more at stake in environmental disputes than in debates over the relative merits of the Yankees and the Dodgers. And by the resolution of these disputes, some people will stand to gain more than others. But even if we admit that deliberation is likely to spawn new conflicts (Lindblom 1990: 126), it would have to be shown that such conflict is inherently undesirable. Moreover, the prevailing environmental consensus provides adequate insurance against such conflict becoming overly divisive.

It is not enough, however, to say that deliberation can build on widely shared values. It does no good to say that we can build if no one is really interested in chipping in. Fortunately, people are interested, indeed they are intensely interested. This may be a surprising claim in an age in which political apathy seems to be setting new records all the time. But it is less surprising if one remembers that voting and deliberating are two very different acts. People have lots of reasons to stay away from the polls. They likewise have lots of reasons to want to deliberate about public policy, environmental policy in particular.

I repeat that, although I did not keep an official count, I believe that in lining up 46 interviews, I had fewer than half a dozen refusals (and a couple of those individuals pleaded busy schedules). None of my participants was a close friend or even an acquaintance. Obviously, anyone willing to spend upwards of four hours on an interview like mine must really want to do it. Almost half of those I asked to complete a short follow-up questionnaire did so; a few of them amending their responses with authentic letters. Most participants also asked to be informed about the results. Furthermore, only about one in four participants seemed either disinterested or plainly dogmatic during the interview. Indeed, perhaps half of the others approached the interview with what can be described only as gusto: it was work, yes, but many found it satisfying or fun (or both) as well. How else can one explain the fact that six or seven interviews extended to 8, 10, even 12 hours? Halfway into our second meeting, Deena Champney paused and exclaimed, "I love talking like this." Michelle Washington, who described herself as a person who mainly keeps to herself, hesitated to give any reasons for her positions on the first set of policy proposals. Slowly, and then quite clearly, she began to loosen up and, by the time we were into the second half, was obviously relishing the whole thing. Washington, like a number of others, needed only a little (self-) reminding that she was fully capable of deliberating; once she (re)discovered that, she jumped in head first. Five minutes into the interview, Val Gotti responded to one of my challenges this way: "God, you got me. You're getting me to where I don't even know. You're making me think so many things I never thought about. This is good [*laughs*] for me. I don't know about your little [*tape recorder*]. But for me, it's good."

One final indicator of this group's enthusiasm for environmental deliberation is perhaps most telling of all: participants were usually conscious (in a general way, at least) of the very gains I described in the preceding sections. They not only willingly deliberated but were also happy with the process—and the results. The postinterview questionnaires speak for themselves:

It was hard to put feelings in words. The good part was I actually learned more info from the questions. (data analyst and former RN Suzette Schell)

I recall the interviews being an enjoyable time to discuss my particular concern, the Oak River Marsh, as well as an opportunity to sort out and then articulate some larger environmental views. The one impact I felt was how very long it had been since I was urged to do some critical thinking about a topic outside of my own professional realm or personal interests. (social worker Teresa Hirschler)

I enjoyed the interview for the most part—pretty long though. The good part for me is that it got me thinking of the other side of the issues—possibly changing opinions/attitudes on subjects. Other issues I knew little about, I learned about. It didn't exactly change my life, but I did learn a lot and am also willing to discuss the issues with those who have other opinions. (college senior Erik Johannsen)

The interview increased my awareness of current issues. I now look for more information and do more leisure reading on the subject. I realized needed to watch this issue more carefully. (legal secretary–accountant Karen Brunson)

It was a very good interview; it also gave me insight on what can be harmful to us in the system, as we know it right now. (young mother Jill King)

I think it raised my consciousness about environmental issues, though it didn't change my opinions. (premed student Julie Binns)

A chance for me to develop in detail some of my ideas. (dairy farmer Paul Zalens)

Induced me into further inquiring. (math tutor Edward Hollister)

The series of questions forced me to face the paradoxical and contradictory aspects of giving simple answers to complex questions. [The interview was] very good. No one has ever encouraged me to expand so widely on such a broad front of questions. I found myself ruminating often on the previous interview simply because of my own appreciation of the complexity of the issues discussed being heightened. The interview did have a lasting impact. Simply put, we finally began recycling our waste materials. In a broader sense, I took a more active stance toward forcing local land use questions to referendum. I also became motivated to relocate my family to California, to gain professional opportunity and greater job satisfaction. (industrial chemist Tim Behringer)

The interview was longer and more detailed than I thought it would be. Also, very thought provoking. (corporate lawyer Carol Chapman)

The interviews helped me clarify and organize my own thoughts on the subject, and I believe made me more willing to get involved (see enclosed news article). (actor and boat dweller Mark Allen, referring to his recent participation in a local protest against river polluters)

As impressive as they are, do these indicators apply to the world out-side an academic interview? Yes, they do. Tim Behringer, the young family man, told me at one point that "America is a problem-solving culture." His coparticipants proved his point, and in several different ways. Recall from chapter 4 that only 13 participants called for handing more environmental decision-making power to experts. The environment poses a problem, but for this group it is clearly the *public's* problem. Second, despite the fact that this group harbored a good deal of skepticism about public institutions and processes, it clearly believed that politics can be more than a simple clash of interests. Over 90 percent made one or more of the following kinds of statements: (1) environmental issues involve no fundamental value clashes; (2) an essential element in meeting the environmental challenge is increased public awareness, learning, discussion, or involvement; (3) public solutions to any given issue must involve uniting the best of the opposing sides. Third, participants generally had a very positive view of the system's ability to translate public concern into policy; most (35/46) argued that the level of U.S. environmental policy has historically been a function of popular demand.

On this issue at least, we can say that, while Americans may not be by nature political animals, politics comes rather naturally to them. Lindblom was right when he wrote, "Societies do not need to urge citizens to probe; they need only permit them to do so" (1990: 230; see also Reich 1990a: 146). This conclusion, I should add, is diametrically at odds with that James Fishkin arrives at in his work *Beyond Subjective Morality* (1984). He found a public unconvinced of the objectivity of moral judgments and hence largely unwilling to transfer them to the public domain. My participants did so freely, and with some relish, and yet simultaneously maintained skepticism about their own views and about the objectivity of the system itself. How does one explain the difference? To answer that question, we must return to the crucial distinction between ethics and politics that underlies this whole study. Fishkin's participants were reasoning about largely private matters, mine about clearly public ones. I would argue, not that Fishkin was wrong about his participants' views, but rather that he asked them the wrong questions, that he made a category mistake: people's views on the objectivity of private morals and public ends logically can be, and in reality are, very different. American culture may in fact deprecate the objectivity of private moral standards, as Fishkin argued, but not the capacity of political claims to be more or less reasonable. Quite the opposite in fact: it requires that political claims be shown, in public, to be reasonable. American political culture does not threaten but supports deliberation.

Skeptics may remain unconvinced. They might object that it is one thing to suggest that individuals support deliberation or that (in at least some respects) ours is a deliberative culture, quite another to claim that the interview itself resulted in deliberation. Isn't it equally possible that the deliberative "gains" recorded here resulted not from the nature of the interview but from the peculiar character of the interviewer? Moreover, the skeptics might continue, if participants responded not to the substance of the questions but to the more or less distinctive personality of the researcher himself, whatever "deliberation" that did in fact occur during this experiment can hardly be reproduced in society as a whole.

A general response to this two-pronged objection is that it is not so much wrong as misdirected. Yes, as a researcher I influenced the outcome of my study. That was, after all, the point. At the same time, however, that influence was largely independent of any special characteristics that I brought to the interview situation. The results the interview produced were likewise largely independent of any strictly personal effect I may have had on them. In other words, they show a deliberative response to the interview, not an affective response to the interviewer. It follows, then, that there ought to be no insuperable barrier to re-creating the same influence throughout American culture as a whole.

My role as "cause" of the deliberative "effects" I have discussed can quite easily be played by others. To appreciate why, we need to look carefully at both of the roles that made up the interviews I conducted: my own and that played by my participants. Let me state from the outset that there is no question here of a "Hawthorne effect" (i.e., of my causing the effects that I set out to investigate in the first place); I consciously aimed to influence or create those effects; I *was* very much their cause. The real question is whether the effects I have reported here are *reproducible*, not in a scientific sense, but in a practical, political one. To argue that they are is to argue that the interview situation I helped create—or a functional facsimile—can be reproduced elsewhere. It is to argue that my role as interviewer and each participant's role as interviewee, can be reproduced elsewhere, by other political actors. If both roles can be re-created, my own interviews must be seen as a specific instance not of a general rule but of a much wider realm of possibility.

The first question that must be answered here is: Can my own role as deliberative spur be filled by others, or did it depend crucially on skills, knowledge, aims, and personality traits unique to me? I do not believe I need to reduce myself to a sociological abstraction to answer the first part of this question affirmatively. Certainly my knowledge of environmental policy and philosophy set me off from the population as a whole. Certainly my primary interest was in deliberation, not in propaganda, misinformation, or reeducation. And it is true that my training as a teacher may have made me well-suited to the role of interviewer. My personality may even have contributed to the interview's impact. But there is absolutely no way to be certain that these were uniquely responsible for the results I obtained. On the other hand, it is at least plausible that some of my own traits (my relative youth, my position as an "expert") may have actually discouraged deliberation. Moreover, given the *generally* deliberative results I obtained, it appears highly unlikely that my personality traits alone, rather than the role I was playing, occasioned the results I have discussed. If it was the questioner rather than the questions that encouraged deliberation, why was the effect of the interview almost universally in the direction of deepened deliberation? Surely no researcher can claim such widespread popularity. Finally—and this consideration is crucial—short of reproducing my personality itself, those interested in encouraging deliberation can reproduce every other facet of the interview situation I organized. They can do this, moreover, while implementing their own judgments about what makes such situations work in different contexts. If one believes that my participants responded primarily to my own deliberative intent, one can adopt an openly deliberative agenda. If one believes that these participants responded to the prolonged attention I gave them, one can focus on maintaining sustained contact with would-be deliberators. If, to give but one more example, one is convinced that my own participants responded favorably because they saw in me a source of up-to-date information, then one's first step is clear: get the facts and the arguments down (neither of which is particularly difficult). My personality aside, there is nothing in the interview situation I have described that could not be re-created (or improved upon) by others.

What of the participants' role—can it so easily be filled by other citizens? Again the answer is yes, for reasons I have already given. Certainly my participants' endorsement of deliberation went beyond endorsing deliberation with *me*: some 90 percent of those I contacted consented to the interview without hesitation, without having ever laid eyes on me before. In perhaps as many cases, participants not only deliberated but did so actively, even enthusiastically. Moreover, as I tried to show in chapter 3, these citizens tended to frame environmental politics in a deliberative, inquisitive way and asked numerous questions along the way. Finally, in open-ended questions, a large plurality of this group called for more public information, education, and involvement in environmental protection, all of which closely parallel the deliberative prescription I am offering here. Will other Americans be so eager to fulfill this role? Yes, they will. Again, demographic data show little variance in environmental policy attitudes. Moreover, my own group was made up of people from a wide range of demographic and political categories. And, with only a handful of exceptions, they *all* benefited from the short deliberative experience I offered them, often to a degree inversely related to their socioeconomic status or educational level.

Why Deliberation Must Be Political

In arguing that deliberation is the ultimate environmental solution, I may appear to be simply adding my voice to an already enormous chorus calling for a change in our environmental consciousness. And in one sense, that is true. We *do* need to think differently about the environment. But that is not enough. That new thinking must be political if it is to do any good. An ethical revolution will not save the environment; what is needed is a new political philosophy of the environment. And the only way we can teach ourselves that philosophy is politically.

Since John Muir first called the wilderness nature's university, environmentalists have held out the hope that, if enough of us just get out into the woods more often, we'd all come to love trees enough to save them (see, for example, Devall and Sessions 1985: chapter 10). The idea is plausible, but fatally flawed. I happen to think that Muir and Leopold were right in thinking that to know Nature is to love her, but one can love in private, which is to say that this line of argument mistakes love of the environment for preservation of the environment. Preservation of the environment requires collective action. And one can spend the rest of one's days camping in Yosemite and never even conceive of the idea of regulations, laws, taxes, incentives, courts, or subsidies. In fact, it is rather likely that one never will (hence the frequency of environmentalists' plea for moral regeneration). Direct experience of nature may produce love of or respect for nature, but one simply cannot directly experience that which experiences of nature presuppose: environmental protection (for a more general version of this argument, see Lindblom 1990: 79).

Nor can we place our faith, as Aldo Leopold and so many after him have, in public education (Leopold [1949] 1970; see also Callicott 1989: 10, 237). In the first place, we must ask, with Marx: Who is to educate the educators? In the second place, our schools are having a hard time delivering the basics: "The number of functional illiterates that our free public education produces does not make us sanguine about educating a majority of the public to respect for the earth, a harder form of literacy" (Stegner 1987: 245). Third, present research indicates that education begins to have a real impact on environmentalism only after students have completed four years of college (Milbrath 1984). Fourth, and most crucial, even completely functional schools would not be up to the task. The "key log" in a stable environmental edifice is not, as Leopold thought, to begin thinking about the land in ethical rather than purely economic terms; it is to begin thinking about it in *political* terms.

Can teaching environmental protection in public schools be justified philosophically? I think so. It is universally important, and need not be any more doctrinaire than U.S. history. Are students likely to learn anything from it? That is less clear. Developmental psychologists, it is true, have in recent years revised downward their estimates of the age of cognitive maturity. Perhaps students in their last two years of high school would be ready for it. It is also true that they are likely to be well motivated. Perhaps the biggest problems are practical: convincing school boards, fitting it into the school day, and the like. But even if all of these challenges could be met, it is hard to see how anyone but individual teachers could guarantee that classroom instruction yields deliberation rather than passivity (see Norton 1991: 194, 236, 255; Gorham 1992: 173–177).

For similar reasons, we ought not to expect organized religion to bring about the necessary change in environmental thinking. Religion and deliberation are hardly antitheses, but it is fair to say that most religious observance involves far more belief, acceptance, and affirmation than challenge, argument, and examination. And, although an ecological ministry has been growing rapidly in America's houses of worship, it is largely directed at reforming individual behaviors. As laudable as that may be, the message is, if anything, implicitly antipolitical. That could change, but one cannot count on it. Nor can one force such a change on institutional religion for rather obvious legal, philosophical, and practical reasons.

Perhaps we can simply wait for the required change to occur, assisted by all the mechanisms of popular culture, especially the mass media. After all, when *Time* magazine's "Man of the Year" is Planet Earth, can a wholesale change in mass consciousness be far behind? Well, yes. The problem is not only the legally protected autonomy of the mass media or that we think there are good reasons to protect that autonomy. A more basic dilemma is that the mass media's capacity to encourage environmental rationality presupposes a more environmentally rational audience (see Entman 1989). Moreover, the mass media's current bias toward "objectivity" probably promotes cognitive quiescence rather than active deliberation (Linsky 1990). Even more debilitating is the fact that the mass media are not interactive (the occasional letter to the editor and the pretensions of talk show hosts notwithstanding): they speak, but they cannot listen. They are simply not deliberative. We may, on the contrary, trust our environmental futures to the culture as a whole. Unfortunately it contains no institution sufficiently environmental, sufficiently broad-based, and sufficiently deliberative to warrant such trust.[6]

The Limits of Expanded Deliberation

The 240 hours I spent deliberating over environmental issues with individuals all over southern Wisconsin left me tired, but more than a bit euphoric. For a long time I drove around wondering why I felt so good about what I was hearing. At first I chalked it up as a kind of immersion-style baptism in the democratic faith. It was only much later that I pieced together the analysis I have presented here. Unfortunately that analysis has not been able to sustain the excitement of those early encounters, but it provides us all with something far more important: solid empirical grounds for believing in the efficacy of political deliberation on environmental questions. Those grounds are not unshakable. Only an army of researchers interviewing a statistically representative sample of Americans could provide indisputable evidence. But they are firmer grounds than such interviews typically provide, for several reasons. In the first place, as I explain more fully in the Appendix, I intentionally sought a representative group of participants. And, as I have repeatedly noted, there is little demographic variance in Americans' environmental beliefs. It is thus doubly probable that my participants represent a fair cross-section of American environmental policy thinking. Second, as I reported above, the interview led to at least half a dozen immediate behavioral changes. Third, there is at least some survey evidence to indicate that, however tortuous or tenuous, there *is* a link between environmental beliefs and political action (Merchant 1989: 20; Starrett 1990; Gill et al. 1986; Dunlap and Van Liere 1978: 16n9; O'Riordan 1976). Fourth, and most important, it must be remembered that these interviews constitute less a series of observations than an experiment. As a result, the data they generated are not just theory-laden, they are theory-*saturated*: they tell us at least as much about the more deliberative polity I envision as they do about the political world we inhabit now.[7] My initial optimism, they show, should be infectious.

However, as effective as deliberation may be, it is no cure-all. There are certain to be occasions upon which it is either partly or wholly impotent. As in all political realms, some environmental questions involve conflicts of interest that simply will not yield to discussion—of any kind, in any setting. Other environmental problems may simply be too pressing to allow time for much talk. Deliberate responses to crises are by definition impossible. Moreover, we ought not to expect deliberation to produce miraculous cures to our environmental ills. All the deliberating in the world cannot transcend the inherent limits on human reason. We will never understand our environment completely, much less be able to predict what it will be like a millennium or even a century from now. Nor is any citizenry other than one made up of angelic political economists ever likely to be able to wholly resist thinking of the environment in individual terms. Despite these limitations, we can expect a great deal from expanding citizens' opportunities to deliberate about environmental policy. Just how we might go about doing that is the subject of the final chapter.

7

Expanding Environmental Deliberation

> I guess I would just like to say that this has helped me to become more aware of how I felt about certain things that I might not have considered or might not have really thought about and that it's too bad that everybody can't be forced to address these issues so that they can formulate some ideas and policies in their mind, because I think it really is a bad situation with our environment right now (world, local, and national) and that we need to take preventative action rather than retroactive because it won't work that way.
>
> —prelaw student Lynda Evans,
> looking back on our interview

Our best environmental hope is to expand the agora—in two ways. At the theoretical level, we must widen our view of democratic deliberation to recognize the many semipublic and private places in which it occurs. We must then act on that awareness by encouraging deliberation in all those places. We need, in short, to stimulate deliberation *wherever* it occurs.[1]

Democratic Deliberation: Both Radical and Practical

Deliberative democracy embodies a radical ideal. As I explained in the first chapter, it calls for encouraging citizens to deliberate about public issues wherever they find themselves. Democratic deliberation envisions a citizenry unwilling to confine their public deliberation to particular places or particular times. Yet deliberative democracy is also a practical theory, since the changes it calls for are changes in degree, not kind. It calls upon citizens to deliberate more, not to deliberate differently. It asks them to do more of something that we know they already do at least occasionally and that, given the findings I reported in the previous four chapters, they can be expected to do more of if given the opportunity. By definition, no ideal can be fully realized in practice. But some ideals are so far removed from the world of practice that they have little capacity to move or guide us. Deliberative democracy, on the contrary, offers us an ideal which not only grew out of practice but was also tested in practice. That test neither achieved nor realized pure deliberation, but it did show that expanding deliberation can have real results. We need only look around us to find ways of doing so.

As I described it in chapter 1, the basic building block of deliberative democracy is not a particular kind of group, neighborhood, or organization, but a dialogue or conversation between two persons. That is where deliberation occurs; that is the locus of deliberation. Hence deliberative reform, if it is to be truly democratic, will have innumerable loci, not just one, two, or five. The deliberative democrat's agenda is limited only by her or his energy and creativity. She or he can stimulate public deliberation almost anywhere—in almost any institutional setting and in many noninstitutional settings, too. Deliberative democracy is an ongoing process threaded throughout the lives of its citizenry. It need not be limited to the outwardly "political" hours spent at meetings, fundraisers, and demonstrations. Deliberation has no program, only a manifesto, and a short one at that: challenge more; respond more. Deliberative democracy is not a constitutional arrangement so much as a way of approaching political life, a political *modus vivendi*.

Democratic deliberation, I argued earlier, is essentially dyadic; that is, democratic deliberation is like a conversation or, more accurately, a dialogue. It is fundamentally a two-person phenomenon. This means that, to stimulate or encourage democratic deliberation, all one really needs is a partner. One can engage in dyadic dialogue almost anywhere, regardless of the institutional setting. As a result, no list of deliberative reforms, including the one I present later in this chapter, can really be exhaustive. Nor can it be authoritative. No matter how erudite or insightful, the individual theorist can know only so much, can see only so far. In many ways people know their own backyards best. It is there that people must look for opportunities to encourage deliberation. I know only that they will find them.

Some will no doubt be frustrated that, despite the numerous deliberative reforms I suggest below, I have not offered more in the way of concrete proposals here. Understandable as this may be, it must also be understood that my own belief in deliberative democracy imposes real limits on recommending changes that might further the deliberative ideal. This may sound surprising, but it follows very directly from the nature of deliberative democracy itself. To issue specific instructions about how the dyadic model of deliberation might be made relevant to contemporary society would amount to a patent contradiction. The dyadic model of deliberation sees deliberation happening everywhere, at least potentially. To recommend particular reforms is to suggest that only certain places, only certain settings, really matter. I want very much to resist that conclusion. It is for that reason, then, that I offer the recommendations below, not as a program, but as a set of suggestions—not as a single, privileged response to the deliberative challenge, but as a stimulus to others who are interested in coming up with responses of their own.

Democratic deliberation's expansive view of public deliberation may in one sense be a radical ideal, but it is an ideal that I discovered among real citizens, citizens who showed that, given the opportunity, they were capable of acting upon that ideal. However radical, deliberative democracy is an ideal that American society already approximates, at least to a limited degree. It is already there in nascent form. If it weren't, it would never have grabbed my attention. Hence the very origins of the theory of deliberative democracy were themselves "practical." The theory was rooted in real life, in interactions with real people, from the very start. Even though these individuals are unique, I doubt very much that their comments are. Surely most who read the middle chapters of this book will hear echoes of conversations they have had with a friend, a cousin, a neighbor, or a co-worker. Surely most of us have overheard similar discussions at home, in the mall, on barstools, or by the coffee pot at work. My research was an experiment, but its results are hardly unique. To replicate them on a wider scale we need only reproduce the experiment's key structural elements: challenge and response. As individual citizens, each of us can stimulate deliberation in innumerable ways, both in ourselves and in those around us. Groups can do the same for their members. And traditional politics at all levels can encourage deliberation in still other ways. The possibilities are virtually infinite. Radical or not, democratic deliberation is thus no mere dream of some professor.

Lowering the Price of Admission: Environmental Redistribution

The last chapter identified a series of cognitive barriers to environmental deliberation. Together they explain to a substantial degree why some of my participants failed to take advantage of the deliberative opportunity the interview presented. But such factors do not explain why some had had so few opportunities in the past. The capacity to deliberate is obviously useless if one never has the chance to exercise it. Without exception, those in my group who were denied such opportunities were denied them by economic circumstance. The single biggest structural barrier to deliberation (in the realm of environmental policy, at least) is poverty. With apologies to Anatole France, we might say that the Culture, in all its wisdom, expects both rich and poor alike to deliberate about public issues. The poor no more choose to ignore civic business than they choose to sleep under bridges.

Economic security is no guarantee of deliberation. It is simply a necessary precondition (Spragens 1990: 166; Majone 1990: 160). That rather self-evident truth has, incidentally, been confirmed by a variety of empirical studies. It has been found, for example, that feelings of powerlessness and self-estrangement (not exactly the hallmarks of the deliberative personality) correlate with low socioeconomic status (see Lindblom 1990: 68). This may be all the more true when it comes to environmental policy. In the early 1970s, sociologist Denton Morrison; arguing on the basis of his own survey research, said:

> There is at least some basis for thinking that in the industrialization/modernization process, class conflict is in substantial measure prevented by environmental exploitation. But, if environmental exploitation leads inevitably to the necessity for restraints on such exploitation (as is implicit in environmentalists' claims), then it follows that environmental exploitation will be an important causal factor in an increase in class conflicts in the long-run. It also follows that a society that is able to de-emphasize social stratification based on material wealth differentiations (there are of course many other bases for social stratification) should have a much higher probability of developing sound environmental policies. (1973: 83)

One of the reasons that this is so, I might add, is that reduced inequality allows more people in on the issue of what to do about the environment.

That is certainly the message I got from my poorer respondents, or from those who had once been poor. Gramscian theory aside, these people hadn't bought into any hegemonic view of the environment; they had no view of the environment one way or another, and told me so. Most of my less well-off participants were black. But upper-middle-class Julie Chandler made it clear that race had little to do with blacks' apparent indifference to environmental problems:

> Where I grew up [in New York], being an environmentalist or conservation—any of that stuff was seen as really uncool, stuff that other folks thought about and did. And we figured they had

enough that they *could* conserve. It wasn't an issue. What was an issue of more importance to us was the *social* environment, not so much the physical environment. I guess when you have freedom in your social environment, then you have the luxury to think about the other, physical, environment. But when you don't have jobs, you don't have food, when, you know, you're discriminated against, you don't have equal opportunity, you don't think about things like the environment. That's not the first priority on your list. . . .

.   .   .

If an environmentalist was really interested in gaining support among the black community, what that environmentalist should do is, first and foremost, advocate jobs, education, and those kind of social programs that are going to help allow blacks to be in a position to become environmentalists?

Right, right. That would be a good strategy to gain support. It's sort of like having a discussion with someone about whether you're going to buy a silk dress at Neiman Marcus or you're going to buy a silk dress at Prange's and you got a person on the side thinking, "Gee, I'd just like to be able to buy a dress!" And that's the analogy I see when you talk to blacks about the environment. You know, they'll say, "Yeah, that's good, that's important." Well, whatever's the right thing to do, they want to do the right thing. But I would suspect urban blacks don't have a lot of profound opinions on the environment, unless they come into contact with it in their jobs.

And she couldn't have been more right, at least in the case of two of the four African Americans I interviewed, for whom the environment—as a recognizable realm, as a discrete political problem, as a concept—simply did not exist.

My analysis here is hardly new. A decade ago Jennifer Hochschild (1981) observed that normative thinking about distributive issues is a luxury some people simply can't afford. Robert Paehlke has recently made a similar point with respect to environmental policy attitudes (1989: 276). One needn't be a Maslowian to recognize that, when one's personal life is a series of pressing crises, it's hard to worry much about the crises taking place "out there." One cannot be environmentally rational without thinking collectively; one cannot think collectively without some measure of individual security. Moreover, the argument that, in the present context, a more environmentally deliberative society requires some redistribution of wealth meshes neatly with three other ecological arguments for greater distributive equality. The first is suggested in the final lines of Morrison's argument above: maximize the minimum income level to enable the least well-off to live with any new environmental limits society imposes. The second and third both imply a minimum-maximum distribution rule: first, because such a rule is a requirement of environmental justice (big consumers inflict big environmental damage) and, second, because such a rule is instrumental in minimizing the overall level of consumption (Daly 1983: 249).

Participation and Deliberation: Sufficient but Not Necessary

Environmentalists have increasingly argued that democracy is good for the environment. Their central contention is that, the more people are involved in environmental decisions (i.e., the greater their number and the greater their involvement), the better off the environment will be. At best this is only partly true. As I suggested in chapter 2, the key variable is not participation, but deliberation: direct decision-making need not yield quality decisions. Deliberation, meanwhile (as we saw in the last chapter), at least improves the quality of decisions. We will become more environmentally rational, not by concentrating our activity close to home, but by expanding our thoughts.

This deliberative approach is at once more radical and more conservative than that of the participatory environmentalists because its view of what counts as participation is at once more expansive and more skeptical than the conventional view. The deliberative perspective on participation is more expansive because it recognizes the possibility of global participation. If participation functions to encourage environmentalism, why restrict it to the locality, especially given the obvious environmental need for supralocal institutions? Citizens can be encouraged to think globally not just by acting locally but also by acting globally—that is, by making decisions whose consequences extend literally around the globe. Moreover, the alternative view I am suggesting recognizes that people can deliberate without being in public, in a group, or even face-to-face (see Spitz 1986: 199). Deliberation, as I noted in the last chapter, requires that individuals both speak and listen, that they justify their positions and pay attention to competing views. Public meetings can perhaps guarantee that each person in attendance has a chance to speak, but not that anyone will be listening. Participatory environmentalists, like most theorists, have ignored this central problem (though, see Lindblom 1990: 48, 233). It is difficult to see why. No deliberative body I have ever heard of did all its business during face-to-face meetings. In fact, most of it is done between meetings in smaller groups, in one-on-one encounters, or when members are alone with their thoughts. And it is precisely thought that counts in the end. Otherwise we would have to say that what judges do doesn't qualify as deliberation, or that leaving a prerecorded debate playing to an empty lecture hall does.

Democratic deliberation occurs anytime a citizen either actively justifies her views (even to herself) or defends them against a challenge (even from herself). The more demanding the audience, the more powerful the challenge, the better the resulting deliberation. Public meetings are likely, in this view, to provoke deliberation both because an audience of many is likely to be more demanding than an audience of one and because they are likely to provide stronger and more varied challenges than one could provide oneself (Spragens 1990: 151). But that is certainly not universally true. Nor does it mean that justification and defense cease when the gavel sounds.

At the same time, this deliberative view is more skeptical than the traditional view because it insists that we look beyond who is making decisions to how they are likely to be made. The deliberative view considers direct participation as useful only to the extent that it is likely to encourage deliberation. But deliberation and participation are not coextensive, especially in the realm of environmentalism. There is no guarantee that participation will always be preceded by or lead to deliberation. In fact, purely local participation is far more likely to impede both holistic and collective thinking. As I noted in chapter 2, there are good historical reasons to think that purely local action will tend to be chauvinistic. The point bears repeating. Consider the intercommunal strife that plagued the golden age of Greece (Hansen 1991). Or consider the history of the Roman Empire, during which loyalty to individual communities "produced fierce rivalries between neighboring cities for titles of honor or possession of border lands" (Starr 1982: 100). This tendency is further aggravated by the interconnectedness that is one of the defining characteristics of environmental problems. As a result, this deliberative view also doubts the need for any thoroughgoing decentralization of society.

Ultimately, deliberation is useless if it does not issue in actual decisions. But those decisions need not be made directly. Participatory theorists would have individual localities across the country spend their weekends building solar panels. Is it any less sound environmentally to purchase solar panels designed by government scientists at the behest of Congress? Of course it's not. Nor will that second option seem so implausible once national environmental policy becomes more an object of public deliberation.

This central limitation aside, there is certainly room for more local participation in environmental policy-making. Local participation does offer advantages. For one, it is easier to see its effects. People participate in politics for any number of reasons: from the most pathological to the most disinterested. But unless one views politics as a game or as a prelude to canonization, it is difficult to remain active for very long unless one feels that one is making a difference. And while making a tangible difference on a small scale is almost always easier to see, it is also usually just as psychologically satisfying as making an imperceptible difference on a grand scale. Another advantage is that, at the local level, self-interest generally dictates environmental watchfulness and, when problems arise, a deliberate search for solutions.[2]

Still, we need to remember that expanding local participation does not in any way undermine the value of deliberation in larger collective processes, in decisions over which separate individuals have little direct control. After all, that is what the vast majority of political philosophers from Plato on have been forced to do. We don't dismiss the thought that went into *The Republic* because its author failed to reform Syracuse. We would be even more gravely mistaken to dismiss the public's deliberation in every instance it does not exercise power directly. At the same time, participation in higher levels of government offers some distinct advantages of its own. Psychologically, distance affords a kind of emotional armor: one can accede to the force of a better argument without appearing to give in. And the higher the level of government, the greater the demand that one approximate the collective and holistic ideals of environmental rationality.

Environmental Deliberation and the Economy

It follows from what I have just said that the key political goal of any environmental restructuring of the economy must be to encourage, not participation, but deliberation. Sometimes participation will encourage deliberation, sometimes not. And sometimes participation, whether it encourages deliberation or not, will clearly be at odds with environmental ends. For example, handing the timber companies over to the loggers in the Pacific Northwest is not likely to do the spotted owl any good. On the other hand, smaller-scale economic units whose environmental impacts are especially noticeable or threatening close to home are good candidates for participatory arrangements (see Lane 1979). Probably more workable, because more in keeping with Americans' continued attachment to entrepreneurialism, are community-administered small business loans. They could include state-imposed environmental qualifications to ensure some degree of uniformity while allowing a great deal of flexibility at the local level. My own participants overwhelmingly favored expanding such programs, from conservative Republicans to those arguing from the smallis-sustainable perspective. Most important, community-administered loans would encourage public debate, public thinking. Workers' cooperatives and participatory firms cannot make such a claim.

On the consumption side, two reforms are as obvious as they are essential. People need (and in fact want) to think more about what they buy. Germany already has an environmental labeling system in effect; we should follow suit. I personally favor a government scheme: to ensure uniformity,[3] to reinforce the idea that society considers informed shopping on a par with informed voting, and, most important, to make it clear to all consumers that their decisions are in large or small degree *public* decisions.

However, labeling is not enough. We need to have positive incentives to use less. As a society, we're only beginning to climb up on the first rung of the environmentalists' ladder of "Reduce, Reuse, Recycle." If we discourage use, we will simultaneously encourage reuse. How? Redistribution is the first step. But wholesale redistribution seems unlikely to fire anyone's imagination soon. And, in any case, it would require taxing the wealthy more heavily. A more direct and more acceptable route would be simply to tax consumption.[4] European economists, notably in Germany, have already begun the ultimately philosophical problem of calculating the environmental cost of virtually everything. Despite the practical and theoretical problems of such an endeavor, it is easy enough to imagine an environmental tax table at least as rational as our current tax structure (see Repetto et al. 1992). Implementation aside, such a tax would—if labeled, say, the environmental damage tax—act as a powerful stimulus to deliberation, in two ways. First, it would be the object of unending complaining. Complaints call forth justifications, and deliberation ensues. At the same time, it would remind people of the purpose of the tax, which will precipitate thinking about the positive environmental values that such a tax serves or could serve, thus reinforcing deliberation.

A parallel with another kind of tax suggests a separate rationale for an environmental damage tax. Property taxes are arguably the most hated taxes in the United States—so much so that they appear to be on their way out as the primary funding mechanism for public schools. Still, I would argue that they have lasted as long as they have primarily because of the wide consensus on the overriding importance of the use to which they were and still are put—education. Such a consensus exists on the importance of environmental protection as well. And more than a few of my respondents said they would feel much better about paying, say, an additional 5 percent in taxes if they knew the money would be used for environmental purposes. Taxes inevitably lead to complaints, and that is not all bad. But an environmentally designated tax is unlikely to meet real resistance.

Environmental Deliberation and Politics

There are many things that can be done in the political sphere to widen the public's opportunities to deliberate on environmental questions. With the possible exception of the ones I discuss first and last, they have all been suggested by other theorists, and for what are essentially the same reasons.

A theme running through all my interviews was that localities' abilities to protect their own environment ought to be strengthened. Why? Because ultimately everyone has a special interest in his or her own locality, was the constant refrain. From a theoretical standpoint, one can formulate this in various ways. Perhaps we should recognize a community's right to a certain level of protective control over its local environment. Perhaps, as one of my participants suggested, we should "allow the locals the least power to damage, and the greatest power to protect the environment." In practice, this could mean allowing municipalities either greater veto powers over certain uses of the environment or, as another of my participants hinted, greater access to the courts in order to demand enforcement of existing statutes and regulations. At a time when so many political theorists are concerned with community, we simply can't forget that all communities depend on a physical infrastructure and that, for many people, community is absolutely inseparable from place. The following comments from my participants illustrate this rather poignantly (see also Seamon 1989; Hiss 1991):

> I just think it's part of the total community; wetlands are part of the total community—particularly here. I just now walked by City Hall and there's this duck [*laughs*] on a manhole, right on the sidewalk. (I'm sure it was warm.) But there is . . . Can you imagine? There's this *duck*, sitting right . . . No one could care.

He couldn't care less, and no one else could care less. (I don't think he voted today, but . . .)

My parents have a place up north. I just love it up there. I'd get active if anything happened to that. I'd be pissed if acid rain ever did anything to the lake, because I'd be affected directly.

And then, too, this is a river-kind-of-town.

Those mountains out West, they're just a pile of rocks; *these* hills, now there's something *to* them. You're from the Driftless Area; you should understand what I mean.

    What part of Hawaii? Oh, I'm from Oahu—the Windward side, the prettiest side.

A perfect environment? Oh, I suppose, it would be like around here! I'd like to go home. Up north. Even if no one's there? Just the environment—is that the thing that'll satisfy me? I'm satisfied here, too. But this isn't *home*. That's home up *there*.

When I leave [here] it's like saying good-bye to mom and dad and maybe you're never going to see them again, you know. And I really don't want to say good-bye.

You know, people will be listening to this tape will sit back and wonder what kind of day it is today. The sun is on our backs. The moon is in front of us. The water is in front of us. Trees and valleys and hills that we see in front of us, and we can feel the wind. It's about 40 degrees out here? And the wind behind us. And we see maybe one, two, three, [*continues counting*] four or five eagles flying around. Making noise, some crows, over to the left of us. It's a sense of peace and quiet and harmony, a sense of beauty and balance. That bird looks like he stopped right in mid-air. He's just there. That's balance; that's beauty and balance, all in itself.

Expanding localities' protective powers by definition constitutes an expansion of environmental policy. Would it also contribute to deliberation? I think so. The great majority of my participants, like Americans more generally, were only tangentially involved in environmental politics, if at all. But when I asked them what might push them to get involved, almost without exception they cited one or another threat to their local environment (like acid rain, in the quote above).

As Carole Patement argued some time ago, the debate between participation and representation is often overdrawn: one can improve participation within the kind of representative structure that, as I argued in chapter 1, is indispensable (Pateman 1970: 109). On this score, let me add my voice to the small chorus already calling for at least some movement toward proportional representation. Perhaps defenders and critics of the present winner-take-all system have ignored the possibility of institutional hybrids. I am hardly an expert on electoral systems. But I strongly believe a more representative system would encourage deliberation by widening the political agenda here. And one of the first things that would be included in this widening would almost surely be the ecological point of view. In addition, proportional representation offers expanded opportunities for citizen participation in the only institution I can think of that can possibly allow a citizen truly to Think Globally, Act Locally—namely, political parties. Political parties link the individual to larger concerns while allowing action close to home (see also Spragens 1990: 211).

Other, less radical, political reforms might be even more effective in stimulating public deliberation about environmental issues. First, and most obvious, the state can greatly stimulate environmental deliberation simply by working harder at cultivating the volume and quality of public information. Even a society of angels, all committed to environmental beatitude, would need to be told how to fulfill their environmental obligations (Ophuls 1977: 149, 153). Or, to mix metaphors: without high-quality information, deliberation has no fuel (Dahl 1989: 339). Now, I do not think that "high quality" can be defined except in a procedural way. That is, no can one say *a priori* which sources of environmental information are likely to be best. But I think we can say that, largely because of economic clout, some sources are unfairly advantaged in the present system. Hence I am sympathetic to Lindblom's recent suggestion that some kind of limits be placed on corporate access to the broadcasting spectrum (1990: 297–298) and to the oft-repeated calls for expanding public-access radio and television (Max M. Kampelman in Fishkin 1991: 101). Likewise, a system of "representative vouchers," whereby citizens are given a predetermined amount of money to distribute among interest groups of their own choosing, strikes me as a reasonable way to diminish the present domination of political action committees (Fishkin 1991: 99–100). Furthermore, procedural requirements for environmental impact statements should be broadened to include regional impacts. More should be done to facilitate the flow of information from government agencies to interested citizens and groups, and to ensure that agencies take advantage of opportunities to encourage public deliberation (Reich 1990a). And the president ought to be required to present the country with a State of the Environment address every other year, preferably in the springtime so that it receives special scrutiny during election years. Finally, and in keeping with what I said about an environmental tax, the Council on Environmental Quality should be required to make public (on a quarterly basis, say) an "index of leading environmental indicators." Keeping the environment in mind is the first step in minding the environment.

The deliberative gains produced by these reforms at the national level could be easily reinforced by other changes closer to home. Individual states, for example, could create an elected statewide post responsible for enforcing environmental law. The ongoing operation of the office would spur deliberation on a routine basis, and the additional deliberative boost provided by election coverage would likely be even more potent than usual because, presumably, a greater diversity of candidates would be in position to contest such an office. Incidentally, at least one nationwide poll shows that creation of such a post is already supported by an overwhelming number of Americans (*Wisconsin State Journal*, June 12, 1990).

The final reform I would like to recommend has nothing at all to do with public institutions. It has, rather, to do with publicly minded private organizations—environmental groups, to be exact—and their reform strategies. Environmental groups come in all shapes and sizes; their specific aims range from saving the American chestnut tree to saving the world. And they often work both inside government and in the larger society. But they almost all have an educative mission. And that is as it should be. The question is: How should that particular mission be carried out? From all that I heard during my interviews, the answer seems clear: that mission is best served if, in addition to the films, the books, the press releases, and the dramatic banners atop smokestacks, environmental groups also work to stimulate deliberation over environmental policy.[5] Interest in and concern about the environment are not enough. They both can, and often do, remain inert, leading neither to real behavioral change nor even to a positive commitment to environmental protection, to the necessarily collective solutions that the environmental crisis demands. Deliberation does produce that kind of commitment and, often enough, the kind of actions that go with it.

How can environmentalists spur deliberation? First, it is worth remembering that, in the United States at least, environmental organizations have the distinct advantage of being trusted by the public.

Very often their members are politically savvy. They are almost always comparatively well-informed. These important deliberative catalysts already exist in great abundance, then. How might environmentalists put them to use? They can do so by asking questions. The "deliberative entrepreneur" is no salesperson. The goal is not to market environmental policy, but to facilitate environmental-political deliberation. The environmental entrepreneur, in short, can best encourage environmental rationality by encouraging environmental deliberation.

How might this be done? The possibilities are truly as endless as they are exciting. And surely those groups that take this recommendation seriously will invent their own techniques suited to their own agendas, resources, and circumstances. Nevertheless, three concrete suggestions come to mind:

1.   Train members to do "deliberative surveys" of the type I have discussed here. Rather than disseminate literature or appeal for money, volunteers could aim simply to discuss a reduced series of local issues over the course of an afternoon or two—and still cover a lot of ground.
2.   Organize issue-specific debates between opposing panels made up of representative citizens. Debates of this kind would not only benefit participants and their audience directly but, if carried out in a public-spirited fashion, would also communicate the broader message that deliberation on environmental issues is *everybody's* business.
3.   Encourage local radio talk shows: to feature environmental topics, whoever the guest and whatever her or his point of view. Such programing approximates deliberative discourse and, of course, has the advantage of reaching a wide audience.

Environmentalists may object that their human and financial resources are already stretched to the breaking point. And that is no doubt at least partly true. Certainly any deliberative program will entail some costs. Even pending improvement in the financial status of public interest groups,[6] however, such a program is worth pursuing because we have every reason to believe that deliberation really works.

Conclusion

There is very little that is especially new in these recommendations. In fact, with the exception of the modified theory of deliberation I advanced in the opening chapter, my entire argument comes down to a plea that we integrate two bodies of thought that now seem isolated, distant, even at odds with one another. To the conclusions of a wide range of environmental ethicists, I have tried to join a political theory as old in its essentials as Aristotle. To political theory I have imported the central problem in environmental ethics (How shall we treat the environment?), while trying to show that political theory, not ethics, holds the ultimate solution. All I have added is the voices of 46 of my fellow citizens.

Political theorists will have noticed the huge debts I owe to "the tradition." From Aristotle I have taken the notion that political ends can never be abstracted from those who make up the political community: citizens are integral not only in defining the Good Society and Environment; they must, in the end, also be willing to pursue it. That theoretical perspective is a humbling one, but it is also exciting. It sees political theory as open, dynamic, and fundamentally bound up with the endlessly fascinating hopes, fears, and, yes, philosophies of one's compatriots. Rousseau helped me see the environmental-political dilemma in stark outline, as one species of the larger problem of reconciling democratic will and understanding or judgment. That formulation was never far from my mind. Once I began to realize that deliberation holds the key, it was not hard to piece together an explanation; the definition of environmental rationality I gave in chapter 6— that is, my own definition of "judgment"—followed rather easily. Kant's moral realism was perhaps the bedrock underlying all of this. When he descended from the metaphysical heights to address the real world of the turbulent eighteenth century, his message was sober, indeed: Wait not for moral miracles; intelligent devils must learn their way to peace. But Kant's sobriety was theoretically debilitating: he never asked how the learning he predicted might be accelerated. This is where my view leans most heavily on contemporary arguments for what might be called a learning culture. Yet it is a learning *politics* that I envision: a politics that allows everyone to become and remain a student—by keeping the cost of tuition low, by providing different kinds of learning opportunities, and by publicly recognizing the value of both the educational process and the educated citizen.

But my aim here has not been to reweave a series of time-worn doctrines. It has been, rather, to provide a solution to an increasingly urgent set of problems. If we do not adopt it, or something like it, one of two things is likely to happen. Things could get better on their own. But I do not think that anyone seriously believes in the likelihood of that happening. Alternatively, the environment may deteriorate to such a degree that people end up begging for a solution, no matter the cost in freedom, equality, and dignity. Not only do we have every reason to prevent such an eventuality, but also by the time it arrives it might well be too late to save much of anything.

In human beings, evolution has become conscious of itself. We value ourselves, but we now realize we ought to value the continuation of the process of which we are the product. That isn't the issue. The issue, for the 46 Americans I talked to at least, is what to *do* about it. Individually and collectively, we are waiting for an answer. If we can just understand that we have to stop saying, "You go first," and start thinking, "Let's find a way to go together," we will find the answer. If citizens are given substantially greater opportunities to engage in political deliberation about the environment, we are capable of becoming as green as we already know we should be.

Appendix
Notes
Bibliography
Index

Appendix
Normative Theory, Criticism, and
Interpretation: An Organic Method

> An adequate social and political theory must be empirical, interpretive,
> and critical.
>
> —Richard Bernstein, *The Restructuring of Social*
> *and Political Theory*

I first read those words early in my graduate school training in
a course on empirical theory. They were a revelation to me, but they should
not have been. Long before I had any conscious idea of what "politics" or
"theory" is, I had come to admire something not unlike that very kind of political theory. The genesis of the approach I adopted for this study fits Plato's
paradoxical theory of knowledge almost to a tee: the more I worried about epistemology and fretted over "methodology," the more I realized that I was simply
rediscovering and refining something that had been with me for a long time.
I say my approach fit *almost* to a tee because I was "remembering," not something I was born with, but something that I learned about the same time I
became aware of a world larger than myself. That something was simply that
a lot could be learned from talking with and about other people. In fact, if one
were to do both (which, as Aristotle reminded me later, comes naturally to most
people) one could rather easily satisfy Bernstein's three criteria. For Aristotle
the family is emphatically not a political association. Perhaps this is so. But
my uncles and aunts, parents and grandparents, clearly constitute an association of political *scientists*—at least in the sense that they have often engaged
and even delighted in producing theory of a kind not substantially different
from the kind recommended by Bernstein. Their theory is not as systematic,
not as careful, not as learned, but in many essentials is the same nonetheless.
And I am certain that my family, if it is at all unique in this, is remarkable primarily for the unflagging enthusiasm with which it has approached the subject.

When I was young, I often became impatient with the seemingly endless
adult talk about various acquaintances, local history, and the world beyond
our home town. As time went on, however, I became more and more interested.

"Good stories," I remember thinking. Only recently have I come to see that quite often there is very little that separates a good story from a good theory, and that sometimes the two are even identical. Good stories can sometimes be more than interesting. In fact, they may occasionally satisfy all three of the interests Habermas says we have in knowledge (1972: Appendix). That realization can also be methodologically liberating: it turns out that often what we most need to learn is also what seems most interesting to learn.

My argument here assumes the independent legitimacy of the interpretive, critical, and normative enterprises (Habermas 1972; Bernstein 1978; Innes 1987). These are the focus of chapters 2 and 3, 4 and 5, respectively. My argument's central methodological principle is that those enterprises can and sometimes should be pursued simultaneously. Thus chapter 4 concludes by normatively evaluating the interpretations resulting from a set of interviews which were themselves critical; chapter 2's critical discussion is grounded in interpretation and supplemented by normative analysis; and chapter 4's normative theory rests on the interpretation of the critical dialogue resulting from the interviews. My argument for proceeding in this fashion starts from the premise that differing methodological prescriptions are not mutually exclusive, yet it goes beyond the Hegelian view that each type of theory is implicated in the others (Bernstein 1978: 235; Braybrooke 1987), or that each is worth pursuing by itself. For I am arguing that they be *fused*, that each task is perhaps not best but at least well-accomplished in conjunction with the other two. The position I arrive at is not that anything goes, but that *every*thing goes.

The Case for an Organic Method

The case for an organic method starts from the following six propositions:

1. Criticism is a prerequisite for advancing normative theory.
2. Interpretation is a prerequisite for advancing normative theory.
3. Interpretation is a prerequisite of all criticism.
4. Normative analysis is a prerequisite of all criticism.
5. Criticism deepens interpretation.
6. Normative evaluation completes interpretation.

If each of these propositions is true, as I attempt to show in the following sections, it follows that theory, criticism, and interpretation are parts of a larger whole. That shown, the only remaining methodological issue is whether to undertake each task in isolation from the others or to proceed with all of them simultaneously. In the final section I explain the reasons which led me to adopt the latter course—namely, parsimony and practicality.

It is the fusion of these three enterprises (the interpretive, critical, and normative) that justifies calling this approach organic. But this does not mean that the approach adopted here is self-sufficient or complete. It is neither. It excepts a fourth, and legitimate, epistemological component—namely, *explanation*.

Hence the results presented in chapter 2 only *suggest* possible explanations for individuals' environmental policy thinking and for the present shape of American environmental policy. Full explanations for either of these would require either controlled experimentation or a greatly enlarged sample population. Controlled experimentation is incompatible with the openness and interaction required for interpretation and criticism, and large samples are incompatible with the practical demands that criticism and interpretation make on the researcher's time. Thus a choice must be made. Either one explains, or one interprets, criticizes, and theorizes. I chose the latter. I did so simply because, while explanation is not inferior to these other cognitive interests, neither is it superior. Despite this, the explanatory mode has dominated this area of social science as much as any other. Epistemological balance dictated taking a less-traveled methodological road. The paths open were interpretation, criticism, and normative analysis. But, as I argue below, these paths are best seen as different lanes in the same road.

This appendix has three basic parts. In the first, I lay out the epistemological argument that each of the three components of knowledge not only implies but positively depends upon the other two. The next section briefly justifies attempting all of these at once. After that methodological discussion, I explain in greater detail than I do in the text exactly how I applied this method. The formal cast of my presentation should not lead anyone to think for a moment that this project began as a problem in epistemology or empirical theory, progressed to methodology, and only then made it into the field. Nor is the reverse any closer to the truth. Whether I knew it at the time or not, these facets of the project, too, happened simultaneously—or perhaps dialectically. There is thus a deeper organism at work here. But here is hardly the place to dwell on it. Instead, let us turn to the first of the three components of what, for purposes of convenience, I call an organic method.

Normative Theory: Aristotle's Method as Model

> The proper procedure will be the one we have followed in our treatment of other subjects: we must present phenomena (that is, the observed facts of moral life and the current beliefs about them), and, after first stating the problems inherent in these, we must, if possible, demonstrate the validity of all the beliefs about these matters, and, if not, the validity of most of them or of the most authoritative. For if the difficulties are resolved and current beliefs are left intact, we shall have proved their validity sufficiently.
>
> — Aristotle, *Nichomachean Ethics* (1145bI)

There are, of course, any number of ways to approach normative political theory. Even if one agrees that, to engage in political inquiry is always to engage in normative theorizing (or at least the invocation of norms), there is always the question of how normative theory itself is best accomplished. Here I am assuming that Aristotle was essentially correct about how to go about this; his normative approach is captured in the above epigraph (Moline 1986; Nussbaum 1982). Nussbaum explains how, in Aristotle's view, we are to begin: "First the philosopher must 'set down' the relevant appearances. These will be different (and differently gathered) in each area. But in all areas we are to include both a study of ordinary beliefs and sayings and a review of previous scientific or philosophical treatments of the problem, the views of 'the many and the wise' " (Nussbaum 1982: 275). In this view of normative theory, then, individual beliefs are the proper starting point for ethical inquiry. They may also improve our ethical conclusions. As Aristotle would say later in a famous passage of the *Politics*, "Each individual may, indeed, be a worse judge than the experts; but all, when they meet together, are either better than experts or at any rate no worse" (III, xi, 14). Notice the qualifier "when they meet together": in the absence of a deliberative setting, beliefs are deprived of their epistemic weight. Nevertheless, "ta legomena" (the things said) are hardly sufficient by themselves to yield ethical truth (Nussbaum 1982). If they were, the philosopher would soon be out of a job. Rational evaluation of popular beliefs is thus a necessary element of ethical inquiry (Nussbaum 1982: 276).

But, then, even that is not enough, in Aristotle's view. Before we may consider an ethical inquiry complete, we must return to "the things said" (Nussbaum 1982: 277). Again, the most striking instance of this claim in Aristotle's writing is in the *Politics*: "A house, for instance, is something which can be understood by others besides the builder: indeed the user of a house—or in other words the householder—will judge it even better than he does. In the same way a pilot will judge a rudder better than a shipwright does; and the diner—not the cook—will be the best judge of a feast" (III, xi, 14). Hence in Aristotle's view, ethics begins with the everyday and ends there. In between there is the lonely job of rational criticism. But as I argue further on, even rational criticism need not be lonely.

With this sketch of the nature of normative theorizing in place, let us turn to the first of the six propositions that form the epistemological backdrop for the method I employed.

Proposition 1. Criticism is a prerequisite for advancing normative theory.

First, let me make clear that, by "criticism" I mean "critical dialogue." When Aristotle referred to "the things said," he added the qualifier "when they meet together." Having said that, it is easy to see why this first proposition is true. Critical dialogue increases the number of things said by inviting those not party to theoretical debates to join in. As a result, deliberative dialogues, or what I am here calling criticism, can be treated as a source of Popperian conjectures or as suggesting what Duncan MacRae has called normative hypotheses (1976). This benefits theory in two fundamental ways: it increases the number of available premises, and it widens the argument about known premises.

On the other hand, critical dialogue prevents neither attention to the particular nor rational evaluation (hence it is not incompatible in any way with the two other steps involved in Aristotle's method).

Proposition 2. Interpretation is a prerequisite for advancing normative theory.

If it is true that critical dialogue is a necessary ingredient of normative theory and that true dialogue presupposes understanding, then normative theory must necessarily be grounded, at least to a degree, in interpretation. The syllogism is inescapable. Yet there are deeper reasons to link interpretive understanding and normative theory.

The immediate aim of interpretation is to reveal the particular; its focus is the individual-in-context. It is because we believe individuals to be intrinsically valuable that interpretation can lay claim to a methodological integrity of its own: what people say counts because individual people count, regardless of whether or not what they say is judged to be an expression of any larger empirical or ethical truth. This is a position to which Aristotle would never have assented. He stressed the importance of "the things said" but never tried to *understand* them. Or, rather, he passed over the problem. To do so requires no essential reworking of the method. Nor does it require that one endorse the modern view that individuals are possessed of an irreducible integrity. Rather, interpretation strengthens Aristotle's method considerably. By deepening our understanding of the particular it provides a kind of test of the general that the theorists alone cannot provide. It can also suggest general truths of its own.

Aristotle would have us ask the dweller how good the dwelling is: the particular tests the general. But must we not interpret the dweller's response? Access to the particular requires interpretation. All theories are partial, and the theorist's vision is always limited. But to supplement it with the vision of others, one must first see the world as others see it.

However, interpretation is more than a test. Its potential contribution to normative theory is positive as well as critical. This is because interpretive understanding allows full scope for citizens to identify normative combinations not yet identified by theorists (unlike, say, surveys, which preselect possibilities). This creative potential is too often wasted. In the area of environmental policy its contribution might be especially large given: the vast number of theoretical possibilities and the fact that the field is so new. Moreover, interpretation is distinct from dialogue and argument because it is experiential, not discursive, and is therefore grounded in a way that dialogue and argument cannot be. More powerful than any argument I might cite in defense of this view are the works of Studs Terkel. Terkel has shown quite clearly what great potential interpretation holds for addressing moral issues. Yes, there is a great deal of "meaning" in his works, but they also pack an unmistakable, if not a very systematic, normative punch. This is because the people he talks to punch and are punched. The works contain no argument, but it is undeniable that they argue. What force they have is not due to the self-evident nature of the premises from which they start. There aren't any. Nor is it due to the rigid logic from which conclusions are derived. One would look in vain for even a hint of a syllogism in his works. The point Terkel is making always depends on individuals' *experience* of a given phenomenon or historical period. As Tallmadge has observed in a different context, this experience is relevant because it shows abstract moral qualities or principles at work in everyday lives; once they are made familiar in this way, we are more open to them. Individuals may become moral examples. In the process, a moral conclusion has been reached. To illustrate, Terkel answers the question "Was World War II a good war?" not by reviewing contemporary theories of international relations or historical evidence. He asks the people who lived through it. And although some of them offer reasons for their opinions, most simply describe their experiences. And those experiences have a moral impact on the reader. If one is describing moral subjects, description will carry normative weight. In interpretation the is-ought gap disappears.

Note, too, that interpretation does not preclude rational evaluation (see Propositions 3, 4). We can understand a person, and still criticize him, understand his views and still find them erroneous.

The Critical Method

Critical theorists . . . contend that we should pursue knowledge through a continuous dialectical process which is essentially conflictual.
—Judith Innes, "Usable Research for Planning Practice"

Criticism, as I have been using the term, or the critical method, requires a dialogue between the respondents and the interviewer. As one practitioner puts it: "[P]ublic preferences, if they are to be relevant and useful in a policy context, should be allowed to change and evolve in a social learning process that is aimed at a discursively achieved rather than a statistically summarized consensus" (Sancar 1985: 118). Being critical in this sense also requires that the investigator challenge the status quo: "The knower has the responsibility to challenge assumptions, to be self-reflective and to participate in action or praxis. . . . the researcher has to be an iconoclast and challenge the dominant paradigm" (Innes 1987: 250–251). Interpretation alone is insufficient for policy design, "because it is built on shared understandings" and thus inevitably reflects "predominant values, existing institutional structures, and power relationships in society" (Innes 1987: 243). For this reason, "the researcher may need in addition to identify disenfranchised interests and help them to get a place in the debates" (Innes 1987: 251). Finally, in order to qualify truly as a critical investigation, "empirical study of practice is not enough. The theorist must also act" (Innes 1987: 251).

How did I try to meet these various requirements? First, to allow real learning and discourse, I separated my interviews into at least two sessions, most often spread out over a course of two weeks or more. I also spent an average of about five hours with each of my 46 respondents. As to the iconoclasm requirement, I worked hard to find unusual individuals to include in my study, and especially sought out critics of the environmental status quo. In addition, both in my lead questions and in my follow-up questions I attempted to test the limits of the accepted. It is, alas, less clear that I satisfied the final of these criteria. After all, who qualifies as an environmental policy "practitioner" is not altogether clear. Is it someone who makes policy, someone who influences policy, or simply someone who is affected by policy? If it is the first, I have clearly failed the test. If the second, my limited involvement in environmental politics would perhaps be enough. If the last, I have clearly met the test. Having defined "criticism" in this way, its relationship to normative theory and interpretation can be reduced to the following two propositions.

Proposition 3: Interpretation is a prerequisite for all criticism.

In an obvious and very fundamental way, criticism cannot even occur without interpretation. To be party to a dialogue, one must first understand the others who are a party to it. At the same time, the better one's understanding, the more relevant one's participation is likely to be. Thus criticism requires interpretation, and valuable criticism presupposes sound interpretation.

The relevant disclaimer here is that neither the need to represent the interests of the disenfranchised nor the requirement that the researcher assume the role of the iconoclast is frustrated by interpretation.

Proposition 4: Normative analysis is a prerequisite of all criticism.

Dialogue presupposes the existence of alternative points of view and the ability to argue them. Hence it requires at least a modicum of normative analysis. Likewise, the identification of the disenfranchised requires at least some familiarity with normative analysis, else one simply won't know who they are. Finally, for the researcher to assume the role of iconoclast she or he must know what such a position entails. This, too, can come only from a familiarity with normative alternatives to the status quo.

The Interpretive Method

We are cultural beings, endowed with the capacity and the will to take a deliberate attitude toward the world and to lend it significance.
—Max Weber, *Methodology of the Social Sciences*

Having held up first Aristotle and then a pair of planning scholars as exemplars in the prior two sections, I want to follow Weber in an equally literal way in this one. I am aware that there is substantial disagreement between those who follow any one of these modes of inquiry, not to mention between the followers of each different mode. But one must begin somewhere. This is not a treatise on methodology, merely an explication of the one I used in this study.

On the basis of the view captured in the above epigraph, Weber argued that sociology has to make room for interpretive understanding. How does that conclusion follow? I think it follows from each part of the categorization considered separately—all the more so when those parts are added up. First, Weber notes that humans are cultural beings. It is hard to imagine culture without language; language requires interpretation. According to Weber, we also possess will and a deliberate attitude. These qualities, too, must be given their due. As Jennifer Hochschild puts the point, democratic norms require that we listen to people and respect them as potential storytellers (1981). If one has a special interest in individuals' normative orientations, as I do, this is all the more true. The method had to be open to all the potential bases of the ethic under consideration (reason, intuition, emotion, revelation, or a mix of these). Psychologist Reid Hastie, in a review of various versions of information-processing theory, points out that info-processing models largely ignore emotion and motivational factors (1986: 13). Hence they are ill suited to descriptive ethics.

Third, Weber notes that we all assume an attitude toward the world. Interpretation focuses precisely on the interplay between that attitude and the world, seeing attitudes as always related to particular circumstances. As one interviewer explained, interpretation attempts to improve our understanding of macrolevel issues by examining how they are refracted and reflected in individual life stories (Reinarman 1987: viii; see also Spradley 1979: 207, 212). Simultaneously, however, interpretation attempts to preserve and highlight the local, idiosyncratic, and subjective meanings, for they, too, count as part of what is not only there but also real (Reinarman 1987: 19).

This brings us to the fourth point: the importance of our capacity to lend significance to the world we inhabit. It is no accident, I think, that the words "significant" and "to signify" have the same root. We are creatures with values, and we use language to convey the values we hold. The same connection is revealed by the two senses of the noun "meaning." Because in-depth interviews are sensitive to "meaning" both in the sense of importance and in the sense of denotation/connotation, they are a useful, perhaps indispensable, means of capturing significance.

Proposition 5: Criticism deepens interpretation.

The cultural, or that which is taken for granted, is best revealed in critical dialogue because dialogue necessarily involves the consideration of alternatives to what is taken for granted. Likewise, intentions and values (both actual and potential) are more clearly revealed in dialogue because dialogue allows the researcher to establish their precise boundaries. The relevance and importance of the particularities of context are also more clearly revealed when the respondent is challenged. Finally, the old view that individuals know their own minds "first and best" is, at the least, "dramatically overstated" (Flanagan 1984: 243). Cognitive science shows that "we often know more than we can tell . . . [and] we often tell more than we know" (Flanagan 1984: 197). Hence, as paradoxical as it sounds, what people really mean is not fully available to them without stimulus. That is where dialogue and probing come in.

Criticism makes another crucial contribution to interpretation. The unintrusive "discovery" at which interpretation aims is impossible to achieve (see Chapters 2 and 3): interviews, like other "searchlights," must be pointed somewhere. They are, to put it simply, theory-laden. That can't be fixed. But dialogue helps, because it improves the respondent's chances of escaping the interviewer's categories.

Proposition 6: Normative evaluation completes interpretation.

This is another fairly obvious point, I think. Again, the cultural (that which is taken for granted) is by its very definition invisible except in the presence of alternatives. An individual's values and intentions, too, can be established only by considering a relatively full range of alternatives, and this is a normative task. Incidentally, Weber himself clearly recognized this. In *The Methodology of the Social Sciences* he argued convincingly that understanding (*Verstehen*) can procede "only by relating the empirical data to an ideal limiting case" (1949: 94).

Conversely, normative evaluation does not preclude attention either to the particularities of context or to meaning and values.

The Simultaneous Pursuit of Interpretation, Criticism, and Normative Theory: An Organic Method

From the preceding discussion, it seems clear that each mode of analysis is complemented by the others. This leaves the researcher with only one further design question: Should the focus be on one mode of analysis, or should all three be attempted at once? My first impulse is to say that it does not really matter. All three enterprises are legitimate in and of themselves. Each, moreover, supplements our knowledge in the other areas, making the use of each doubly worthwhile. And, in the end, the fact that one engages in an interpretive study now need not prevent one from engaging in normative theory later. Finally, is it not simply impossible to examine all the facets of social reality at once? Can one interpret, criticize, and theorize simultaneously? My answer, of course, is that it is not only possible and quite natural to do so but also easier and perhaps even more revealing than to attempt to do each individually. It is not just that each mode of analysis is deepened in light of the others, but also that doing everything at once has certain advantages of its own. Briefly put, I see social investigation as analogous, not to sculpting a block of marble, but to making a hologram: the truest representations of a multifaceted subject are not made in discrete stages such as sketching, chiseling, and planing; instead, they emerge all at once out of a complex, but essentially unitary, process.

I began this explanation by assuming the legitimacy of interpretation, criticism, and normative theory. The previous section argued that each presupposes, or at least greatly benefits, the other. Now I want to explain the reasons I had for engaging in all three within the confines of a single study.

The first, and most important, reason is simply that it is impossible *not* to engage in all three modes of analysis when doing social research, unless that research has as its express or implicit aim the out-and-out manipulation of those under investigation. Hence, to interpret, criticize, and theorize actively is to do self-consciously what all but the most autocratic researcher must do anyway. This appears to me to be as obvious as it is important. I take it not as an article of faith but as a demonstrable truth that social science is an irremediably value-laden enterprise (Billig 1976; Stone 1987: 42; Habermas 1972: Appendix; Taylor 1978; MacIntyre 1978). Thus all social science results not just in data but also in normative arguments—or at least normative propositions. Most empirical social scientists realize this, and at least admit, however cautiously, the "value slope" inherent in their research. But why not go further and advocate those values? Doing empirical research does not mean that one has left one's values back there in the ivory tower. Nor need it mean that one leave behind the reasons one has for holding those values. Conversely, one's research is likely to have reinforced, undermined, or rearranged those reasons in one way or another. Hence the empirical researcher, if she is thinking at all, will likely have engaged in some degree of normative theory as a result of her project. Why not turn a necessity into an opportunity? Why not share one's normative conclusions? Even more obvious, I think, is the fact that every social scientist's research means something and that it eventually confronts (and is confronted by) the very citizens who were its object.

There are other, less obvious, reasons to avoid restricting oneself to one mode of political inquiry. I almost feel as though the argument I am about to make is redundant. But then, I am happy to do whatever I can to avoid the day when "intersubdisciplinary" research is frowned upon.

First, and most central, this approach can help one keep methodology in its place. I am, to repeat, no methodological anarchist. But neither do I believe in its authoritarian cousin. There is always a danger that we preclude important findings on an *a priori* basis (Feyerabend 1978). As a corollary to this, I would add that this method or approach may also help prevent us from being satisfied with formal procedures when what we are really after is understanding, knowledge, wisdom. In the end, an "organic" approach helps us remember the point of our study: its goal and why that goal is important. Similarly, Lasswell recommended an interdisciplinary approach as a way to avoid serving the status quo (in Stone 1987: 55).

In the view of knowledge I have borrowed from Habermas, we will always be confronted with the task of making wholes out of parts. Knowledge doesn't come in wholes. They instead must be crafted out of individual parts. The very fact that so few attempt this today is another important reason—perhaps the main reason—I adopted this approach. It would be different if political science were like Plato's Republic, with a group of specialists whose expertise is in being general. As it is, we have too few who strive to knit our divided labors back together again.

There is an even better reason for proceeding this way, I think. It has to do not with the present status of the discipline but with the very notion of a division of academic labor itself. If it is true that full knowledge can come only through a process of synthesis, it seems to me to make at least as much sense to have individual researchers do the job of synthesizing as it does to have them create individual pieces of knowledge and then let those who were not in on that creation do the synthesizing. What one has helped create, one grasps especially firmly. One perhaps sees connections that others would miss. This suggests another point. It is one thing to interpret, criticize, and theorize about a subject, another to engage in those activities at one remove. Is a synthesis constructed from parts drawn from the work of three others any truer than one based on three parts of one's own construction? Is it *as* true?

Last, I wish to anticipate one kind of criticism that might be leveled against this argument if read in isolation from the text. No doubt some will have noticed that the discussion so far mentions neither history nor social structure (of any type). Yet the text of my argument does in fact integrate both modes of analysis, beginning in chapter 1. A more basic theoretical point is that both historical and structural analysis may be subsumed under the four cognitive categories I employed above. Both history and structural analysis tend to be both interpretive and explanatory in essence, however strong the normative admixture.

In conclusion I should point out that I am far from the first to engage in this general type of inquiry. As I suggest in the opening section, it was latent in Aristotle's own method. Many other philosophers since antiquity have also combined moral psychology and ethical inquiry, most notably Hume and Dewey. Within our own discipline this kind of methodological pluralism is not only being advocated (Dery 1984; Cook 1985) but also increasingly practiced (Fishkin 1984; Soltan 1987; Hochschild 1981: 315).

The Organic Method in Action

In this heading I say "in action" rather than "applied" because the method, or at least the reasoning behind it, partly evolved out of listening to my participants. For this reason it is difficult to reconstruct exactly what I did and when. What I say here will thus be less a manual than a road map. And, like most maps, its picture of the terrain will be rather lifeless. Still, it should help anyone interested in following the twists and turns of this project. It may even be of help to those interested in doing similar research in the future. If nothing else, the interested reader will find the danger zones clearly marked. For ease of presentation, I will recount the steps in the project in chronological order. I think this will also help those who are interested in the present study, rather than in one of their own, to follow how my thinking about the study evolved over time. Critics may thus be able to pinpoint my errors more clearly, and those who share my conclusions can more fully determine if the evidence presented here truly supports those conclusions in the way and to the degree I believe it does.

Selection of Participants

I originally set out to interview approximately 40 individuals (the final number was 46). Initial pretesting showed that each interview would last approximately four hours. The chief selection criteria were derived from the two primary aims of the project. The interpretive goal (understanding people) is best served by selecting representative individuals. The critical goal is best served by selecting both representative individuals and outsiders, or what Innes called disenfranchised individuals (1987: 251). The question then becomes: by what measure are these individuals representative? The answer was again dictated by my central interest in critically understanding different political stances toward the environment. "Representative" thus means "typical of the different ways in which Americans think about and experience the environment" (see Reinarman 1987: viii). Regarding experience, I decided to divide my participants into two groups: those whose self-interest is threatened or has been hurt by environmental policy and those whose self-interest has not been implicated in environmental policy in any direct or obvious way. To structure the interview population in this way would also provide a series of potentially very revealing contrasts, for it would guarantee both instances of similarly situated individuals reasoning to very different policy conclusions and instances of very differently situated individuals reasoning to more or less similar policy conclusions.

In regard to thought patterns, existing survey data provided some guidance. I knew that some 20 percent of Americans believe that a basic reorientation toward a more sustainable society is necessary, 20 percent believe the current social trajectory to be wise and sustainable, and about 60 percent have "less clearly worked out beliefs" (Milbrath 1984: 7; see also Dunlap 1987). As it turned out, my group consisted of 46 percent environmental conservatives, 37 percent environmental progressives, and 15 percent environmental radicals. Existing data also told me that about 1 in 100 Americans is an environmental activist (see chapter 3). My own group contained seven such individuals. Furthermore, as I explained in chapter 4, sociological data show that the two most powerful correlates of low environmental concern are materialistic values and a belief in laissez-faire government. I thus sought out individuals that might be expected to fall on either side of these cognitive divides. Demographic variables, by contrast, are far less helpful in explaining environmental concern (Dunlap and Van Liere 1984, 1978; Sandbach 1980). For that reason, and because the explanatory pretensions of this project were necessarily minimal, I relegated background characteristics to secondary status in the selection process. As the profiles below indicate, however, I still managed to cover most of the relevant demographic bases: age, gender, race, income, education, occupation, residence, and so on. Finally, I hoped to include individuals whose environmental self-interest was clearly threatened by the absence of policy, and others whose environmental interest was not so threatened.

Because individuals would be selected from across the environmental spectrum, they themselves would be criticizing each other's views, if unknowingly. Moreover, individuals would be asked at each step to respond to arguments from at least one of the opposing camps.

Finally, because the primary goals of this research were to represent people's views and simultaneously to criticize them, the sample had to contain both the voices and the critics of the silent majority. In selecting those critics—especially on the pro-environment side—I attempted to make room for the differing types of environmental positions now dominant in the literature. In this I was relatively successful: my activist participants were involved in groups that spanned the spectrum from Ducks Unlimited to local citizens' action groups to the Greens to Earth First!

*Demographic Profile of Participants**

* = environmental radical (n = 7)
+ = environmental progressive (n = 21)
0 = environmental conservative (n = 17)
1. By age
   18–25   0+ + **
   26–35   0000+ + + + **
   36–45   00+ + + + **
   46–55   0000000+ + + + + + + *
   >56   00+ + + + +
2. By gender
   Male   000000000+ + + + + + + + + + + + ****
   Female   00000000+ + + + + + + + + ***
3. By race or ethnicity
   White   00000000000000+ *****
   Black   00+ + +
   Hispanic   0
   Native American   *
   Mixed   *
4. By religion
   Protestant   000000+ + + + + + + + + + + + **
   Catholic   00+ + + + + + + +
   Jewish   0
   Animist   *
   Bhuddist   *
   Unaffiliated   0+ + + ****
   Atheist   + + *
5. By income†
   >$75,000   + + + +
   $50,000–75,000   00000+ + +
   $30,000–49,000   00+ + + + **
   $15,000–29,000   0+ + + **
   <$15,000   00+ + + + + + + + + ***

* Omitted from the following profiles is the single participant who remained "unsure" of her overall view of environmental policy.

† Three participants declined to specify their income.

6. By education
   Graduate degree   000++++**
   College/tech school
   degree   000+++++++**
   Some college   0000000+++++**
   High school
   diploma   000++++*
   Some high school   0
7. By occupation
   Extractive (includ-
   ing real estate)   000000+++*
   Manufacturing   00+++++
   Service   00000000++++++++*****
   Retired   ++
   No outside
   employment   0++*
8. By size of
   community
   Metropolis
   (>500,000)   00++
   Large city
   (>150,000–500,000)   00000000+++++++++++*
   Medium city
   (10,000–150,000)   000+++****
   Small city
   (1,000–9,000)   0+*
   Rural area or village   000+++++*

Individual Participant Profiles

The following list provides most of the basic demographic characteristics of each of my 46 participants. The characteristics are given in the following order: age, gender, race or ethnicity, yearly income, educational level, occupation, size of residential community, and religion. The names which appear here correspond to the pseudonyms used in the text.

1. Mark Allen (radical); 54; male; white; "comfortable living simply in a place that floats"; M.Ed. degree; Renaissance actor; medium city; unaffiliated
2. Tim Behringer (progressive); 33; male; white; $35,000; BS degree; quality control chemist; medium city; unaffiliated
3. Julie Binns (progressive); 22; female; white; $2,500; BS degree; premed student; large city; Catholic
4. Doreen Brill (unsure); 35; female; Hispanic; $35,000; some college; real estate agent; large city; Catholic
5. Karen Brunson (progressive); 45; female; white; $50,000; some college; tax preparer; medium city; Lutheran

6. James Burson (progressive); 30; male: white; $20,000; MD degree; psychiatrist; large city; unaffiliated

7. Michael Cerutti (progressive); 57; male; white; $30,000; some college; letter carrier; large city; Catholic

8. Deena Champney (progressive); 43; female; black; $7,000; BA degree; disabled; metropolis; Lutheran

9. Julie Chandler (progressive); 40; female; black; $100,000; BA degree; marketing research manager; large city; Protestant

10. Carole Chapman (progressive); 30; female; white; $55,000; JD degree; corporate lawyer; metropolis; agnostic

11. Gary Chauncey (radical); 31; male; Native American (Potawatomi-Menominee); under $1,000; high school diploma; alcohol and drug counselor; small city; Native American pantheism

12. Lynda Evans (radical); 22; female; white; $25,000; BA degree; prelaw student; medium city; Buddhist

13. Billy Franks (progressive); 29; male; black; $12,000; high school diploma; caretaker for mentally disabled; large city; unaffiliated

14. Louise Fredericks (progressive); 48; female; white; $30,000; some college; office manager; large city; Presbyterian

15. Eliot Gascon (progressive); 48; male; white; $45,000; PhD degree; professor of electrical engineering; medium city; atheist

16. Val Gotti (progressive); 28; female; white; $25,000; some college; clerk; metropolis; Catholic

17. Frank Hauser (conservative); 53; male; white; over $50,000; high school diploma; diversified farmer; rural area; Lutheran

18. Adela Hill (progressive); 94; female; white; $5,000; high school diploma; retired (former farmer, teacher, and waitress); large city; Lutheran

19. Teresa Hirschler (radical); 33; female; white; $31,000; MS degree; social worker focusing on adolescents; medium city; unaffiliated

20. Edward Hollister (conservative); 62; male; black; $6,000; some college; tutor; metropolis; Protestant

21. Erik Johannsen (progressive); 22; male; white; $8,000; college senior; large city; Lutheran

22. Richard Johnson (conservative); 55; male; white; $45,000; some college; farmer and insurance agent; rural area; Congregational

23. Jill King (progressive); 30; female; black; $18,000; high school diploma; homemaker; large city; Baptist

24. Bob Kovalek (progressive); 69; male; white; $9,000; high school diploma; dairy farmer; rural area; Methodist

25. Jay Little (progressive); 25; male; white; $12,000; technical school graduate; owner and manager of auto dealership and repair shop; small city; Catholic

26. Frederick Lorenz (progressive); 51; male; white; $50,000; BA degree; information manager; small city; Greek Orthodox

27. Fred Mechler (progressive); 48: male; white; over $40,000; some college; union officer; medium city; Catholic

28. Betty Mikels (conservative); 48; female; white; $35,000; some college; real estate agent; large city; Catholic
29. Elizabeth Naess (progressive); 55; female; white; over $100,000; college degree; homemaker; large city; Catholic
30. Jim Needham (progressive); 55; male; white; over $500,000; BS degree; developer; large city; Catholic
31. William Noone (progressive); 45; male; white; $85,000; master's degree (planning); urban planner; medium city; Protestant
32. Joe Page (progressive); 43; male; white; $—; high school diploma; farmer; rural area; Lutheran
33. Joseph Palasota (conservative); 50; male; white; $ "significant"; MA degree; developer; large city; Greek Orthodox
34. Judith Sanders (conservative); 42; female; white; $60,000; some college; business manager for nonprofit organization; rural village; Protestant
35. Donna Scheda (conservative); 29; female; white; $9,000; high school diploma; paper wholesaling; large city; unaffiliated
36. Suzette Schell (radical); 47; female; white; $11,000; MS degree; data analyst (former RN); large city; Protestant
37. Jack Schmidt (radical); 56; male; white; $25,000; some college; dairy farmer; rural area; Lutheran
38. Betsy Schon (progressive); 55; female; white; $10,000; some college; home-care provider; rural area; Seventh-day Adventist
39. Fred Springer (conservative); 55; male; white; $60,000; high school diploma; crop duster; rural village; Lutheran
40. Caroline Stowe (progressive); 65; female; white; $8,000; retired (former administrative assistant); large city; Protestant
41. Glen Thorne (conservative); 50; male; white; $65,000; MS degree; environmental compliance officer; medium city; Lutheran
42. Ralph Thorson (radical); 20; male; white; $1,000; some college; cab driver; medium city; unaffiliated
43. Michelle Washington (progressive); 33; female; black; $8,000; some high school; homemaker; large city; Baptist
44. Carmen Wiley (radical); 42; female; black-Hispanic; $32,000; some college; employment placement; large city; atheist
45. Donald Wilson (conservative); 66; male; white; $65,000; MS degree; civil engineer; large city; Jewish
46. Paul Zalens (radical); 39; male; white; $40,000, BS degree; dairy farmer; rural area; unaffiliated

The Interview Questionnaire

The interview questionnaire contained the following substantive elements:

—personal background
—personal and political behaviors relating to the environment

—positions on specific issues and dilemmas (three local, four state, nine national, three international, and four structural)
—individual ideals (personal, sociopolitical, environmental policy)
—explanation for current level of environmental policy
—perceived limits on environmentally conscious behavior
—opportunity to explain inconsistencies

The most abstract of these elements involved questions which asked for descriptive answers. The issue questions, meanwhile, asked for a yes/no response. In every instance I asked for the reasons behind the participant's response. I then asked if the respondent could, unaided, think of why someone might object to his or her view and how they might respond. If the respondent was unable to come up with an opposing argument, I supplied one, in which case he or she was to respond to that. There were thus two moments in every interview: one discursive, one dialectic. If this study deviated from similar ones in the past, it was during this latter, interactive phase.

At each level I asked, too, about potential influences on the respondent's thinking, and about his or her behaviors. The questionnaire concluded by asking the respondent first to speculate about the future course of environmental policy and then to confront any obvious inconsistencies I had noted in his or her responses.

The rebuttal-challenge aspect of the interview was crucial to the critical intent of the project; it was, in effect, the essence of the critical method (as explained above). I searched out a number of individuals who might be able to provide a negative view of current environmental policy. To challenge them was essential if they were to take into account the point of view of the reader who was satisfied with the environmental status quo. Yet it was also an important element in eliciting the kinds of responses that would allow a fair interpretation. As one interviewer once put it: "To think that one knows the appropriate questions to ask presumes too much in a psychological survey" (Gayln 1975: xvi). Finally, only by allowing my respondents to rebut opposing arguments did I have a chance to test the relevance of normative policy theories against the reality of specific circumstances.

Important, too, were those questions that asked why the individual might not behave (personally or politically) in conformity with whatever environmental ethic he or she espoused. Only by asking this question repeatedly would I be in a position to decide to what degree the environment is a structural or an individual problem and what kinds of environmental solutions people might best respond to.

Even a cursory reading of the questionnaire raises an obvious question: Why pose so many concrete dilemmas? Philosophical prejudice, I am tempted to say. I was interested in problem-solving because I am convinced that problem-solving is what matters. But the same answer follows, I think, from ego psychology, cognitive psychology, ethnomethodology, and environmental sociology. For a more explicit answer, I refer the reader to the body of the text.

Interview Schedule

Personal Background
    I.   Gender
   II.   Age: How old are you?
  III.   Race: What is your racial or ethnic identity?
  IV.   Religion
      A. What is your religious orientation?
      B. Are you a member of any organized church or religious group? (Which one?)
   V.   Class
      A. Income: Can you give me an estimate of your annual income over the last five years?
      B. Education
         1. How far did you go in school?
         2. What kinds of things did you focus on in school?
      C. Occupation
         1. What is your occupation? (If unemployed, what kind of job would you like to get?)
         2. Tell me a little about the kind of work you do.
Specific Issue Positions
    I.   Local issues
      A. Personal position on local issues
         1. What are the most important environmental issues in this area?
         2. What causes them?
         3. How do you think they should be resolved?
      B. Personal position in regard to specific local dilemmas
         1. Would it make sense to impose a countywide ban on developing wetlands?
         2. Would you be for or against a comprehensive county plan that attempted to match land use to the environmental characteristics of the land?
         3. Would you be in favor of or against a new factory coming to your town if you knew beforehand that it would add to air and water pollution here but would also add to the tax base and create several hundred new jobs?
   II.   State issues
      A. Personal position on state issues
         1. What are the most important environmental issues in the state of Wisconsin?
         2. What causes them?
         3. How do you think they should be resolved?
      B. Personal position in regard to specific state dilemmas
         1. Should northern Wisconsin be made off-limits to mining companies unless they conform to local regulations?

2. Would you be for or against a state program of low-interest loans to allow communities to purchase land to lease out to individuals and establish small businesses?

3. Some people have suggested that the state should encourage recycling by requiring that all communities do a certain minimum amount of recycling, by banning certain nonrecyclable materials such as Styrofoam, and by subsidizing businesses using recycled materials. Do you think such policies make sense?

4. Do you think students in the public schools receive enough instruction in environmental matters?

III. National issues

A. Personal position on national issues
1. What are the most important environmental issues facing the United States as a whole?
2. What do you think causes them?
3. What should be done about them?

B. Personal position in regard to specific national dilemmas
1. Do you think federal policy should be changed to encourage more environmentally sound farming practices?
2. Should we allow economic activity, like lumbering and drilling for oil, in wilderness areas?
3. Would you be in favor of or opposed to a huge program to re-invigorate cutover forest lands and plant billions of trees to help deal with global warming if you knew that it would increase your federal taxes by 3 percent yeach year over the next five years?
4. Would you be willing to pay 5 percent more for consumer products if the money were spent on controlling air and water pollution?
5. Do you think we need stricter controls on the possible negative environmental consequences of new technologies?
6. Do you think federal energy policy should focus on conservation and renewable energy sources even if the immediate results are higher prices and slowed economic growth?
7. Would it be a good idea to have a national, overall limit on economic growth?
8. Would you favor or oppose a federal program which encourages people to have small families by taxing couples with more than two children?
9. Do you think we need to place overall limits on how much we take out of the nation's forests, ground, and water supply?

IV. A. Personal position on international issues
1. At the global or international level, are there any environmental problems that strike you as being especially important?

    2. What do you think causes those problems?

    3. What part should the United States play in solving them?

  B. Personal position in regard to specific international dilemmas

    1. Should the United States pursue a treaty regulating the amount of greenhouse gases each country is permitted to produce even if we had to reduce ours more than other countries did?

    2. Should the United States provide, say, 3 percent of our GNP in financial aid to less-developed countries to help them protect environmental resources like the rain forests?

    3. Should the United States join with other countries in a treaty to prohibit mining and other economic activity in Antarctica?

V. A. Personal position on structural issues

    1. In general, how do you think we should go about deciding how to treat the environment? Why?

    2. Who do you think should decide how we solve environmental problems?

  B. Personal position in regard to specific structural dilemmas

    1. Do you think the government should have more, less, or about the same control over environmental decisions as it now has?

    2. Should the federal government have more control in environmental area, or should local communities be given more power to make decisions affecting the environment?

    3. Would it make sense to let those who know most about the environment—say, ecologists, policy experts, and administrators—have more power to deal with our environmental problems?

    4. Do you think we need to create an international environmental authority, perhaps through the United Nations, with power to police the global environment?

VI. Influences

Tell me about how you came to view environmental issues the way you do.

VII. Decisions

Has your view of any of these issues ever influenced a personal or political decision you have made?

Individual ideals

I. Personal

  A. Work: How important to you is your job in terms of personal satisfaction?

  B. Family and residence

    1. Are you basically happy with your family life?

    2. Do you like living where you do now?

  C. Leisure

    1. What kinds of things do you like to do in your free time?

    2. Is there anything you'd like to be able to do more often but can't? (Why can't you do this more often than you do now?)

D. Community involvement
   1. Are you involved in any kind of community organizations—social recreational, religious, or political?
   2. How important are these activities to you?
E. General
   1. Overall, what would you say are the most important things or people in your life?
   2. Is there anything you would change in your life if you could? Or are basically satisfied with the way things are?

II. Socio-political
   A. Contemporary society
      1. How would you describe yourself politically—your overall political orientation?
      2. Do you generally approve of American society? Why (not)?
      3. Do you see anything especially good about American society? What, exactly?
      4. How do those things come about? (What caused them?)
      5. Do you see anything especially wrong with American society? What, exactly?
      6. And how did those things come about? (What caused them?)
   B. Social ideal
      1. What might be done to imporove our society?
      2. What kind of society do you think would be best overall? What kind of society would be *ideal*?
      3. What kind of role would government play in such a society? Would it do more than, less than, or about the same as it does now?
      4. Would government do more than, less than, or about the same as it does now in the economy?

III. Environmental policy
   A. "Environment" as a concept: The word "environment" means a lot of different things to different people. When *you* hear the word "environment," what do you think of?
   B. Overall orientation: What is your general attitude toward environmental issues?
   C. State of the environment
      1. Overall, what are the most important environmental problems facing us now?
      2. What do you think causes those problems?
      3. Do you think we are close to damaging the environment beyond repair?
      4. Do you think we need to worry about shortages of raw materials? If so, how soon?
      5. Are we close to exceeding the population level the Earth can maintain?

    6. Do you think our standard of living will continue to improve for the foreseeable future, or will we soon have to get by without many of the things we took for granted in the past?

    7. If things go on as they are going, will the environment get better or worse or stay about the same? Why?

D. Ethic

Many people believe that protecting the environment is a good idea. The question seems to be: How far we should go in that direction?

    1. How much environmental protection do *you* think is enough? In which kind of situations do we need to protect the environment and when is it OK to use it however we want? Why?

    2. What *kind* of environment should we strive to achieve and maintain?

    3. What would you be willing to give up to achieve that kind of environment?

    4. Is there anything you would *not* be willing to give up to achieve that goal?

E. Nonpolitical environmental behaviors

    1. Do you try to take account of how you think the environment should be treated in your day-to-day life? How?

    2. Does the kind of work you do have any direct impact on the environment? How do you feel about that?

    3. Have you ever decided to buy something or *not* buy something because of environmental considerations?

    4. Do you ever discuss environmental issues or problems with other people?

    5. Would the environment ever be a consideration for you in choosing a job?

F. Obstacles to living up to the environmental ideal

    1. Is there anything you would like to be able to do to help protect the environment that you can't do now?

    2. What keeps you from doing this now?

    3. Do you think this is a problem for most people in America?

IV. Fit between environmental and social ideals

    1. Are the kinds of things that go into making a good society ever at odds with what we need to do to protect the environment?

If yes

    2. Where? How so exactly?

    3. If you had to make a choice between _____ and _____ , which would you choose? Why? (Here I filled in the blanks on the basis of prior exchanges in the interview.)

If no

No clash apparent with any previous exchange in the interview (end; move to next section)

Clash apparent with previous exchange(s):

2. What about _____ and _____?
   (Here I filled in the blanks on the basis of interviewee's preceding answers.)

If admits to a conflict
3. If both of these are important, what do you think should be done when they come into conflict?
If denies any conflict
3. Why is there no conflict between these?

V. Environmental policy ideal
   A. Ends
      A little while ago you described your idea of the kind of environment we should create and maintain, and some of the things you do or would like to do to help bring about that kind of environment.
      1. Do you think the *government* should also work toward creating and maintaining that kind of environment?
      2. Is the government doing enough to protect the environment?
      3. Does the government ever go too far in protecting the environment?
      4. In general, how effective is the government when it steps in to protect the environment?
      5. Can you think of any reason someone might think that the government ought to do more/less to protect the environment?

      If yes
      6. For example?
      7. Why would it be wrong for the government to do those things only/too?

      If no
         (I supplied an option at variance with the respondent's view, stressing that position most removed from his or her own; my response challenged both the individual's environment ethic and his or her view of government simultaneously.)
      6. How would you respond to that argument?
      7. Why would it be wrong for the government to do those things only/too?

      8. Has anyone or anything especially influenced the way you think about government's role in protecting the environment?
      9. Political behaviors
         a) Voting
            (1) To what extent do you take the environment into account when voting? Why (not)?
            (2) Have you ever voted for or against someone specifically because of his or her environmental position? When?
            (3) Have you ever voted for a particular political party because of its environmental position?

    b) Political parties

        (1) Do you consider yourself a Democrat, Republican, an independent, or something else?

        (2) Are you a member of any political party?

        (3) Why did you join?

    c) Voicing opinions: Have you ever contacted anyone in the government or in the media about environmental issues? When?

    d) Financial contributions: Have you ever donated money to any environmental organization? To which groups? About how much over the last five years?

    e) Group membership: Are you a member of any environmental organization(s)? Which? For how long? How active are you in _____ ?

    f) Protests: Have you ever participated in any environmental protest or demonstration? Upon what occasion(s)?

    g) Independent action: Have you ever been involved in any environmental issue not directly linked to an established organization?

    h) Anticipating future action: Can you think of any situation in which you *might* do any of these things even if you haven't done them up until now?

B. Means

A short time ago you talked about what you saw as our worst environmental problems.

    1. What should be done to solve these problems, if anything?

    2. Should the government be involved in any way?

    3. Why not try to solve them by _____ ?

        (Here I filled in the blank with that type of measure most at odds with the one favored by the respondent. From high to low governmental involvement, the list I chose from is as follows:

        —centralization and expert planning

        —decentralization and local control

        —altering the market in a systematic fashion to reflect environmental costs

        —increasing regulations and the use of economic incentives

        —leaving everything to the market

    4. Do you think we spend enough on protecting the environment?

    5. Where should we get the money for more environmental protection, or don't we need more?

The Real World

   I. Perceived sources of environmental policy and barriers to its extension

     A. I'm interested in finding out how you think we came to have the amount of government protection of the environment that we now have. Why don't we have more or less?

    B. Do you think government will have more than, less than, or about the same level of involvement in environmental issues in the future?

II. If the world were different

    A. Is there any basic change in either society or the environment that might change the way you think about or relate to environmental issues?

    B. Is there any change in your personal situation that might have that effect?

Reflecting on the Interview

    I. Opportunity to explain inconsistencies

      A. There is one more point I'd like to touch on. At a couple points you admitted that, like most people, you don't always act on your environmental ideals. Why is that?

      B. Do you think that that is a problem most Americans have?

  II. Summary statement

      A. Have you changed your mind about government regulation of the environment in any way since we started this interview?

      B. I'm pretty well done with my questions. Is there anything you'd like to add to what you've said so far?

      C. If you had to sum up your overall view of what government ought to do or *not* do in the environmental area, what would you emphasize?

Notes

Introduction

1. One of the earliest statements of this view, and still the best, is William Ophuls' *Ecology and the Politics of Scarcity (1977)*.

Chapter 1. Democracy, Deliberation, and the Environment

1. One need not be a philosophical idealist to believe in the power of ideas. In fact, it is impossible to be philosophical at all without at least a limited belief of this kind. History, for its part, may not be the record of the Idea becoming manifest in the world, but neither is it the study of pure matter in motion. If it were, we could reduce history to a set of lawlike propositions and predict the future with the same accuracy that we predict eclipses or cancers. (See Karl Popper's well-known version of this argument in the Preface to *The Poverty of Historicism*. [1957].) Finally, even Freudian and behavioral psychology presume some human capacity to reflect upon or at least process incoming impulses. This capacity is, of course, taken far more seriously by cognitive and developmental psychologists (see Flanagan 1984: chapters 5, 6).

2. James Fishkin has recently argued that we "reconcile democracy and deliberation" (1991: 1). I largely agree with Fishkin, but think that his own attempt to do so fails. It fails not because he leaves the concept of deliberation underdeveloped (following David Braybrooke, Fishkin's deliberative model is the "logically complete debate" [1991: 37]), but because, in the end, he abandons the hope that "the people" might become more deliberative and envisions deliberation extending only as far as a group of several hundred representative citizens. I applaud any and all suggestions for deliberative reform, Fishkin's included (see also Reich 1990a; Ingram and Smith 1994), but even the most representative citizen deliberators are still representatives. Democracy and deliberation can be reconciled, in my view, only if deliberation becomes

truly democratic, if the people, not just a select group of them, actually deliberate.

Chapter 2. The Deepest Ecological Question of Them All: Whence Democracy?

1. See for example, the subdiscipline's premier academic journal, *Environmental Ethics.*

2. There are exceptions, of course. See, for example, Holmes Rolston III's "Valuing Wildlands" (1985).

3. Hayek provides a neat summary of this argument in his *Constitution of Liberty* (1960), where he writes:

> Perhaps the best way of concisely stating the chief point is to say that all resource conservation constitutes investment and should be judged by precisely the same criteria as all other investment. There is nothing in the preservation of natural resources as such which makes it a more desirable object of investment than manmade equipment or human capacities; and, so long as society anticipates the exhaustion of particular resources and channels its investment in such a manner that its aggregate income is made as great as the funds available for investment can make it, there is no further economic case for preserving any one kind of resource. To extend investment in the conservation of a particular natural resource to a point where the return is lower than the capital it uses would bring elsewhere would reduce future income below what it would otherwise be. As has been well said, "the conservationist who urges us 'to make greater provision for the future' is in fact urging a lesser provision for posterity." (p. 374)

A similar version of this same argument can be found in David Stockman's "Wrong War? The Case against a National Energy Policy" (1978).

4. In William Ophuls' words, defenders of hierarchy envision "legislating the temperance and virtue needed for the ecological survival of a steady-state society" but end up "exalting the few over the many and subjecting individuals to the unwarranted exercise of power" (1977: 227). Achieving the first while avoiding the second, Ophuls warns, is an "exceedingly difficult problem." The deliberative solution I offer here is meant as a solution to precisely this problem.

5. Their vile legacy goes far beyond the 2,500 square miles of land contaminated by the Chernobyl disaster, the half dozen nuclear submarines sunk above the Artic Circle, and the death of the Aral Sea. In fact, Czech foresters have taken to calling Central Europe the Bermuda Triangle of pollution, and for good reason: between a quarter and a third of the forests in four of the six countries there are showing signs of pollutant-related damage (*New York Times*, March 19, 1990; French 1989: 24). And the list goes on. Consider these Polish statis-

tics: pollution has rendered at least 50 percent of all fresh water unfit even for industrial uses and a quarter of its soil unfit for farming (French 1989: 22, 25); air pollution in almost every major city reportedly exceeds permissible levels by a factor of 50 (French 1989: 22). Other Eastern European environments have fared little better. And perhaps a third of the residents of former East Germany are at risk from environmentally induced disease (*Village Voice*, March 1, 1990). Socialist countries were also abysmally inefficient in their use of natural resources, at least as measured by energy efficiency. Even the most efficient (Yugoslavia) ranked behind the United States, itself a laggard among OECD countries. In 1983, for example, the Soviet Union was barely a quarter as energy-efficient as France (French 1989: 28). See also *To Breath Free: Eastern Europe's Environmental Crisis*, edited by Joan DeBardeleben (1991).

6. Even if one assumes away the human relationships I refer to here, necessary physical relationships remain. All humans need heat, light, space, water, air, and nutrients. At the present time, all of these can be threatened by one's neighbors, often in inverse relation to the size of the territory in which one resides.

7. This observation was made to me originally by Charles W. Anderson. For a theoretically informed discussion of the NIMBY problem the interested reader is advised to consult either Denis J. Brion, *Essential Industry and the NIMBY Phenomenon* (1991) or Charles Piller, *The Fail-Safe Society* (1991).

Chapter 3. Americans in Search of Environmental Protection

1. This is true of virtually every study of the public's environmental policy thinking of which I am aware, whether theoretical, historical, psychological, or sociological (Sandbrook 1986; Fox 1985; Porritt 1984; Nash 1989; O'Riordan and Turner 1983; Rodman 1983; Sandbach 1980; Ophuls 1977). Interviews are essential if we are to learn anything about the meaning people attribute to environmental policy. We can categorize people's beliefs all we want but, as Stephen Cotgrove noted in his well-known statistical study, "there is always the question of meaning" (1982: 25; see also Galyn 1975). In-depth interviews meet most of the shortcomings of traditional survey techniques on this score. They, too, are language-dependent, of course, but at least responsibility for *generating* the language is shared between researcher and respondent. In addition, interviews allow for numerous iterations of the "hermeneutic circle": one iteration is completed each time a new question is asked. The longer the interview, the less likely misinterpretations will be. Interviews are also sensitive to the nuances of language and expression, where surveys are not. What interviews lose in generalizability, they gain in "the particular, idiosyncratic, and local facets of opinions, as well as much of their subjective meaning" (Reinarman 1987: 19). I expand on this point in the Appendix in the subsection entitled "The Interpretive Method."

2. Nash argues that it is difficult to explain the intensity and breadth of concern over the environment in the 1960s and 1970s without considering the "possibility that an ethical attitude toward nature is the latest in a succession

of American concerns for the rights of exploited or oppressed minorities." "Perhaps," Nash goes on, "the gospel of ecology should not be seen so much as a revolt against American traditions as an extension and new application of them—as just another working out of the American revolution" (1985: 249, 255). This is an appealing theory, but one that received virtually no support from the cross-section of citizens with whom I spoke: only two—both college students—regularly adopted "an ethical attitude toward nature," and even then it never dominated their thinking about environmental policy as a whole.

3. See Douglas and Wildavsky 1982. If it is true that one's view of the environment is largely structured by one's view of risk, why do people across the environmental spectrum all seem to cast the environment in the same way: as posing a problem to be solved? More to the point: Why does anyone frame the environment that way? If our environmental attitudes derive from our political beliefs, they ought to be definitive: more like answers than tentative responses accompanied by numerous questions. Conversely, if environmental puzzlement is the product of political puzzlement, there is nothing left to do the structuring.

4. According to historian Samuel Hays, the growth of environmentalism in the late 1960s was due to a generational shift brought on by increased levels of material well-being and education. For Hays, the new environmentalism was primarily underwritten by a trio of values: beauty, health, and permanence (1987: 32–35). The environment has become, according to Hays, another part of the American dream:

> Environmental and ecological values were an integral part of the continuous search for a better standard of living. They reflected changing attitudes about what constitutes a better life. The natural and the developed became intermingled as coordinated, mutually reinforcing aspects of the quality of living. . . . Environmental values were based not on one's role as a producer of goods and services but on consumption, the quality of home and leisure. Such environmental concerns were not prevalent at earlier times. But after World War II, rising levels of living led more people to desire qualitative experiences as well as material goods in their lives. . . . The focus was on changing life-styles, those qualitative concerns associated with increased leisure time and greater ability to use leisure time creatively and enjoyably. (1987: 34–35)

Although there are any number of problems with this analysis, some of which I touch on in later chapters, here I will confine myself to pointing out that, for my participants at least, the environment represents not so much a postbourgeois desideratum as a problem to be solved.

5. This finding accords rather well with the results of one of the two most thorough and sophisticated survey studies ever done of Americans' environmental beliefs, which found that, despite the fact that the public believes a "considerable" amount of political, social, and economic change is needed if we are to cure our environmental ills, and despite the fact that most people believe environmental problems to be quite urgent, "the mass of people do

not have a clear picture of the new society envisioned by the [environmental] vanguard" (Milbrath 1984: 80).

6. Numerous survey researchers have uncovered an unwillingness to make such trade-offs, especially between environmental and economic values (see Gilroy and Shapiro 1986; Mitchell 1984: 56; Reinarman 1987: 32; Cotgrove 1982).

7. At least one survey research team has argued, on the contrary, that (at least in the case of economic vs. environmental values) some three quarters of the American public denies the existence of any significant trade-off (Springer and Constantini 1974).

8. This simply reinforces what is by now perhaps in-depth interviewers' most robust finding: that people resist integrating different realms of experience. For example, in *What's Fair?* (1981), a study of Americans' beliefs about distributive justice, Jennifer Hochschild shows that people tend to separate the political and the economic spheres. Likewise, in *American States of Mind* (1987), Craig Reinarman illustrates how citizens maintain a similar division between their work and domestic lives.

Chapter 4. Why Americans Are Willing to Deliberate about Environmental Protection

1. However else one views this cultural bias toward specifics (against broad labels and categories), it ought to be taken into account in any effort to expand public deliberation on environmental questions. I attempt to do so in the closing chapter.

2. Here I am specifically reporting on the position participants assumed at the outset of our first discussion, as revealed by their first spontaneous generalization about environmental policy, *not* on the views they were defending at the end of our discussions. In chapter 6, I examine at length how participants' views changed over the course of the interviews.

3. I emphasize again that I am reporting participants' first spontaneous generalizations, not what they came to believe as a result of the interview experience. I followed this procedure because, for the moment, I am interested in the beliefs that participants brought to the interview.

4. See Appendix, "Selection of Participants," pp. 221–223.

5. Survey trends may also be read as indicating a steady increase in environmentalism, at least since systematic polls on the subject began in the mid-1960s. In the five years between 1965 and 1970 the public opinion scales were tipped toward those believing pollution to be a serious problem, those endorsing greater federal spending on environmental programs, and those willing to pay a modest increment in taxes to fund them (Erskine 1972a, b). Occasional fluctuations notwithstanding, the pro-environmentalism numbers have continued to grow since that time (see Petulla 1987: 120–121). Given all the available evidence, these numbers plainly indicate, not a dawning radicalism, but the continuing evolution of American environmentalism.

6. Greenpeace is the largest of these; it claims a membership of 2 million (*In These Times*, April 18–24, 1990). By the early 1990s, the Greens (U.S.) were

losing the look of a fringe group, with local groups numbering in the hundreds, local electoral successes mounting, and statewide candidates running in at least several states see *Green Letter,* Summer 1990: 54, 70; see also Porritt 1984; Capra and Spretnak 1984; Tokar 1986). More or less simultaneously, and often drawing on the same constituency, bioregionalism and the Earth First! "movement" have been attracting adherents by the thousands (Alexander 1990: 163; Tokar 1987: 31). Other environmental groups at least occasionally appear to be following these groups' lead, so much so that Gottlieb and Ingram were led to dub the tendency the new environmentalism (1988; Stegner 1987: 240; Wattenberg et al. 1989: 29, 32).

7. The critique typically blames environmental degradation on certain elements of American culture, especially individualism (Lynton Caldwell in Dunlap and Van Liere 1984: 1013), the faith in economic growth ("immutably fixed in our consciousness"—Bookchin 1989: 21), materialistic values ("the key log" that must be moved—Leopold [1949] 1970; see also Reinarman 1987: 190; Bellah et al. 1985), a belief in progress (our "secular religion"—Ophuls, 1977: 185), the frontier mentality and manifest destiny (Wisenhunt 1974; Wyant 1982; Ekirch 1963), or a combination of all of these (Barbour 1980: chapter 2). A representative survey of historical treatments of American attitudes toward nature would include the following: Ekirch 1963; Wisenhunt 1974; Glacken 1966; McHarg 1969; Tuan 1974; Hargrove 1983; Wyant 1982; Rodman 1977; Worster 1985; Fox 1985; Nash, 1989.

Philosophical critiques are too numerous to list, but among the more important are those accusing Western thought of being *dualistic* (see, for example: Heidegger [1954] 1977; Baudrillard 1981: chapter 10; Tuan 1974: 63, 247; Salleh 1984; Dodson Gray 1979; Warren 1987: 6; Zimmerman 1987: 28, 34; Tokar 1987: chapter 1), *reductionistic* (see Schumacher 1974: 29, 71, 75; Habermas 1972, 1976; Kohak 1984; Bookchin 1987: 8, 60, 362ff.; 391, 409; Mishan 1970: 3; Perrings 1987; ; Daly 1976; Commoner 1976; McHarg 1969; Boulding 1966), *anthropocentric* (see Leopold [1949] 1970: xviii; L. White 1971; Callicott 1989: 136–139, 64n3; Shaiko 1987: 245; Rolston 1975: 101, in Callicott 1989: 64n3; Tuan 1974; Black 1970; Glacken 1966; Barbour 1980; Leiss 1972; Ehrenfeld 1978; O'Riordan and Turner 1983; Taylor 1986), *overly individualistic* (see Ophuls 1977; Schumacher 1974: chapter 3), or *all of these at once* (Callicott 1989: 182–183, 191; Tokar 1987). The problem with all such critiques is that, as undeniably persuasive as they often are, it is almost never possible to link the enemies they identify to negative attitudes toward nature in the public as a whole. In most cases, there is no empirical evidence that most people think in the way posited or that thinking that way actually leads people to deprecate environmental protection. In many cases, empirical support of both kinds is lacking. In addition, the wealth of evidence pointing to positive orientations, not just to nature, but to nature protection, makes it all the harder to lend them much credence.

8. See also: Dunlap 1987; Stegner, 1987; Allen and Popkin 1988; Enloe 1975; Andrews 1984: 174.

9. In addition, Americans have generally denied that economic growth was responsible for the energy problems of the 1970s (Hays 1987). Other polls

showed that at least half of the public believed the energy crisis was susceptible to a purely technological "fix" (Richman 1979). Americans were also reluctant, even in a time of scarce energy supplies, to accept either of the energy plans advanced during the Carter administration, and they opposed government-orchestrated conservation incentives (Richman 1979). Nor did the energy crisis of the 1970s elicit widespread individual attempts to limit energy consumption. Finally, most Americans appear to favor offshore oil drilling to keep oil imports down (*New York Times*, July 1, 1990). Similar results are reported in Milbrath 1984; by Robert Cameron Mitchell in Hays 1987: 32; Petulla 1987: 120; Stanislaw and Yergin in the *New York Times*, July 1, 1990; CBS News Poll in the *New York Times*, April 17, 1990; Dunlap and Van Liere 1978: 13; and Dunlap and Van Liere 1984.

10. Neither do Americans appear naive about the costs of maintaining present energy supplies. A majority of Americans believed that the primary purpose of Operation Desert Storm was to preserve energy sources, not to deter Saddam Hussein or free Kuwait (*Capital Times* [Madison], January 8, 1991). See also Cotgrove 1982: 97n7.

11. The total membership of the 19 largest national groups exceeded 5.5 million even before experiencing the growth of the early 1980s (Sandbach, 1980: 13). And this does not count the perhaps 40,000 local environmental groups that existed nationwide when the decade began (Sandbach 1980: 13). In all, probably 1 in 10 Americans—some 20 million—belong to some environmental group. Of these, perhaps 1 in 10 is active (Milbrath 1990: 285; Milbrath 1984: 73). In addition, 1984 surveys showed that the public trusts environmental groups to provide accurate information on public policy more than it trusts government regulators or corporations and that national political leaders consider environmental groups to be far more effective than their business counterparts (Hays 1987: 327, 493). Polls also show that approximately 100 million Americans, upwards of 60 percent of the adult population, sympathize with these groups (Mitchell, 1984: 60, 72). Finally, a 1989 Harris survey showed that 76 percent of those queried called themselves environmentalists (*Harper's*, November 1989). Such subjective reports may not be too wide of the mark, for there is at least some evidence that people tend to take action on an individual basis more often than in groups (Milbrath 1984: 87).

12. There is an already large body of literature on "green consumerism." There is little doubt now about its importance—more than half of all Americans claim that they at least occasionally take environmental considerations into account when shopping—but lots of disagreement about its meaning (*Capital Times*, November 6, 1990). For some representative views, see: *Greenpeace*, May/June 1990; Makower 1990: 48–49; *Los Angeles Times*, March 15, 1990).

13. A recent report prepared for the Wisconsin Department of Natural Resources, for example, indicated that "Over 80 percent of the state adult population participated in a nonconsumptive activity" during the course of 1987 and that, "in general, all wildlife users prefer wild, undeveloped lands to

developed wildlife lands, even if development might increase the likelihood of seeing wildlife" (Petchenik 1989: 38, 37). See also Hays 1987: 110, 558fn30.

14. Suffice it to say here that the theme has gone beyond being a subject for newscasters and has now entered mainstream programming: "thirtysomething" characters complained about disposable diapers, plastic drycleaning bags, and waste incinerators. And Turner Broadcasting recently began airing a new children's series, *Captain Planet* (*Vis-a-Vis*, April 1990: 57). At the same time, two-thirds of the top 25 programs aired by the Public Broadcasting Service in 1989 dealt with the environment in some capacity or another (Lewis 1990: 580). Meanwhile, like others who are even more directly involved, television professionals banded together in 1989 to form their own environmental caucus, the Environmental Media Association (*Vis-a-Vis*, April 1990: 57).

15. See, for example, *Sierra*, July/August 1990, and the *Serious Investor*, April 2, 1990. There are other signs that a major environmental reorientation is underway. One might point to the rapid spread of alternative farming, or sustainable agriculture as it is more commonly called, whose practitioners more than doubled during the 1980s (*WorldWatch*, November/December 1988, 8), or to the so-called New Forestry movement within the Forest Service bureaucracy, which has grown despite the threat it represents to the status quo and the consequent dangers participation poses to the careers of those who are promoting its goals of diversity and sustainability (Ryan 1990). Or one might point to the fact that environmental ethics has, in the space of little more than a decade and a half, become an institutionalized academic enterprise, replete with its own journal (*Environmental Ethics*) and advanced-degree programs.

Or consider the greening of American religion. Already in 1979, the National Council of Churches emphasized that, in the Christian commandment to "love thy neighbor," "neighbor" is to be understood as including nonhumans as well as future generations (Barbour 1980: 89; see also *Firmament*, the newsletter of the North American Conference on Christianity and Ecology; *ISEE Newsletter*, Summer 1990; and the *Utne Reader*, November/December 1989).

16. Historian Samuel Hays points out that in evaluating Americans' environmental commitments in the post-1970 period, one must keep in mind the energy crises and economic difficulties of the 1970s, the vast amounts of money spent on environmental protection, and the anti-regulatory climate of the1980s. His own conclusion is that the ability of environmentalists to achieve some limited successes despite Reagan's opposition "reflected the depth of public support on which they drew" (1987: 513, 533). Finally, he notes that, given the political inequality between environmentalists and developers, one must be "taken aback" by environmentalist successes, which could never have occurred in the absence of public support (534). For several parallel analyses, see also Vig and Kraft 1984b.

Chapter 5. Accelerating the Evolution of American Environmentalism

1. While it is true that outward consistency may indicate nothing more than the repetition of slogans (W. R. Neumann in Reinarman 1987: 217n10), it must be remembered that during the course of the interview participants were constantly challenged to explain—and defend—their beliefs. With that procedure any facile attempts at diverting my attention from inconsistent beliefs was rendered rather transparent in most cases.

2. There was even greater diversity among participants at the metaethical level. That is, if their values were diverse, the ways in which they grounded or justified those values were more diverse still. For example, many participants invoked future generations as a justification for one or another policy reform. But that justification was itself supported by everything from a belief in a temporally extended human family to the notion of intergenerational rights. A college professor declared simply, "I don't want to be cursed by my grandchildren for the stupidity I used," and a chemist mused, "Do I want to know that my charitable efforts right now are futile—ultimately futile, ridiculous, laughable? No."

Although I shall not dwell on them here, the implications of such metaethical and ethical diversity for environmental ethics are profound, indeed. They suggest not only that we need not knock ourselves out finding (and then justifying) inherent value in nature, but also that any reasonably compelling environmental ethic will be complex or, to use the now fashionable term, pluralistic.

At the same time, these findings directly contradict Nash's ethical evolution thesis (1989), for not only did all my participants cite many nonethical reasons for preserving nature, but also (as table 5.3 on p. 135 shows) the concept of "rights in nature" surfaced far less frequently than did other norms.

3. This finding is not as different from those of the various paradigm studies as their label might suggest. It turns out that some 60 percent of Milbrath's respondents endorsed neither the DSP nor the New Environmental Paradigm; he argues that this group's responses also contain "paradigm-like structures" (1984: chapter 3). But the empirical basis for the claim is weak. Cotgrove's findings are largely similar: most endorsed a mix of economic and noneconomic values (1982: 19). Nor do Van Liere and Dunlap's findings differ greatly (Dunlap and Van Liere 1984). And, as Milbrath himself points out, a number of other studies support these findings (Milbrath 1984: chapter 3). Either there exist many such clusters, or there is a third (and fourth?) paradigm out there. If many such clusters exist, they cannot rightly be called paradigms; if other paradigms exist, they ought to be described. The only defense one might make on behalf of the paradigm thesis is that, in the long term, the dissonance thus created is likely to be reduced (Dunlap and Van Liere 1984). A second problem with the empirical findings of the paradigm studies is that, even among those who agreed that major changes are needed, large differences surfaced as to what *type* of changes are needed (technological or lifestyle). And Cotgrove's findings showed that individuals' view of resource shortages clearly separated radical from conservative environmentalists (1982: 15). Again, no paradigms here.

Finally, it must be pointed out that the correlations revealed by these studies are between the NEP and environmental concern. But environmental concern, as numerous scholars have observed, is a weak indicator of values, much less of how one balances competing values (Gill et al. 1986; Dunlap 1985; Van Liere and Dunlap 1980). What is more, the various measures of environmental concern conflate the reasons people have for being concerned (Cotgrove 1982: 99). Little wonder that research shows a poor correlation between environmental concern and willingness to endorse reform measures (Martinson and Wilkening in Sandbach 1980: 9). My own study, by contrast, required participants not only to endorse or reject reform measures, but also to justify and then defend their positions.

4. Genetic theories of environmental policy-thinking can be grouped into three basic types: historical, sociological, and psychological. Their explanatory ambitions vary from pinning down the roots of environmental concern to locating the determinants of entire thought structures such as the New Environmental Paradigm, which I discuss below.

5. In 1980 Van Liere and Dunlap concluded a review of 21 such studies by noting "the limited utility of demographic variables in explaining variation in environmental concern." Their conclusion: cognitive determinants must be at least as important as demography in determining environmental concern (1980: 193). Subsequent research by that team and others has tended to confirm that hypothesis (see Dunlap and Van Liere 1984; Cotgrove 1982; Milbrath 1984, 1990; Allen and Popkin 1988; Watts 1988; Shaiko 1987).

6. Likewise, Shaiko's recent study of religious environmentalists found that "adherents of both [stewardship and mastery of nature] perspectives are able to coexist within the environmental movement" (1987: 259; see also Barbour 1980: 27). Bryan Norton has recently argued that such value pluralism characterizes American environmentalists as a whole (1991: 60, 197). Such findings ought not surprise us. Rational choice theorists, for example, have for some time argued that heterogeneity of group norms encourages collective action (see also Lindblom 1990: 147–154). According to a number of different theorists, we ought to welcome such a policy-consensus–normative-disensus. Deep ecologist Arne Naess has observed that a variety of motives are consistent with an ecological "gestalt" and that, as a result, one ought not be too precise in stating environmental norms (1989: 153; see also Devall and Sessions 1985: 225). Bryan Norton likewise argues that the the environmental movement's strength lies in its ability to appeal to a wide variety of value positions (1991: 12, 93). Martin Lewis' recent attack on "eco-radicalism" is motivated by much the same belief (1992; see also Paehlke 1989: 278). My own position differs from these views, I think, only in its specificity. Whereas these authors rightly argue that there is a positive connection between consensus and environmental*ism*, I am arguing that we ought to focus on the positive connection between consensus and environmental *deliberation*.

7. This interpretation squares neatly with existing research on the relationship between political individualism and environmental attitudes. Milbrath found that environmentalists apparently have higher trust in government than

the public as a whole, but they are also critical of government efforts to deal with environmental problems (Milbrath, 1984: 93, 85–87; see also Hays 1987: 206; *New York Times*, April 17, 1990). At the same time, he found no correlation between individuals' left-right position and their environmental orientation (Milbrath 1984: 85). Several years earlier, Van Liere and Dunlap's literature review showed that previous investigations had discovered only a slight relationship between the two (1980). And, reporting the results of their own study, those authors conclude that individualism per se is not significantly correlated with hostility to environmental regulations, environmental spending, or the NEP (Dunlap and Van Liere 1984). Cotgrove, whose results include the United Kingdom, found that leftists were actually *less* concerned than their political counterparts about the environment. That lead him to argue that politics is not a good predictor of environmentalism, despite the strong participatory sentiments he uncovered among many environmentalists (Cotgrove 1982: 134, 31).

Even the modern environmental movement, critical as it has been of the socio-political status quo, has generally preferred individual over public action (Hays 1987: 206). Moreover, despite the fact that polls have for some time shown that majorities believe voluntary action by industries or individuals insufficient by itself to cope with environmental problems (Rickson 1972), the public appears to consider *itself* largely innocent of any environmental wrongdoing (Allen and Popkin 1988, Simon 1985; Murch 1974; Erskine 1972b). The public's reaction to the Exxon *Valdez* oil spill in 1989 cast this almost Hobbesian acceptance of the need for collective action into high relief: attention focused on the recklessness of the pilot, not on society's demand for oil. As a Greenpeace ad put it, people blamed Captain Haselwood's driving, not their own (much less society's, I would add). What was the preferred solution? It was a technological fix (double-hulled tankers), perhaps coupled with more vigilant regulation of tanker operations. From this moralistic perspective, environmental degradation has much in common with good old-fashioned criminal behavior; to prevent it one installs locks on the door, hires more police, and builds bigger jails. As a result, the structural or social causes of the behavior are largely ignored.

8. This view is strongly supported by the numerous cognitive connections revealed by the various paradigm studies. Cotgrove found that "the most consistent predictors of environmental concern generally" are anti-materialism, anti-industrialism, the rejection of scientific expertise, and, most centrally, an aversion to economic individualism. Dunlap and Van Liere found that commitment to economic growth, a laissez faire political economy, and property rights "explain considerably more variation in levels of environmental concern than do the demographic variables" (1984: 1023). Lester Milbrath has also tested the paradigm hypothesis in a national study published in the early 1980s. His conclusion was that the two ends of the environmental-concern spectrum are divided primarily according to attitudes toward limiting growth and economic planning; also of some importance are the strength of faith in science and technology and the level of trust in the government (1984: 93, 140). In other words, environmental concern has numerous cognitive correlates, not just one or two.

And, as Cotgrove rightly concludes, "it is the complex *pattern* of beliefs and values which explains support" (my emphasis; Cotgrove 1982: 134). Logically, we can expect people's environmental policy norms to be even more complex. These authors err primarily in ascribing similar, well-integrated belief patterns to most people. A truer picture would be one in which a huge variety of individual schema, none of which is particularly well developed, overlap to produce similar policy conclusions. The reason for the discrepancy in interpretations on this score is again rooted in the associational nature of the paradigm data versus the ability of interviews actually to confirm or disconfirm "causal" links in people's thinking.

9. Although my findings provide strong warrants for believing this to be the case, I am certainly not the first to come to this conclusion (see, for example, Piasecki and Asmus 1990). At the same time, this remains very much a minority view. The conventional environmental wisdom has always been that saving nature depends on moral regeneration. Numerous examples can be found in virtually any issue of the journal *Environmental Ethics*.

Chapter 6. Deliberation, Environmental Rationality, and Environmental Commitment

1. In fact, three of the four occasions on which the interview produced something like a genuine epiphany occurred while the participant was out of the room, mulling over something we'd been discussing. Deliberation must be public, but ultimately thought takes place in its own, often very private, space. On this point see Barber 1984: 175.

2. The goal I have in mind is not fundamentally different from James Fishkin's notion of a "self-reflective political culture." For Fishkin, social reform ought to focus on bringing "the self-purging dimension of liberal thought experiments home to the environment people actually live in, rather than merely to one they are asked to imagine" (1986: 57). See also his recent work *Democracy and Deliberation* (1991). My own theory diverges from Fishkin's at two important points. First, I explicitly link deliberation to a substantive notion of rationality, that is, environmental rationality. By invoking the norms of equality and nontyranny in the latter work, Fishkin implicitly admits to such a link as well. But the connection is never articulated, much less defended. Second, whereas Fishkin stresses representative, group processes, or deliberative fora, I stress universal, undifferentiated ones. (The difference here is really one of emphasis: the two kinds of process are not mutually exclusive. It is just that the latter kind has been too often overlooked [see Chapter 7]).

3. Paleontologist Stephen Jay Gould has observed, "It takes a particular kind of genius or deep understanding to transcend this most pervasive of all conceptual biases and to capture a phenomenon by grasping a proper scale beyond the measuring rods of our own world" (1990: 24).

4. Political psychologist Timothy Cook has argued recently, "Only when politics becomes more central in one's existence would a pull provided by one's

environment impel one to a higher level of reasoning and understanding" (1985: 1085). These results certainly confirm that view.

5. Hence the interviews as a whole strongly support the "primary postulate" of Lindblom's "self-guided model," that is, "that masses of people probe and can greatly improve their probing" (1990: 229). It is worth pointing out in this connection that it was my least well-educated participants that appeared to benefit most from the interview. Thus, because my sample was better educated than the public at large, my results probably understate the value of deliberation. I thank John Tryneski for bringing this point to my attention.

6. See, for example, Richard M. Merelman's *Making Something of Ourselves* (1984). Merelman argues, persuasively I think, that American culture is presently unable to transmit any single political ideology or vision. Following Durkheim, he recommends the reinvigoration of agencies capable of transmitting such a vision. I agree with his analysis, as far as it goes. But, like the argument between hierarchy and democracy, I believe this crucial cultural issue cannot be reduced to institutions per se—that, instead, the central issue is the nature of the challenges and opportunities with which those institutions are confronted.

7. It is important to remember, in other words, that these data are part of a larger normative argument. At the same time, however, relying on experimental data in the construction of a normative theory is hardly standard practice (in either environmental ethics or political theory). The conventional approach to normative theory is, rather, to advance and defend a theoretical ideal and then to compare that ideal with the status quo. My own approach was importantly different in that it compared an environmental ideal (here, environmental rationality), not with how people think or act now (as viewed by an "impartial" observer), but with how they come to think under certain ideal political conditions. Rather than comparing "pure theory" and "pure practice," then, my approach literally combined them.

Chapter 7. Expanding Environmental Deliberation

1. My argument is thus formally similar to that advanced recently by Herbert J. Gans, for whom the reinvigoration of representative democracy depends, not upon increased participation per se, but on making institutions more accountable. See his *Middle American Individualism* (1991).

The key phrase in my text is "wherever it occurs": I do not believe anyone can fully specify in advance just where deliberation does occur in our complex society—much less where it might have a chance of flourishing in the future. The practical suggestions I make in this chapter are thus to be taken as points of departure, not as a definitive program. They are at least partly intended to show that expanding democratic deliberation is institutionally possible. To state precisely how that possibility might be realized would not only take me well beyond the scope of my argument but would also actually contradict its principal conclusion. I have argued that our best environmental strategy is to enhance public deliberation. Means-ends consistency requires that I likewise endorse a deliberative search for the means to enhanced deliberation, not specific recipes. Theory and research can help in this search, but they should never be confused with the search itself.

2. Likewise, participation can help thwart the power of highly organized private interests, many of which, history suggests, are anti-environmental. See Paehlke, 1989: 174–176.

3. One of the private seals of environmental approval, Green Cross, has already come under fire from environmental critics for being misleading (Knight-Ridder News Service, October 1, 1991).

4. On the political economy of value-added taxation, see Charles E. McLure, Jr., *The Value-Added Tax* (1991).

5. Professor Ann Khademian inspired this recommendation, and the label deliberative entrepreneur, by drawing a parallel between my deliberative prescription and recent work in policy analysis.

6. The financial status of public interest groups could be improved through a change in their tax status, for example. See Paehlke 1989: 279; Repetto et al. 1992.

Bibliography

Albrecht, Stan L., Clay W. Hardin, and Armand L. Mauss. 1975. "Population." In Armand L. Mauss, ed., *Social Problems as Social Movements*. Philadelphia: Lippincott.

Alexander, Donald. 1990. "Bioregionalism: Science or Sensibility?" *Environmental Ethics* 12, no. 2 (Summer): 161–173.

al Kouri, Frid. 1990. "Historical Notes about Christian Community with Some Ecological Implications." *Firmament* 2, no. 2 (Summer): 10.

Allen, Frederick W., and Roy Popkin. 1988. "Environmental Polls: What They Tell Us." *EPA Journal* 14, no. 6 (July/August): 10–11.

Anderson, Charles W. 1990. *Pragmatic Liberalism*. Chicago: University of Chicago Press.

Andrews, Richard N. L. 1984. "Deregulation: The Failure at EPA." In Norman J. Vig and Michael E. Kraft, eds., *Environmental Policy in the 1980s: Reagan's New Agenda*, 161–180. Washington, D.C.: Congressional Quarterly Press.

Bailes, Kendall E. 1985a. "Critical Issues in Environmental History." In Kendall E. Bailes, ed., *Environmental History: Critical Issues in Comparative Perspective*, 1–21. Lanham, Md.: University Press of America.

Bailes, Kendall E., ed. 1985b. *Environmental History: Critical Issues in Comparative Perspective*. Lanham, Md.: University Press of America.

Baldwin, John H. 1985. *Environmental Planning and Management*. Boulder, Colo.: Westview Press.

Barber, Benjamin R. 1984. *Strong Democracy: Participatory Politics for a New Age*. Berkeley: University of California Press.

Barbour, Ian G. 1980. *Technology, Environment, and Human Values*. New York: Praeger.

Barnes, S., and M. Kaase, eds. 1979. *Political Action: Mass Participation in Five Western Democracies*. Beverly Hills: Sage Publications.

Bartlett, Robert V. 1986. "Ecological Rationality: Reason and Environmental Policy." *Environmental Ethics* 8, no. 3 (Fall): 221–239.

Baudrillard, Jean. 1981. *For a Critique of the Political Economy of the Sign.* St. Louis, Mo.: Telos Press.

Bellah, Robert N., Richard Madsen, William M. Sullivan, Ann Swidler, and Steven M. Tipton. 1985. *Habits of the Heart: Individualism and Commitment in American Life.* New York: Harper and Row.

Bennett, W. Lance. 1980. *Public Opinion in American Politics.* New York: Harcourt, Brace, Jovanovich.

Berberet, William G. 1988. "Earth Day and Environmental Education: Retrospect and Prospect." University of Wisconsin–Madison Institute for Environmental Studies. *Monograph* no. 1.

Bernstein, Richard. 1978. *The Restructuring of Social and Political Theory.* Philadelphia: University of Pennsylvania Press.

Billig, Michael. 1976. *Social Psychology and Intergroup Relations.* London: Academic Press.

Billig, Michael. 1982. *Ideology and Social Psychology: Extremism, Moderation, and Contradiction.* New York: St. Martin.

Black, J. H. 1970. *The Dominion of Man: The Search for Ecological Responsibility.* Edinburgh: Edinburgh University Press.

Bookchin, Murray. [1964] 1988. *Ecology and Revolutionary Thought.* Reprint. Burlington, Vt.: Green Program Project.

Bookchin, Murray. [1969] 1986. *The Power to Create! The Power to Destroy!* Reprint. Burlington, Vt.: Green Program Project.

Bookchin, Murray. 1987. *The Modern Crisis.* 2nd ed. New York: Black Rose Books.

Bookchin, Murray. 1989. "Death of a Small Planet." *The Progressive* 53, no. 8 (August): 19–23.

Bookchin, Murray. 1991. *The Ecology of Freedom: The Emergence and Dissolution of Hierarchy.* Montreal: Black Rose Books.

Botkin, Daniel. 1990. *Discordant Harmonies: A New Ecology for the Twenty-first Century.* New York: Oxford University Press.

Boulding, Kenneth E. 1966. "The Economics of the Coming Spaceship Earth." In Henry Jarrett, ed., *Environmental Quality in a Growing Economy: Essays from the Sixth RFF Forum,* 3–14. Ann Arbor, Mich.: Books on Demand.

Braybrooke, David. 1987. *Philosophy of Social Sciences.* Englewood Cliffs, N.J.: Prentice-Hall.

Braybrooke, David, and Charles E. Lindblom. 1963. *A Strategy of Decision: Policy Evaluation as a Social Process.* New York: Free Press.

Brenner, Michael J. 1973. *The Political Economy of America's Environmental Dilemma.* Lexington, Mass.: Lexington Books.

Brion, Denis J. 1991. *Essential Industry and the NIMBY Phenomenon.* New York: Quorum Books.

Bruvold, William H. 1973. "Beliefs and Behavior as Determinants of Environmental Attitudes." *Journal of Social Psychology* 5: 202–218.

Bumiller, Kristin. 1987. "Victims in the Shadow of the Law: A Critique of the Model of Legal Protection." *Signs* 12, no. 3 (Spring): 421–439.

Buttel, Frederick H., and William L. Flinn. 1976. "Economic Growth versus the Environment: Survey Evidence." *Social Science Quarterly* 57 (September): 410–420.

Buttel, Frederick H., and William L. Flinn. 1978. "Social Class and Mass Environmental Beliefs: A Reconsideration." *Environmental Behavior* 10 (September): 43–50.

Cahn, Robert. 1978. *Footprints on the Planet: A Search for an Environmental Ethic.* New York: Universe Books.

Caldwell, Lynton Keith. 1970. *Environment: Challenges to Modern Society.* Garden City, N.Y.: Natural History Press.

Callicott, J. Baird. 1989. *In Defense of the Land Ethic: Essays in Environmental Philosophy.* Albany: State University of New York Press.

Capra, Fritjof, and Charlene Spretnak. 1984. *Green Politics.* New York: E. P. Dutton.

Chubb, John E. 1983. *Interest Groups and the Bureaucracy: The Politics of Energy.* Stanford, Calif.: Stanford University Press.

Commoner, Barry. 1976. *The Poverty of Power: Energy and the Economic Crisis.* New York: A. E. Knopf.

Commoner, Barry. 1990. "Don't Control Pollution; Prevent It." *USA Today*, April 20.

Converse, Jean M., and Howard Schuman. 1974. *Conversations at Random: Survey Research as Interviewers See It.* New York: John Wiley and Sons.

Converse, Philip E. 1964. "The Nature of Belief Systems in Mass Publics." In David Apter, ed., *Ideology and Discontent*, 206–261. Glencoe, Ill.: Free Press.

Cook, Thomas D. 1985. "Postpositivist Critical Multiplism." In R. Lance Shotland and Melvin M. Mark, eds., *Social Science and Social Policy*, 21–62. Beverly Hills, Calif.: Sage.

Cook, Tim. 1985. "The Bear Market in Political Socialization and the Costs of Misunderstood Psychological Theories." *American Political Science Review* 79, no. 4 (December): 1079–1093.

Cotgrove, Stephen. 1982. *Catastrophe or Cornucopia: The Environment, Politics and the Future.* New York: John Wiley and Sons.

Dahl, Robert A. 1989. *Democracy and Its Critics.* New Haven, Conn.: Yale University Press.

Daly, Herman E. 1976. "The Steady-State Economy." In K. D. Wilson, ed., *Prospects for Growth*, 263–281. New York: Praeger.

Daly, Herman E. 1983. "The Steady-State Economy." In Timothy O'Riordan and R. Kerry Turner, eds., *An Annotated Reader in Environmental and Management*, 237–253. Oxford: Pergamon Press.

Daly, Herman E., and John B. Cobb, Jr. 1990. *For the Common Good: Redirecting the Economy toward Community, the Environment, and a Sustainable Future.* Boston: Beacon Press.

DeBardeleben, Joan, ed. 1991. *To Breath Free: Eastern Europe's Environmental Crisis.* Baltimore, Md.: John Hopkins University Press.

Dery, David. 1984. *Problem Definition in Policy Analysis.* Lawrence, Kans.: University Press of Kansas.

Devall, Bill, and George Sessions. 1985. *Deep Ecology: Living as if Nature Mattered.* Salt Lake City, Utah: Gibbs Smith.

Dodson Gray, Elizabeth. 1979. *Why the Green Nigger? Re-Mything Genesis.* Wellesley, Mass.: Roundtable Press.

Douglas, Mary, and Aaron Wildavsky. 1982. *Risk and Culture: An Essay on the Selection of Technical and Environmental Dangers.* Berkeley: University of California Press.

Drysek, John S. 1990. "The Environmental Politics of the Good Society." Paper presented at the Annual Meeting of the American Political Science Association, San Francisco.

Dunlap, Riley E. 1981. "Public Opinion in the 1980s: Clear Consensus, Ambiguous Commitment." *Environment* 33 (October): 10–15, 32–37.

Dunlap, Riley E. 1985. "Public Opinion: Behind the Transformation." *EPA Journal* 11, no. 6 (July/August): 15–17.

Dunlap, Riley E. 1987. "Public Opinion on the Environment in the Reagan Era." *Environment* 29 (July/August): 6–11, 32–37.

Dunlap, Riley E. 1991. "Trends in Public Opinion toward Environmental Issues: 1965–1990." *Society and Natural Resources* 4: 285–312.

Dunlap, Riley E., and Kent D. Van Liere. 1978. "The 'New Environmental Paradigm': A Proposed Measuring Instrument and Preliminary Results." *Journal of Environmental Education* 9 (Summer): 10–19.

Dunlap, Riley E., and Kent D. Van Liere. 1984. "Commitment to the Dominant Social Paradigm and Concern for Environmental Quality." *Social Science Quarterly* 65, no. 4 (December): 1013–1028.

Ehrenfeld, David. 1978. *The Arrogance of Humanism.* New York: Oxford University Press.

Ekirch, Arthur A. 1963. *Man and Nature in America.* New York: Columbia University Press.

Enloe, Cynthia H. 1975. *The Politics of Pollution in a Comparative Perspective: Ecology and Power in Four Nations.* New York: David McKay.

Entman, Robert M. 1989. *Democracy without Citizens: Media and the Decay of American Politics.* New York: Oxford University Press.

Erskine, Hazel. 1972a. "The Polls: Pollution and Its Costs." *Public Opinion Quarterly* 36, no. 1 (Spring): 120–135.

Erskine, Hazel. 1982b. "The Polls: Pollution and Industry." *Public Opinion Quarterly* 36, no. 2 (Summer): 263–280.

Feyerabend, Paul K. 1978. *Against Method: Outline of an Anarchistic Theory of Knowledge.* London: Verso Edition.

Fishkin, James S. 1984. *Beyond Subjective Morality.* New Haven, Conn.: Yale University Press.

Fishkin, James S. 1986. "Liberal Theory: Strategies of Reconstruction." In Alfonso J. Damico, ed., *Liberals on Liberalism,* 54–64. Totowa, N.J.: Rowman and Littlefield.

Fishkin, James S. 1991. *Democracy and Deliberation*. New Haven, Conn.: Yale University Press.

Flader, Susan L. 1989. "Citizenry, State, and Environmental Policy." Aldo Leopold Lecture, delivered November 15 at the University of Wisconsin-Madison.

Flanagan, Owen J. 1984. *The Science of the Mind*. Cambridge, Mass.: MIT Press.

Fowler, Robert Booth. 1991. *The Dance with Community: The Contemporary Debate in American Political Thought*. Lawrence: University Press of Kansas.

Fox, Irving K. 1971. "Water Resources Management in the Soviet Union and the United States: Some Similarities, Differences, and Policy Issues." In Irving Fox, ed., *Water Resource Law and Policy in the Soviet Union*, 3–20. Madison: University of Wisconsin Press.

Fox, Stephen. 1985. *The American Conservation Movement: John Muir and His Legacy*. Madison: University of Wisconsin Press.

Freeman, John, et al. 1973. *Environmental Economics*. Standord, Calif.: Stanford University Press.

French, Hilary F. 1989. "Industrial Wasteland." *WorldWatch* (November/December): 21–30.

French, Hilary F. 1990a. "Environmental Protection Breaches the Berlin Wall." *WorldWatch* (April/May): 6–7.

French, Hilary F. 1990b. "You Are What You Breath." *WorldWatch* (May/June): 27–34.

Galston, William A. 1986. "Liberalism and Public Morality." In Alfonso J. Damico, ed., *Liberals on Liberalism*, 129–146. Totowa, N.J.: Rowman and Littlefield.

Gans, Herbert J. 1991. *Middle American Individualism: Political Participation and Liberal Democracy*. New York: Oxford University Press.

Gaus, Gerald F. 1983. *The Modern Liberal Theory of Man*. New York: St. Martin's Press.

Gayln, Willard. 1975. *Partial Justice: A Study of Bias in Sentencing*. New York: Vintage Books.

Gill, James D., Lawrence A. Crosby, and James R. Taylor. 1986. "Ecological Concern, Attitudes, and Social Norms in Voting Behavior." *Public Opinion Quarterly* 50, no. 4 (Winter): 537–554.

Gilroy, John M., and Robert Y. Shapiro. 1986. "The Polls: Environmental Protection." *Public Opinion Quarterly* 50, no. 2 (Summer): 270–279.

Glacken, Clarence J. 1966. "Reflections on the Man-Nature Theme as a Subject for Study." In F. Fraser Darling and John P. Milton, eds., *Future Environments of North America*, 355–371. Garden City, N.Y.: Natural History Press.

Gorham, Eric B. 1992. *National Service, Citizenship, and Political Education*. Albany: State University of New York Press.

Gottlieb, Robert, and Helen Ingram. 1988. "The New Environmentalists." *The Progressive* (August): 115.

Gould, Stephen Jay. 1990. "The Golden Rule—A Proper Scale for Our Environmental Crisis." *Natural History* (September): 24–30.

Greenwood, F. 1989. "A More Sustainable Society Is Possible." *Utne Reader* (July/August): 54–60.

Habermas, Jurgen. 1972. *Knowledge and Human Interests.* Boston: Beacon Press.

Habermas, Jurgen. 1976. *Theory and Practice.* London: Heinemann Educational Books.

Hage, Jeremy, and Remi Clignet. 1982. "Coordination Styles and Economic Growth." *Annals of the American Association of Political Science* 459 (January): 77–92.

Hansen, Mogens Herman. 1991. *The Athenian Democracy in the Age of Demosthenes.* New York: Cambridge University Press.

Hargrove, Eugene C. 1983. "Anglo-American Land Use Attitudes." In Donald Sherer and Thomas Attig, eds., *Ethics and the Environment*, 121–148. Englewood Cliffs, N.J.: Prentice-Hall.

Hastie, Reid. 1986. "A Primer of Information-processing Theory for the Political Scientist." In Richard R. Lau and David O. Sears, eds., *Political Cognition*, 11–40. Hillsdale, N.J.: Laurence Erlbaum Associates.

Hayek, Friedrich A. 1960. *The Constitution of Liberty.* South Bend, Iowa: Gateway Editions, Ltd.

Hays, Samuel P. 1987. *Beauty, Health, Permanence.* Cambridge and New York: Cambridge University Press.

Heidegger, Martin. [1954] 1977. *The Question Concerning Technology and Other Essays.* Translated and with an introduction by William Loritt. New York: Harper and Row.

Heilbroner, Robert L. 1974. *An Inquiry into the Human Prospect.* New York: Norton.

Hiss, Tony. 1991. *The Experience of Place.* New York: Alfred Knopf.

Hochschild, Jennifer. 1981. *What's Fair? American Beliefs about Distributive Justice.* Cambridge, Mass.: Harvard University Press.

Humphrey, Craig R., and Frederick H. Buttel. 1986. *Environment, Energy, and Society.* Malabar, Fla.: Krieger Publishing Company.

Ingram, Helen, and Steven Rathgeb Smith, eds. 1994. *Public Policy for Democracy.* Washington, D.C.: Brookings Institution.

Innes, Judith E. 1987. "Usable Research for Planning Practice." *Design Methods and Theories* 22, no. 3: 243–252.

Joppke, Christian. 1990. "Decentralization of Control: The U.S. Nuclear Power Controversy since Three Mile Island." Paper presented at the annual meeting of the American Political Science Association in San Francisco, Calif.

Kelley, Donald R., Denneth R. Stunkel, and Richard R. Wescott. 1976. *The Economic Superpowers and the Environment: The U.S., the Soviet Union, and Japan.* San Francisco, Calif.: W. H. Freeman and Co.

Kenski, M., and F. Kenski. 1984. "Environmental Attitudes." *Public Opinion Quarterly* 32, no. 2: 54–67.

Kohak, Erazim. 1984. *The Embers and the Stars: A Philosophical Inquiry into the Moral Sense of Nature.* Chicago: University of Chicago Press.

Kraft, Michael E. 1984. "A New Environmental Policy Agenda: The 1980 Presidential Campaign and Its Aftermath." In Norman J. Vig and Michael E. Kraft, eds., *Environmental Policy in the 1980s: Reagan's New Agenda*, 29–50. Washington, D.C.: Congressional Quarterly Press.

Lane, Robert E. 1964. *Political Life: Why People Get Involved in Politics.* 3rd ed. New York: Free Press of Glencoe.

Lane, Robert E. 1979. "Capitalist Man, Socialist Man." In Peter Laslett and James Fishkin, eds. *Philosophy, Politics and Society*, 57–77. New Haven, Conn.: Yale University Press.

Lau, Richard R., and David O. Sears. 1986a. "An Introduction to Political Cognition." In Richard R. Lau and David O. Sears, eds., *Political Cognition*, 3–10. Hillsdale, N.J.: Laurence Erlbaum Associates.

Lau, Richard R., and David O. Sears, eds. 1986b. *Political Cognition.* Hillsdale, N.J.: Laurence Erlbaum Associates.

Leiss, William. 1972. *The Domination of Nature.* New York: Beziller.

Leopold, Aldo. [1949] 1970. *A Sand County Almanac.* New York: Ballantine Books.

Leopold, Aldo. 1991. "The River of the Mother of God." *Wilderness* 54, no. 192 (Spring): 19–26. Excerpted from *The River of the Mother of God and Other Essays by Aldo Leopold*, ed. Susan L. Flader and J. Baird Callicott, Madison: University of Wisconsin Press, 1991.

Lewis, Anne C. 1990. "Education and the Environment." *Phi Delta Kappa* (April): 580–581.

Lewis, Martin W. 1992. *Green Delusions: An Environmentalist Critique of Radical Environmentalism.* Durham, N.C.: Duke University Press.

Lindblom, Charles E. 1990. *Inquiry and Change: The Troubled Attempt to Understand and Shape Society.* New Haven, Conn.: Yale University Press.

Linsky, Martin. 1990. "The Media and Public Deliberation." In Robert B. Reich, ed., *The Power of Public Ideas*, 205–227. Cambridge, Mass.: Harvard University Press.

Lipset, Seymour Martin. 1986. "Beyond 1984: The Anomalies of American Politics." *PS* 19, no. 2 (Spring): 222–236.

Lovins, Amory. 1977. *Soft Energy Paths.* Cambridge, Mass.: Ballinger.

Lowenthal, David. 1966. "Assumptions behind the Public Attitudes." In Henry Jarrett, ed., *Environmental Quality in a Growing Economy*, 128–137. Baltimore: Johns Hopkins University Press.

Lukas, A. 1988. "American Greens." *Green Letter* (Summer): 12.

Lundqvist, Lennart J. 1974. *Environmental Policies in Canada, Sweden, and the United States: A Comparative Overview.* Beverly Hills, Calif.: Sage.

McClure, Charles E., Jr. 1991. *The Value-added Tax: Key to Deficit Reduction?* Washington, D.C.: American Enterprise Institute.

McEvoy, James, III. 1972. "The American Concern with Environment." In William R. Burch, Jr., Neil H. Cheek, Jr., and Lee Taylor, eds., *Social Behavior, Natural Resources, and the Environment*, 214–236. New York: Harper and Row.

McHarg, Ian L. 1969. *Design with Nature.* Garden City, N.Y.: Natural History Press.

McLaughlin, Andrew. 1990. "Ecology, Capitalism, and Socialism." *Socialism and Democracy* (Spring/Summer).

MacRae, Duncan. 1976. *The Social Function of Social Science.* New Haven, Conn.: Yale University Press.

Macy, Joanna R. 1983. *Despair and Personal Power in the Nuclear Age.* Philadelphia: New Society Publishers.

Majone, Giandomenico. 1990. "Policy Analysis and Public Deliberation." In Robert B. Reich, ed., *The Power of Public Ideas,* 157–178. Cambridge, Mass.: Harvard University Press.

Makower, Joel. 1990. "The Green Revolution." *Vis-a-Vis* (April): 48–54.

Mansbridge, Jane. 1983. *Beyond Adversary Democracy.* Chicago: University of Chicago Press.

Martinson, Oscar B., and E. A. Wilkening. 1975. "A Scale to Measure Awareness of Environmental Problems: Structure and Correlates." Paper presented at the annual meeting of the Midwest Sociological Society, Chicago.

Merchant, Carolyn. 1989. *Ecological Revolutions: Nature, Gender, and Science in New England.* Chapel Hill: University of North Carolina Press.

Merelman, Richard M. 1969. "The Development of Political Ideology: A Framework for the Analysis of Political Socialization." *American Political Science Review* 63: 750–767.

Merelman, Richard M. 1971. "The Development of Policy Thinking in Adolescence." *American Political Science Review* 65: 1033–1047.

Merelman, Richard M. 1983. "The Concept of Ideology in Political Socialization and Political Sociology." Paper presented at the conference "Socialisations et idéologies: Approches nouvelles et recherches recentes." Departement de Science Politique, Université Laval, Quebec, Canada.

Merelman, Richard M. 1984. *Making Something of Ourselves.* Berkeley: University of California Press.

Milbrath, Lester W. 1984. *Environmentalists: Vanguard for a New Society.* Albany: State University of New York Press.

Milbrath, Lester W. 1990. "Environmental Understanding: A New Concern for Political Socialization." In Orit Ichilov, ed., *Political Socialization, Citizenship Education and Democracy,* 281–293. New York: Teachers College Press.

Mishan, E. J. 1970. *Technology and Growth: The Price We Pay.* New York: Praeger.

Mitchell, Robert Cameron. 1984. "Public Opinion and Environmental Politics in the 1970s and 1980s." In Norman J. Vig and Michael E. Kraft, eds., *Environmental Policy in the 1980s: Reagan's New Agenda,* 51–74. Washington, D.C.: Congressional Quarterly Press.

Moline, Jon N. 1986. "Aldo Leopold and the Moral Community." *Environmental Ethics* 8, no. 2 (Summer): 99–120.

Morris, David. 1989. "The Materials We Need to Create a Sustainable Society Lie Close to Home." *Utne Reader* (November/December): 84–90.

Morrison, Denton E. 1973. "The Environmental Movement: Conflict Dynamics." *Journal of Voluntary Action Research* 2: 74–85.

Murch, Arvin. 1974. "Who Cares about the Environment? The Nature and Origins of Environmental Concern." In Arvin W. Murch, ed., *Environmental Concern*, 9–42. New York: MSS Information Corporation.

Naess, Arne. 1989. *Ecology, Community, Lifestyle.* Cambridge, England: Cambridge University Press.

Nash, Roderick. 1985. "Rounding Out the American Revolution: Ethical Extension and the New Environmentalism." In Kendall E. Bailes, ed., *Environmental History*, 242–257. Lanham, Md.: University Press of America.

Nash, Roderick. 1989. *The Rights of Nature: A History of Environmental Ethics.* Madison: University of Wisconsin Press.

The New York Times. March 19, 1990; April 17, 1990; April 23, 1990; July 1, 1990.

Norton, Bryan. 1991. *Toward Unity among Environmentalists.* New York: Oxford University Press.

Nussbaum, Martha Craven. 1982. "Saving Aristotle's Appearances." In Malcolm Schofield, ed., *Language and Logos*, 267–293. New York: Cambridge University Press.

Organization for Economic Cooperation and Development (OECD). 1985. *The State of the Environment 1985.* Paris: OECD.

Organization for Economic Cooperation and Development (OECD). 1988. *Environmental Policies in Finland.* Paris: OECD.

Ophuls, William. 1977. *Ecology and the Politics of Scarcity.* San Francisco: W. H. Freeman.

O'Riordan, Timothy. 1976. "Attitudes, Behavior, and Environmental Policy Issues." In Irwin Altman and Joachim F. Wohlwill, eds., 1976. *Human Behavior and Environment: Advances in Theory and Research*, 1–36. Vol. 1. New York and London: Plenum Press.

O'Riordan, Timothy, and R. Kerry Turner, eds. 1983. *An Annotated Reader in Environmental Planning and Management.* Oxford, England: Pergamon Press.

Ostrom, Elinor. 1990. *Governing the Commons.* New York: Cambridge University Press.

Paehlke, Robert C. 1979. *Environmentalism and the Future of Progressive Politics.* New Haven, Conn.: Yale University Press.

Park, Christopher C., ed. 1986. *Environmental Policies: An International Review.* London: Croom Helm.

Partridge, Ernest. 1982. "Are We Ready for an Ecological Morality?" *Environmental Ethics* 4, no. 2 (Summer): 175–190.

Pateman, Carole. 1970. *Participation and Democratic Theory.* Cambridge: Cambridge University Press.

Perrings, Charles. 1987. *Economy and Environment: A Theoretical Essay on the Interdependence of Economic and Environmental Systems.* Cambridge: Cambridge University Press.

Petchenik, Jordan B. 1989. "Wisconsin Wildlife Constituency." Results of a statewide mailed questionnaire prepared for the Wisconsin Department of Natural Resources, draft version.

Petulla, Joseph M. 1987. *Environmental Protection in the United States: Industry, Agency, Environmentalists.* San Francisco: San Francisco Study Center.

Piasecki, Bruce, and Peter Asmus. 1990. *In Search of Environmental Excellence: Moving Beyond Blame.* New York: Simon and Schuster.

Pierce, John R. 1972. "Communication." *Scientific American* 227, no. 3 (September): 31–41.

Piller, Charles. 1991. *The Fail-Safe Society: Community Defiance and the End of American Technological Optimism.* New York: Basic Books.

Piore, Michael J., and Charles F. Sabel. 1984. *The Second Industrial Divide.* New York: Basic Books.

Pope John Paul II. 1990. "Peace with God the Creator—Peace with All of Creation." *Earch Ethics* 1, no. 3 (Spring): 11.

Popper, Karl. 1957. *The Poverty of Historicism.* Boston: Beacon Press.

Porritt, Jonathan. 1984. *Seeing Green: The Politics of Ecology Explained.* New York: Basil Blackwell.

Reich, Robert B. 1983. "The Next American Frontier." *Atlantic Monthly* (March): 42–108, and (April): 97–108.

Reich, Robert B. 1990a. "Policy Making in a Democracy." In Robert B. Reich, ed., *The Power of Public Ideas,* 123–156. Cambridge, Mass.: Harvard University Press.

Reich, Robert B., ed. 1990b. *The Power of Public Ideas.* Cambridge, Mass.: Harvard University Press.

Reinarman, Craig. 1987. *American States of Mind: Political Beliefs and Behavior among Private and Public Workers.* New Haven, Conn.: Yale University Press.

Repetto, Robert, Roger C. Dower, Robin Jenkins, and Jacqueline Geoghegan. 1992. *Green Fees: How a Tax Shift Can Work for the Environment and the Economy.* Washington, D.C.: World Resources Institute.

Richman, Al. 1979. "The Polls: Public Attitudes toward the Energy Crisis." *Public Opinion Quarterly* 43, no. 4 (Winter): 576–585.

Rickson, Roy E. 1972. "Self-Interest and Pollution Control." *Journal of Environmental Education* 4: 43–48.

Riesman, David. 1965. *Faces in the Crowd* Abridged ed. New Haven, Conn.: Yale University Press.

Rodman, John. 1977. "The Liberation of Nature?" *Inquiry* 20: 83–145.

Rolston, Holmes, III. 1985. "Valuing Wildlands." *Environmental Ethics* 7, no. 1 (Spring): 23–48.

Ryan, John C. 1990. "Timber's Last Stand." *WorldWatch* 3, no. 4 (July/August): 27–34.

Sale, Kirkpatrick. 1985. *Dwellers in the Land: The Bioregional Vision.* San Francisco: Sierra Club Books.

Salleh, Ariel Kay. 1984. "Deeper Than Deep Ecology: The Eco-Feminist Connection." *Environmental Ethics* 6, no. 4 (Winter): 339–345.

Sancar, Fahriye Hazer. 1985. "Towards Theory Generation in Landscape Aesthetics." *Landscape Journal* 4, no. 2 (Fall): 116–124.

Sandbach, Francis. 1980. *Environment, Ideology, and Policy.* Montclair, N.J.: Allanheld and Osmun.

Sandbrook, J. Richard. 1986. "Toward a Global Environmental Strategy." In Christopher C. Park, ed., *Environmental Policies: An International Review,* 289–303. London: Croom Helm.

Sarkar, Saral. 1990. "Accommodating Industrialism: A Third World View of the West German Ecological Movement." *The Ecologist* 20, no. 4 (July/August): 147–152.

Scherer, Donald, and Thomas Attig, eds. 1983. *Ethics and the Environment.* Englewood Cliffs, N.J.: Prentice-Hall.

Schnaiberg, A. 1973. "Politics, Participation, and Pollution: The Environmental Movement." In J. Walton and D. Carns, eds., *Cities in Change: A Reader on Urban Sociology.* Boston: Allyn and Bacon.

Schon, Donald. 1971. *Beyond the Stable State.* New York: Random House.

Schrader-Frechette, Kristin. 1985. "Environmental Ethics and Global Imperatives." In Robert Repetto, ed., *The Global Possible: Resources, Development, and the New Century,* 97–127. New Haven, Conn.: Yale University Press.

Schumacher, E. F. 1974. *Small Is Beautiful.* New York: Abacus Books.

Seamon, Robert. 1989. *Community and the Politics of Place.* New York: St. Martin's.

Shaiko, Ronald G. 1987. "Religion, Politics, and Environmental Concern: A Powerful Mix of Passions." *Social Science Quarterly* 68, no. 2: 244–262.

Shapiro, Robert Y., and John M. Gilroy. 1984a. "The Polls: Regulation—Part I." *Public Opinion Quarterly* 48, no. 2 (Summer): 531–542.

Shapiro, Robert Y., and John M. Gilroy. 1984b. "The Polls: Regulation—Part II." *Public Opinion Quarterly* 48, no. 3 (Fall): 666–677.

Simon, Herbert. 1985. "Human Nature in Politics: The Dialogue of Psychology with Political Science." *American Political Science Review* 79: 293–304.

Soltan, Karol. 1987. *The Casual Theory of Justice.* Berkeley: University of California Press.

Spitz, Elaine. 1986. "Citizenship and Liberal Institutions." In Alfonso J. Damico, ed., *Liberals on Liberalism,* 185–199. Totowa, N.J.: Rowman and Littlefield.

Spradley, James P. 1979. *The Ethnographic Interview.* New York: Holt, Rinehart, and Winston.

Spragens, Thomas A. 1990. *Reason and Democracy.* Durham, N.C.: Duke University Press.

Springer, J. Fred, and Edmond Costantini. 1974. "Public Opinion and the Environment: An Issue in Search of a Home." In Stuart S. Nagel, ed., *Environmental Politics,* 195–224. New York: Praeger.

Starr, Chester. 1982. *The Roman Empire: 27 B.C.—A.D. 476: A Study in Survival.* New York: Oxford University Press.

Starrett, Ray. 1990. Personal communication, March 15.

Stegner, Wallace. 1987. "The Legacy of Aldo Leopold." In J. Baird Callicott, ed., *Companion to A Sand County Almanac,* 233–245. Madison: University of Wisconsin Press.

Steinbrunner, John D. 1974. *The Cybernetic Theory of Decision.* Princeton, N.J.: Princeton University Press.

Stockman, David A. 1978. "The Wrong War? The Case against a National Energy Policy." *Public Interest* 53 (Fall): 3–44.

Stone, Christopher D. 1987. *Earth and Other Ethics: The Case for Moral Pluralism.* New York: Harper and Row.

Taylor, Charles. 1978. "Neutrality in Political Science." In Alan Ryan, ed., *The Philosophy of Social Explanation*, 139–170. London: Oxford Universtiy Press.

Taylor, Paul. 1986. *Respect for Nature: A Theory of Environmental Ethics.* Princeton, N.J.: Princeton University Press.

Tokar, Brian. 1987. *The Green Alternative: Creating an Ecological Future.* San Pedro, Calif.: R. and E. Miles.

Trop, Cecile, and Leslie L. Roos, Jr. 1971. "Public Opinion and the Environment." In L. L. Roos, Jr., ed. *The Politics of Ecosuicide*, 52–63. New York: Holt, Rinehart and Winston.

Tuan, Yi-Fu. 1974. *Topophilia: A Study of Environmental Perception, Attitudes, and Values.* Englewood Cliffs, N.J.: Prentice-Hall.

Tyler, Tom R. 1986. "Justice and Leadership Endorsement." Richard R. Lau and David O. Sears, eds., *Political Cognition*, 257–278. Hillsdale, N.J.: Laurence Erlbaum Associates.

United Nations Environmental Program. 1989. *Our Planet.* Nairobi, Kenya: United Nations.

Van Liere, Kent D., and Riley E. Dunlap. 1980. "The Social Bases of Environmental Concern: A Review of Hypotheses, Explanations and Empirical Evidence." *Public Opinion Quarterly* 44, no. 2 (Summer): 181–197.

Verba, Sidney, Norman Nie, and Jae-on Kim. 1978. *Participation and Political Equality.* Cambridge: Cambridge University Press.

Vig, Norman J., and Michael E. Kraft. 1984a. "Environmental Policy from the Seventies to the Eighties." In Norman J. Vig and Michael E. Kraft, eds., *Environmental Policy in the 1980s: Reagan's New Agenda*, 3–26. Washington, D.C.: Congressional Quarterly Press.

Vig, Norman J., and Michael E. Kraft, eds. 1984b. *Environmental Policy in the 1980s: Reagan's New Agenda.* Washington, D.C.: Congressional Quarterly Press.

Ward, Dana. 1986. "Comments on 'Cognitive Functioning and Socio-Political Ideology Revisited.'" *Political Psychology* 7, no. 1: 141–147.

Warren, Karen J. 1987. "Feminism and Ecology: Making Connections." *Environmental Ethics* 9, no. 1 (Spring): 3–20.

Wattenberg, Ben J., et al. 1979. "Environmental Activism: Here We Go Again." *U.S. News and World Report* (April 17): 29, 32.

Watts, Nicholas J. 1983. "Environmental Complaint and Concern in the European Community." In David Canter, Martin Krampen, and David Stea, eds., *Environmental Policy, Assessment, and Communications*, 55–73. Aldershot, England: Avebury.

Weber, Max. 1949. *Methodology of the Social Sciences*, ed. Edward A. Shils and Henry A. Finch. Glencoe, Ill.: Free Press.

Wenz, Peter S. 1988. *Environmental Justice.* Albany: State University of New York Press.

Werner, Oswald, and G. Mark Schoepfle. 1987. *Ethnographic Analysis and Data Management.* Newbury Park, Calif.: Sage.

White, Gilbert F. 1966. "Formation and Role of Public Attitudes." In Henry Jarrett, ed., *Environmental Quality in a Growing Economy*, 105–127. Baltimore: Johns Hopkins University Press.

White, Lynn, Jr. 1971. "The Historical Roots of Our Ecological Crisis." Reprinted in Thomas Detwyler, ed., *Man's Impact on the Environment*, 27–35. New York: McGraw Hill.

Wisenhunt, Donald W. 1974. *The Environment and the American Experience.* Port Washington, N.Y.: Kennikat Press.

Wolfe, Alan. 1983. "Why Is There No Green Party in the United States?" *World Policy Journal* 1: 159–180.

Wolfson, Zeev. 1992. "The Massive Degradation of Ecosystems in the USSR." In John Massey Stewart, ed., *The Soviet Environment: Problems, Policies and Politics.* New York: Cambridge University Press.

Worster, Donald. 1985. "Conservation and Environmentalist Movements in the U.S.: Comment on Hays and Nash." In Kendall E. Bailes, ed., *Environmental History: Critical Issues in Comparative Perspective*, 258–263. Lanham, Md.: University Press of America.

Wyant, William K. 1982. *Westward in Eden: The Public Lands and the Conservation Movement.* Berkeley: University of California Press.

Zimmerman, Michael E. 1987. "Feminism, Deep Ecology, and Environmental Ethics." *Environmental Ethics* 9, no. 1 (Spring): 21–44.

Index

263